25 Years of Rock

John Tobler and
Pete Frame

Introduction by
Elton John

This edition produced exclusively for

WHSMITH

Published in the UK exclusively for W H Smith

Published by
The Hamlyn Publishing Group Limited
London · New York · Sydney · Toronto
Astronaut House, Feltham, Middlesex, England

Copyright © The Hamlyn Publishing Group Limited 1980
ISBN 0 600 37638 9

Filmset in England by Photocomp Limited, Birmingham
Printed in Spain
by Printer, industria gráfica sa   Sant Vicenç dels Horts
Barcelona D.L.B. 11539-1980

endpapers: Kiss
half-title page: Little Richard
title page: Steven Tyler of Aerosmith

Acknowledgments

The quotation on page 37 is taken from *Revolt into Style : The Pop Arts in Britain* (1970), page 39, © George Melly (1970), and is reprinted by permission of Penguin Books Ltd.

The publishers would like to thank the following for providing illustrations for use in the book: Arista, Asylum, Beserkley, Tony Brainsbury, Capricorn, Charisma, Chrysalis, Decca, EMI, Epic, Island, MCA, Melody Maker, New Musical Express, Polydor, Tamla Motown, United Artists and Vertigo.

Thanks are also due to the following people who supplied material from their collections: John Beecher, Neil Foster, John Goldman of Bygone Record Sales, Jan and Ian Hunter, Leigh Jones, Adam Komoroski, Barry Lazelle, Kim Ludlow, Jennie Morris, Philip Morris, Bernard White of Luigi and the Boys.

The following illustrations are reproduced by courtesy of Communication Vectors and the Rock Art Studios, London. All rights reserved © 1979. Page 220 top by Chris Burke © The Artist; page 220 bottom by Carey Kirkland © The Artist (Media & Graphic Creations); page 224 by Kathy Wyatt © The Artist; page 243 top right by Hunt Emerson © The Artist (Media & Graphic Creations); page 243 bottom by Brett Ewins © The Artist (Media & Graphic Creations); page 246 centre by Jeremy Soar © The Artist (Rogers and Company).

The illustrations on pages 29, 113, 132, 163, 170, 205, 214 and 244 are by Kipper Williams.

Photographs
Colour
Cyrus Andrews, London 38 top left, 51, 58 top, 58 bottom, 71, 75 bottom, 78 bottom, 82, 83 top, 86 top right, 98 top right; Frank Driggs Collection, New York 15 bottom, 19 bottom, 153 centre left, 153 centre top, 153 bottom right; Flair Photography, London 75 top right; Pete Frame, London 192 bottom, 194 top right, 203 bottom, 206 top left, 213 bottom, 235 centre; Tim Graham, London 161 top, 207 bottom; Hamlyn Group Picture Library 14 top left, 18, 35, 54, 55, 83 bottom, 102, 103, 152, 153, 198, 199 bottom right, 242, 243 top left, 243 centre left; Dezo Hoffman, London 66, 95; London Features International, London* 59, 117 bottom left, 130 bottom, 135 top, 138 bottom left, 146 top right, 146 centre left, 146 bottom, 159, 173 inset, 176 top, 177 bottom, 188 top right, 188 bottom, 189 top right, 192 centre right, 199 right, 202 bottom right, 203 top, 209 top right, 221 bottom, 230 top left, 230-231, 231 top right, 234 bottom left, 239 top left, 239 centre right, 246 bottom left, 247; NASA 151 top left; Photofeatures International, London endpapers, title page, 111 top right, 142, 158 bottom left, 158 bottom right, 164, 172 bottom, 176 bottom, 177 top left, 181 top, 181 bottom right, 185, 189 top left, 189 bottom, 192 top left, 192 top

right, 194 top left, 195, 202 top, 202 bottom left, 203 centre, 206 top right, 207 top, 209 top left, 209 bottom right, 212 top left, 212 top right, 212 centre, 213 top, 216 top, 217 top, 217 bottom, 220 centre, 221 top left, 221 top right, 226 top left, 226 top right, 226 centre, 226 bottom, 227 top, 227 bottom left, 230 bottom, 231 bottom, 234 top, 235 top, 238 top, 239 bottom left; Barry Plummer, London 158 centre, 161 bottom, 172 top, 246 top left; David Redfern, London 131 top left, 131 top right, 158 top, 165, 173 top left, 173 bottom, 180, 181 bottom left, 216 bottom, 217 centre; Rex Features, London 15 top left, 15 top right, 38 top right, 38 bottom, 39 top left, 39 top right, 39 bottom, 43, 47, 50, 63, 67, 70, 78 top, 86 top left, 86 bottom, 87 top, 87 centre, 91, 94 top, 94 bottom, 98 top left, 99, 106, 110, 111 top left, 113 centre right, 116, 117 top left, 117 top right, 117 centre, 117 bottom right, 120-121, 121, 124, 128 top, 128 bottom, 130 top left, 130 centre top, 130 centre bottom, 135 bottom, 138 top left, 139 top right, 143, 146 top left, 146 centre right, 147 top, 147 centre, 147 bottom, 151 top right, 168 left inset, 168 centre inset, 168 right inset, 168-169, 173 top right; Bernard White 130 top right.

Black and White
Cyrus Andrews, London 16 top left, 41 bottom, 43 bottom, 47 bottom left, 71 top, 77 bottom, 106 bottom, 118-119, 145 bottom right, 166 bottom right; Associated Press, London 68, 88, 112; BBC, London 100 bottom right; British Airways, London 45 top, 215 top; British Film Institute, London 13 top left, 13 top right, 19 top left, 25 bottom right, 29 bottom, 30, 34-35, 36 top, 44-45, 52 right, 69 top, 69 bottom left, 69 bottom right, 80, 81 bottom, 89 bottom right, 101 top right, 140, 150, 160 centre left, 163 top right, 170 bottom right, 171 bottom right, 183 top left, 183 top right, 197 top, 205 top, 205 bottom right, 215 bottom left, 237 top right, 237 centre, 245 bottom left; Camera Press, London 123 bottom, 182, 183 bottom, 187 bottom, 245 top left; Frank Driggs Collection, New York 13 bottom, 14 top right, 16 bottom, 17 top, 21, 23 bottom right, 25 centre left, 25 centre right, 26 top right, 31 centre, 32 top right, 43 top, 47 top left, 48, 49 top, 49 bottom, 51 bottom, 59 bottom, 62 top, 65 top, 66 top right, 73, 87 bottom, 90 bottom, 96-97, 105 bottom, 107 bottom, 108 top left, 108 top right, 111 bottom, 113 bottom, 119 top, 120 top left, 120 top right, 121 bottom, 142 bottom, 164 bottom, 211; Flair Photography, London 22, 23 top right, 23 bottom left, 26 top left, 27 top, 27 bottom, 31 top left, 31 top right, 31 bottom left, 32 top left, 33 top left, 33 top right, 36 bottom, 40, 41 top, 42, 50 top right, 66 top left, 77 top, 91; Pete Frame, London 125 top, 125 bottom, 126 bottom, 127 top, 138 top right, 138 bottom right, 138-139, 145 top, 145 bottom left, 148 right, 149 top, 149 bottom, 160 top right, 179 right, 194 centre right, 200, 210, 228 centre top; Hamlyn Group Picture Library 15, 60, 101 top left, 133; Dezo Hoffman, London 26 bottom, 31 bottom right, 63 bottom, 65 bottom right, 98 bottom; Ron Howard 171 top; Keystone Press, London 24, 81

top; London Features International, London 20, 56, 72, 119 bottom, 139 bottom, 156, 157 bottom, 160 bottom right, 166 top, 180 top left, 180 centre 234 bottom right, 241, 248 top; Photofeatures International, London 190; Barry Plummer, London 125 centre, 134 bottom left, 136, 137, 144 top, 148 left, 153, 167 left, 167 right, 179 left, 185 inset, 188 top left, 188 centre top, 193 top, 193 bottom right, 195 bottom, 208 top, 208 bottom, 215 bottom right, 219, 228 top left, 228 top right, 232 top, 233, 239 centre right, 239 bottom, 240 top; David Redfern, London 152, 174, 181 centre bottom, 194 bottom; Rex Features, London 28, 37, 53 top, 53 bottom, 61, 62 bottom, 79 top, 89 top right, 89 bottom left, 92, 95 top, 96 top left, 97 top right, 99, 101 bottom, 104 top left, 104 centre top, 104 top right, 104 bottom, 105 top, 108 bottom, 109, 110 bottom, 113 centre left, 114 top, 114 bottom, 118, 126 top, 129, 132 bottom, 133 bottom left, 134 top, 134 centre, 134 bottom right, 141 top, 141 bottom, 143 bottom left, 143 bottom right, 144 bottom, 162, 171 bottom left, 180 bottom right, 186, 197 bottom left, 197 bottom right, 225 top left, 225 bottom, 235 bottom, 237 bottom, 245 bottom right; Screen Gems – EMI Music Ltd, London 157 top; Syndication International, London 236 bottom; John Tobler 160 top left, 175, 180, 184 centre, 191, 222, 248 bottom; Twentieth Century-Fox Film Co Ltd, London 19 top right, 43 centre, 89 top left, 163 bottom, 225 top right, 245 top right; Bernard White 84.

*LFI Photographs are by Adrian Boot, Paul Canty, Cloads Studio, Fin Costello, Henry Ditz, Jill Furmanowsky, Frank Griffin, Neil Jones, Neil Preston, Michael Putland, David Redfern.

The publishers have made every attempt to contact the owners of the illustrations appearing in this book. In the few instances where they have been unsuccessful, they invite the copyright holders to contact them direct.

Finally, the authors and publishers would like to thank the following for their kind assistance: Laura Beggs, Catherine Blackie, Caroline Bone and Leigh Jones.

foreword

In 1954 Bill Haley recorded *Rock Around the Clock,* which has since become the anthem of rock'n'roll. That is not to say that rock'n'roll was not recorded before this date, it was, in the form of 'rhythm and blues' which was the exclusive preserve of such black artists as Fats Domino, Joe Turner, and Ruth Brown. What *Rock Around the Clock* did was combine 'rhythm and blues' with Country Music to form the music with the beat that we know as rock'n'roll.

Rock'n'roll started a revolution in popular music. Its new and alien form caught the imagination of young people all over the world. Pop music was born and has remained an almost exclusive domain of the young, only crossing into the area of adult popularity when it has had the rough edges smoothed off it.

Rock'n'roll didn't happen in isolation. To catch the mood of the music as it happened, we have included 25 spreads, highlighting the fashions and fads, the news and the films of the year, with a list of number ones in Britain and the United States. And, at the start of each year, there is a list of the new stars to burst on the scene that year.

In a book of this length it is only possible to deal with major themes and artists. That is not to say that the authors are unaware of the minor influences and artists and their contribution to music. They are. But if we included everyone it would need a book a thousand times the size of the one you are now holding. We would like to apologise if you feel that your favourite artist or music has not been given the attention they merit. There just wasn't room!

So here it is – the first twenty-five years of rock. If the next twenty-five years are as exciting as the last we confidently can expect to rock well into the next century.

Adrian Scott

Introduction

To précis 25 years of rock'n'roll into a book of this size and remain faithful to minute detail is well nigh impossible. Pete Frame and John Tobler have achieved the impossible because of their experience as excellent journalists and their incredible knowledge of what's gone down. I mean, if you want to know what Neil Young eats for breakfast they probably know. If they could tell me I'd be very grateful as I've had a constant battle with my weight.

In a sense this book is the ultimate textbook on the history of rock – a reference book which, unlike any other textbook, you can read time and time again. For those of you who thought that Elvis Presley, the Beatles, the Rolling Stones and Bob Dylan were the backbone of rock'n'roll throughout the years, you're in for a big shock. Credit is given where credit is due – and about time. Speaking as a musician, it's very rare to find journalists who really know their way around, but these guys know what they're talking about. For example, their analysis of styles and in-fluences is extremely accurate, as in the case of Fats Domino who, for me, was every bit as important as Jerry Lee and Little Richard.

A lot of artists who never made the big time are remembered with great reverence by the authors, which pleased me no end. Time and time again a big artist has lifted a song from an obscure R&B record and made it famous – a prime case being *Piece Of My Heart*, which became a Janis Joplin standard. How many people know that Erma Franklin (Aretha's sister) had done a much superior version earlier? However, I honestly believe that the British public have always had a great deal of affection for the lesser known artist. Artists like Bobby Bland, Garnet Mimms, David Ackles, and the late Tim Buckley are much better known in the U.K. than in the U.S.A. – Tom Paxton's emotional reaction to his incredible reception at the Dylan Isle of Wight concert springs to mind.

So if you are a vinyl junkie or a novice, you're going to love this book. The choice of photographs is excellent and the reading is irresistible. Well done lads, can't wait for the next 25 years.

Elton John

'55

'Rock Around The Clock'

Johnny Ace · LaVern Baker · Hank Ballard and the Midnighters · Chuck Berry
Pat Boone · The Cadillacs · Ray Charles · The Clovers · The Crew Cuts
The Crows · Bo Diddley · Fats Domino · The Drifters · Stan Freberg
Alan Freed · Bill Haley and the Comets · Roy Hamilton · Etta James
B. B. King · The Penguins · The Platters · Elvis Presley · Sonny Til
and the Orioles · Joe Turner

As the year opened, rock'n'roll was making only the mildest impact on the rigid patterns of popular music in Britain.

Established pop, adult-oriented though seldom adult-minded, was characterised by songs reflecting idealistic romance and good clean fun. Any ebullience was controlled, any thoughts of love were 'honourable' rather than passionate. Ballads and balladeers held sway, and the Tin Pan Alley establishment felt no sense of threat or alarm about the fact that Bill Haley and the Comets stood at number four on the hit parade with their bowdlerized version of a crude blues called *Shake, Rattle And Roll*. Haley, they thought, was a flash in the pan and he, along with his brash, noisy novelty hit, would soon go away and let things get back to normal. They thought wrong.

A generation of war babies had reached teen age and were busily rejecting the values of the previous generation, whose lives had largely been shaped by the effects of World War Two. One thing was certain: they weren't about to accept music approved by their parents. They already had film stars with whom they could identify: James Dean, the rebel without a cause, the victim of adult misunderstanding; and Marlon Brando, the aggressive black leather biker and mixed-up kid. 'What are you rebelling against?' Brando was asked in *The Wild Ones*, a film released in 1953. 'What've you got?' he replied.

If mid-fifties teenagers were going to listen to music, it was going to be raucous and rhythmic; it was going to have a solid beat, suitable for dancing or stomping; and it was going to express the way they felt or wanted to feel. The audience was ready and waiting. Temporary exultation was all that mattered; to escape the drabness of everyday life and the gloomy prospects of a well-defined dead-end future.

Rock'n'roll was almost here.

In America, rock'n'roll and rhythm'n'blues (R&B) had been rumbling for several years, though their early popularity was localised and almost entirely restricted to black urban communities.

Among singles which managed to achieve national success during 1953 were *Crazy Man Crazy* by Bill Haley, *Crying In The Chapel* by Sonny Til and the Orioles, and *Money Honey* by the Drifters. In 1954, *Gee* by the Crows, *Work With Me Annie* by Hank Ballard, *Sh'boom* by the Chords and the Crew Cuts, *Shake, Rattle And Roll* by Bill Haley, *Hearts Of Stone* by the Charms, *Sincerely* by the Moonglows, and *Earth Angel* by the Penguins were among a slew of country-wide rock hits and by the start of 1955 it was evident that rock'n'roll fever was about

to sweep the States. And when a nice Jewish songstress like Georgia Gibbs scored hits by covering singles by the black and overtly sexual LaVern Baker, it was obvious that the shrewder entrepreneurs had not only accepted rock'n'roll but were bending to its force.

Rock'n'roll changed everything: suddenly it was the performance, rather than the song, which mattered. Teenagers weren't prepared to tolerate good songs being murdered by old fogies, and a wave of new heroes emerged to displace the crooners (mostly Italianate) and cocktail orchestras. In the forefront was a kiss-curled shouter from Detroit, Bill Haley.

Haley, who had been singing and playing guitar with a country and western combo since 1940, when he was 15 years old, was one of the first white singers to realise that blues and country music could be rocked up to great effect. His first big record, made in 1951, was called *Rock The Joint* – a fairly prophetic title, it might be said.

Quite why Haley and his group, the Comets, decided to emphasise the backbeat of their music, in a typically 'black' manner, is uncertain, although it has been suggested that Haley noticed the young whites in his audience adopting black ghetto slang, clothing and dancing, and decided to produce music from similar cultural roots. Whatever the reason, in April 1954 Haley and the Comets recorded a pair of songs which would become generally accepted as the first rock'n'roll records, or at least the first rock'n'roll records to gain mass popularity with the more affluent white audience.

One of the songs had just become a R&B hit for Joe Turner, but the Haley version of *Shake, Rattle And Roll* was far more raucous and exciting to a public who didn't appreciate the subtleties of the blues, and provided Haley with his first international top twenty hit. It was the other track, however, a novelty dance song called *Rock Around The Clock*, which really clinched it for rock'n'roll. The song had actually been recorded and released to little response by another artist a couple of years earlier. The story goes that one of the song's co-writers was Haley's manager, who had just negotiated an advantageous record contract for him. To express his thanks Haley recorded the song. It was actually released before *Shake, Rattle And Roll*, but sold only moderately.

A little later, however, Haley's manager was apparently roped in as technical adviser on *Blackboard Jungle*, one of the earliest films focussing on teenage rebellion, and *Rock Around The Clock* was used over the opening credits. The plot of *Blackboard Jungle*, revolving around the problems

Opposite left: The Wild Ones, especially Marlon Brando, seemed to many to be a pattern for a generation of juvenile delinquency.

Opposite right: Glenn Ford loses control of his rock-crazed charges in *The Blackboard Jungle.*

Opposite below: Young, raw and powerful – the early Elvis in action.

of a young school teacher (played by Glenn Ford), was a mirror of the times, the most memorable scene being one where Ford, in a final desperate bid to bridge the generation gap between himself and his pupils, brought his treasured collection of jazz 78s into class. His pupils showed their understanding and appreciation by smashing them to pieces.

As a result of its exposure to a huge cinema audience, *Rock Around The Clock* became *the* great anti-establishment song and teenage anthem, and made Haley the first rock'n'roll star. By the end of 1955, it was the best-selling single in both America and Britain.

Haley's detractors accused him of watering his music down to reach a wider audience – a criticism which could hardly be levelled at his principal rival, the up and coming Elvis Presley.

Elvis Aaron Presley, born on 8th January 1935 to a poor family from Tupelo Mississippi, moved to Memphis Tennessee with his parents in 1948. After school, he drifted through various menial jobs, choosing to concentrate his attention on leisure activities – including listening to country music and R&B on the local radio stations and occasionally singing with a gospel group, the Blackwood Brothers.

It is said that Presley's idol at the time was the super smooth Dean Martin, and it seems probable that when he first entered the premises of the Memphis Recording Company to make a private tape of the late forties ballad *My Happiness* (originally recorded by the Pied Pipers, one of whom was Jo Stafford) he was trying to emulate Martin, as the record was to be a birthday present for his mother.

Presley made use of the studio several more times over the next year without attracting attention until an assistant at the studio, Marion Keisker, detected something unique in the 19 year old's voice and persona and mentioned the fact to her boss, Sam Phillips. Phillips owned not only the studio but also his own label, Sun Records, which at this time was concentrating on blues artists like Rufus Thomas,

It's The Greatest! Get With It!...

NEW NEW NEW

"RHYTHM AND BLUES REVUE"

KALEIDOSCOPE WONDERCOLOR

COUNT BASIE JOE TURNER SARAH VAUGHAN HERB JEFFRIES

FAYE ADAMS

AMOS MILBURN LIONEL HAMPTON

NAT "KING" COLE

RUTH BROWN

THE LARKS

Plus
DELTA RHYTHM BOYS
MARTHA DAVIS
BILL BAILEY
MANTAN MORELAND
& "NIPSEY" RUSSELL
FREDDY & FLO ROBINSON
LITTLE BUCK
PAUL "HUCKLEBUCK" WILLIAMS & His Orchestra
M. C. WILLIE BRYANT

A STUDIO FILMS PRODUCTION

Top: This typical low budget money-spinner featured a varied collection of black artists, many of whom had little connection with the rock'n'roll breakthrough.

Above: Boss of Sun Records, the legendary Sam Phillips.

Top right: The country roots of rock'n'roll, Bill Monroe and his Bluegrass Boys. Elvis supercharged Monroe's music and gave it teen appeal.

James Cotton and Little Milton, and a gospel group the Prisonaires – so called because they were inmates at Tennessee State Penitentiary. He seems to have been more interested in black music than white, but his growing reputation caused aspiring songwriters to send him songs in the hope that one of his acts would record them. One such song was *Casual Love Affair* with which Phillips decided to give Presley (then driving a truck) a chance – mainly because he had no-one suitable for the song, apparently a Dean Martin styled affair.

The session was not a great success but some time later Phillips introduced Presley to a couple of other young musicians who hung around his studio: guitarist Scotty Moore and bassplayer Bill Black. When the three of them (Presley on vocals and acoustic rhythm guitar) recorded upbeat versions of Arthur Crudup's *That's All Right (Mama)* and Bill Monroe's *Blue Moon Of Kentucky*, Phillips heard the sound of gold. The two songs were released as a single in August 1954 and reaction to local air-play was immediate – although sales were mainly confined to the South.

Sun issued a total of five Presley singles and though none reached the national charts, they remain amongst the finest rock'n'roll records ever made. Each had an R&B song on one side and a rocked up country ballad on the other. Apart from Crudup's *That's All Right*, the R&B cuts were Roy Brown's *Good Rockin' Tonight*, an old blues song – *Milk Cow Blues,* Arthur Gunter's *Baby Let's Play House*, and Junior Parker's *Mystery Train* – while most of the country songs were fairly straight before they received the 'treatment' from Presley, Moore and Black.

By the middle of 1955, Presley's reputation had spread to the extent that several of America's biggest record companies were bidding for his contract. Columbia (C.B.S.) dropped out at $20,000, Atlantic went to $25,000, and in November 1955, R.C.A. signed him for the unprecedentedly large

sum of $35,000. Presley's adviser in the deal was the self-styled 'Colonel' Tom Parker, who had seen Elvis performing down the bill on various country music packages and heard him on the influential radio show *Louisiana Hayride*, before taking over the role of manager from Memphis D.J. Bob Neal.

Presley's appeal lay not only in his wild music but also in his totally uninhibited, sexually-oriented stage presence, which was considered disgusting by an older generation totally unused to the hip-swivelling, the snarling, the sexuality and the (to them) incomprehensible lyrics. This was the cue for the arrival of the complete antithesis to the threatening Presley . . . the charming, well-mannered, married, religious Charles Eugene (Pat) Boone, the complete All-American Boy from his well-trimmed hair to his buckskin shoes.

In 1955, Pat Boone was 21 years old and had already become a regular guest on the popular Arthur Godfrey T.V. show (for which Elvis had failed an audition in 1954), and it was at this point that he was signed to Dot Records by the label's president, Randy Wood; it was under his direction that Boone covered a string of songs first recorded by blacks, beginning with his version of Fats Domino's *Ain't That A Shame*, which made the British and American top tens in late 55.

The following year, Boone scored with his versions of Little Richard's *Tutti Frutti* and *Long Tall Sally*, Ivory Joe Hunter's *I Almost Lost My Mind*, and his biggest U.K. hit, *I'll Be Home* – originally recorded by the Flamingoes.

During his early career, he was second only to Presley as a prolific hitmaker, though many of his records were far from rock'n'roll. In fact, Boone achieved over 30 chart entries between his first hit in March 1955 and his final top twenty appearance in late 1962, and became the first rock star with that elusive 'all round appeal'. As such, he was despised by hard-core rock'n'rollers, who saw him as 'one of them': if their parents approved of this smiling

become divided along generation lines. Generally speaking, if parents were repelled by a song or singer, it was instantly an attractive proposition to teenagers. Thus, rhythm and blues moved out of the ghetto as several black artists made a dramatic crossover into white markets. One of the first to do so was Antoine 'Fats' Domino, a native of New Orleans, who made his vinyl debut, *The Fat Man*, as early as December 1949.

Domino's percussive piano-playing and vocal technique were derived from the dixieland jazz for which New Orleans was famed, though according to informed sources difficulties in recording *The Fat Man* led to its unusual style; it was never intended that his piano and voice should be so dominant in the ensemble sound. This record was arguably the very first million-seller in rock'n'roll, achieving that distinction some four years after release, since

smoothie who wouldn't even kiss his leading lady in a film, then he couldn't be the genuine article. However, it must be said in his defence that a great many more people than care to admit it heard their first, albeit ersatz, rock'n'roll on Pat Boone records.

Since his hitmaking career ended, Boone has devoted his life to religious entertainment, making several religious albums for specialist labels, while his children (Debbie in particular) have also entered the recording field with some success. Despite all this, several of his hits from the fifties, including *Friendly Persuasion*, *Love Letters In The Sand*, *A Wonderful Time Up There* (an early hint at his post-hit career) and *Speedy Gonzales*, remain well known 20 years later and his overall impact cannot be denied.

Previously divided (like America itself) along regional and colour lines, pop music had by 1955

Ruby Murray was an Irish songstress who was totally unaffected by the onset of rock'n'roll. In one week in March 1955 she had five records in the top twenty and would continue to achieve British hits well into 1959.

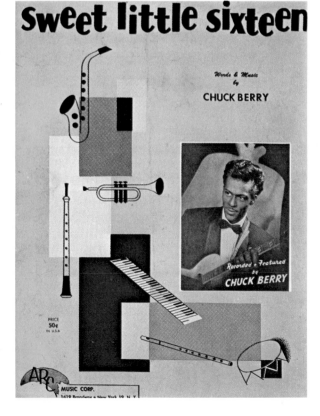

Sheet music for *Sweet Little Sixteen*, one of the earliest rock'n'roll classics.

classical music and concentrate instead on rhythm 'n' blues), *School Days* (the first and probably best anti-school song ever written), *Sweet Little Sixteen*, *Johhny B. Goode* and *Rock And Roll Music*.

During the early sixties, Berry served a short prison sentence for transporting a girl across a state line for immoral purposes, and his career might have ended had not the Beatles and especially the Rolling Stones championed his music so fervently during his absence. At the age of nearly 40, Berry enjoyed a renaissance both financial and artistic which continues today, although his apparent lack of interest in anything other than money has led to a very noticeable decline in musical quality and a further prison spell for tax evasion.

Ray Charles, the 'genius of soul' as he was dubbed, also came to the fore in 1955. Born in Georgia, Charles moved to Florida with his family when he was still a baby, and at the age of six contracted an illness which left him blind. Despite this handicap, and the fact that he became an orphan at 15, he taught himself piano and became a professional musician. His tragic life no doubt contributed to his extraordinarily soulful R&B style, displayed in 1955 on his first big hit *I Got A Woman*, and in 1959 on his top tenner *What'd I Say*, one of the most copied songs from the era.

Left: Armed with a succession of bizarrely shaped electric guitars, Bo Diddley (born Elias McDaniel on 30th December 1930) turned out a succession of great songs after signing for Chess Records in 55. His characteristic rhythmic pattern has become one of the standard sounds of the music and was used by great admirers of his, the Rolling Stones, on *Not Fade Away.*

Sheet music for La Vern Baker's 1956 hit, *Jim Dandy*, which was written by Lincoln Chase, who also penned *Such A Night* for the Drifters and several hits for sixties soul star Shirley Ellis.

when Fats has accumulated over 20 million-sellers. He remains one of the few artists from the birth of rock'n'roll who is still working today, although his current activities rarely result in hit records.

The same is true of Bo Diddley and Chuck Berry who both started their recording careers in Chicago, though they had been born further south.

Diddley acquired his nickname when he was a teenage amateur boxer, but his love for music eclipsed his interest in sport and by the mid-fifties he had perfected a distinctive guitar rhythm around which he constructed a song also called *Bo Diddley* in early 1955. This was to be the first of a series of classic Diddley songs which nearly all used that same unmistakable beat, but none of them provided their originator with the chart success he so obviously deserved. Bo was also a great showman, using exotically shaped custom-built guitars of his own design and looking far larger than life in extravagant stage clothes, and his influence on many succeeding generations of musicians from Buddy Holly to the Rolling Stones and the Clash has been immense.

Chuck Berry's influence was even greater: there is not a rock musician alive who has failed to fall under his spell at one time or another. It was the great bluesman Muddy Waters who suggested that Berry audition for Chess Records, for whom the vast majority of his catalogue of memorable teen epics were made. In fact, Berry was getting on for 30 but an intuitive comprehension of the teenage condition enabled him to write some of the most exuberant, and certainly the most durable songs of the mid-fifties: *Maybelline*, *Roll Over Beethoven* (an archetypal rebellion song requesting a D.J. to forget

JIM DANDY

50c

By LINCOLN CHASE

Recorded by
LA VERN BAKER ATLANTIC RECORDS

RALEIGH MUSIC CO.
1650 Broadway, New York 19, N.Y.

Many of the finest R&B and 'doo wop' groups took their names from species of birds. *Earth Angel*, by the Penguins, was one of the first R&B hits to cross over to the national pop charts.

A blues singer who did manage to find controversial yet commercial success, was Detroit-born Hank Ballard, populariser of suggestive lyrics and the inspiration behind 'answer songs'. The first song to put Ballard and his group, the Midnighters, on the map was the thinly-veiled sexual invitation *Work With Me Annie* in April 1954. As well as enjoying healthy sales, it provoked an answer record, running along similar lines, called *Roll With Me Henry* by Etta James. Ballard's subsequent hit, *Annie Had A Baby* continued the story – as did one of Buddy Holly's first records, *Midnight Shift*, which found the legendary Annie engaged in a modelling career.

Because black acts were often denied airplay and because their acceptance was still untenable in some areas, many white artists made a killing by recording de-horned copies (known as 'cover versions') of songs which were bubbling on regional R&B charts. Early examples of this practice were: the Chords' *Sh'boom* covered by the Crew Cuts, who also covered *Earth Angel* by the Penguins; *Sincerely* by the Moonglows, covered by the McGuire Sisters; LaVern Baker's *Tweedle Dee* covered by Georgia Gibbs, who also covered Etta James' *Roll With Me Henry* as *Dance With Me Henry*; Gene and Eunice's *Kokomo* covered by Perry Como, and of course we've already mentioned the supreme copycat Pat Boone, who ripped off black music without the least twinge of conscience.

An artist who did survive being 'covered' was the first lady of rock'n'roll, the Chicago born LaVern Baker. LaVern was a well-built and undeniably sexy black girl, who learnt to sing in church before gravitating into night clubs, where it's rumoured she instructed Johnnie Ray in the art of blues singing. However, unlike her contemporaries, including Sarah Vaughan and Dinah Washington – black singers who inclined towards the jazzier side of R&B – LaVern was a rocker.

After losing her *Tweedle Dee* battle to Georgia Gibbs, LaVern eclipsed her closest rival, Etta James, to become the most consistent female rock'n'roller of the fifties, scoring hits with *Jim Dandy, Jim Dandy Got Married* and her biggest *I Cried A Tear,* before retiring to Japan with her husband.

One of LaVern's major rivals was another black girl with a gospel background, Ruth Brown from Portsmouth Virginia. Ruth, on the Atlantic label, enjoyed numerous R&B hits during the fifties, among them the million-selling *5–10–15 Hours* in 1952, *Mama He Treats Your Daughter Mean* in 1953 and *Lucky Lips* in 1957 – the last of which was also a million seller for Cliff Richard when he revived it in 1963. By mid-1960 she had left Atlantic Records and since then has only occasionally performed in public.

The year also saw the rise to prominence of several black vocal groups: the Orioles, the Crows, the Clovers, the Penguins, the Harptones, the Spaniels, the Cadillacs, the Five Royales, the Moonglows and many others. Most of these groups relied on a single lead voice with three or four harmony singers providing occasional emphasis and background 'oohs' and 'aahs', which led them to be termed 'doo wop' groups – 'doo wop' being a favourite background chant. All saw varying degrees of chart activity, but their success was

Considerably less enduring was the ill-starred Johnny Ace. Born in Memphis, Ace returned from service in the U.S. Navy to play piano in the Beale Streeters, a late forties band which also included subsequent blues legends Bobby Bland and B. B. King. His speciality was the 'beat ballad', where he used the rhythms of R&B to decorate something rather more controlled and less frantic than the output of his contemporaries, but he didn't live to witness his greatest success. After recording *Pledging My Love*, a chart topper in early 55, he blew his brains out playing Russian roulette – thus becoming the genre's first and most dramatic fatality.

Ace's erstwhile cohort B. B. King began recording around 1950 and within a few years had become one of the most influential guitarists in the field, cutting an almost uninterrupted string of R&B (although not national) hits through the decade and creating music which would later strongly influence the major figures emerging during the British blues boom of the sixties – Eric Clapton, Jimi Hendrix and Carlos Santana in particular.

'55 the year

Events

1 Apr. Worst outbreaks of violence in Cyprus since 1931.

5 Apr. Sir Winston Churchill resigns as British Prime Minister; Sir Anthony Eden succeeds him.

16 May Rocky Marciano, world heavyweight boxing champion retains his title with a ninth round knockout of Briton Don Cockell.

27 July The Conservatives win the U.K. General Election with a 59 seat majority.

19 Sept. General Peron resigns as President of Argentina.

18 Oct. Scientists at Berkeley announce that they have artificially created anti-protons; this confirms the existence of anti-matter.

26 Oct. Ngo Dinh Diems proclaims South Vietnam as an independent republic and declares himself president.

2 Dec. The American Federation of Labour (A.F.L.) and Congress of Industrial Organizations (C.I.O.) merge; combined membership is over 16 million.

22 Dec. France decides to send 60,000 more troops to Algeria.

Films of 55

Bad Day At Black Rock · Blackboard Jungle · Love Is A Many-Splendoured Thing · Marty · Oklahoma · Rebel Without A Cause · The Seven Year Itch · A Star Is Born

Opposite top left: James Dean in *Rebel Without A Cause.*

Opposite top right: Tom Ewell and Marilyn Monroe in *The Seven Year Itch.*

U.S. CHART TOPPERS – WEEKS AT TOP

Mr. Sandman	Chordettes	2
Let Me Go Lover	Joan Weber	2
Hearts Of Stone	Fontane Sisters	1
Sincerely	McGuire Sisters	6
The Ballad Of Davy Crockett	Bill Hayes	5
Cherry Pink And Apple Blossom White	Perez Prado	10
Rock Around The Clock	Bill Haley and the Comets	8
The Yellow Rose Of Texas	Mitch Miller	6
Love Is A Many Splendoured Thing	Four Aces	5
Autumn Leaves	Roger Williams	2
Sixteen Tons	Tennessee Ernie Ford	5

U.K. CHART TOPPERS – WEEKS AT TOP

Finger Of Suspicion	Dickie Valentine	1
Mambo Italiano	Rosemary Clooney	3
I Need You Now	Eddie Fisher	2
Softly Softly	Ruby Murray	3
Give Me Your Word	Tennessee Ernie Ford	7
Cherry Pink And Apple Blossom White	Perez Prado	2
Stranger In Paradise	Tony Bennett	2
Cherry Pink And Apple Blossom White	Eddie Calvert	4
Unchained Melody	Jimmy Young	3
Dreamboat	Alma Cogan	2
Rose Marie	Slim Whitman	9
The Man From Laramie	Jimmy Young	4
Hernando's Hideaway	Johnston Brothers	2
Rock Around The Clock	Bill Haley and the Comets	5
Christmas Alphabet	Dickie Valentine	3

The Drifters suffered many line-up permutations over the years, although without affecting their popularity significantly. Johnny Moore (second left) replaced Clyde McPhatter as lead singer and fronted the group until 1980, despite several years absence in the late fifties and early sixties.

fleeting compared to that of the Drifters from New York and the Platters from Los Angeles.

The Drifters have continued to operate in one form or another (sometimes in several forms at the same time) since first getting together in 1953 under the management of George Treadwell. Treadwell and his wife, Faye, who took over on George's death in 1967, have always owned the rights to the name of the Drifters and many singers have passed through the group over the years.

The first of several impressive lead vocalists was Clyde McPhatter (previously with another seminal group, Billy Ward and the Dominoes, in which he was replaced by the equally influential Jackie Wilson), who prior to being drafted into the Army sang on their first hit, *Money Honey*. His replacement, Johnny Moore, whose best performance was on the mid-1956 R&B hit *Ruby Baby*, was also called up, and by late 1958 the original group had disbanded.

Treadwell, determined to capitalise on his ownership of the name, signed up another group called the Five Crowns – led by Ben E. King – renamed them the Drifters and under the aegis of the young songwriting/producing team of Jerry Leiber and Mike Stoller, who were independently contracted to Atlantic Records, they entered their most successful period with a string of international

hits. The first of these classics, *There Goes My Baby* – widely cited as the first R&B song with a string arrangement – was a million seller in 1959, and by 1964 they'd had 11 top twenty hits, including *Save The Last Dance For Me*, *Sweets For My Sweet* and *Up On The Roof*.

Of course, there had been numerous personnel changes in the interim: after six hits, Ben E King had left the group for a solo career in 1960, and had been replaced by Rudy Lewis, from Clara Ward's gospel group. He sang lead on the next dozen singles, most of which were successful, before Johnny Moore returned to garner more chart action with *Under The Boardwalk*, *One Way Love*, *At The Club* and *I'll Take You Where The Music's Playing* among others. By 1968, however, the all-conquering Drifters were reduced to cabaret work – which is not to say they were finished, as subsequent chapters reveal.

In late 1955, *Only You* by the Platters reached number five in the U.S. charts despite a cover version by one of Randy Wood's white groups, the Hilltoppers (which also made the top ten). It was to be the first of well over a dozen hits, including four number ones and five gold discs (indicating sales in excess of a million).

Guided by their perceptive manager, Buck Ram, the Platters achieved national success only after 15 year old Zola Taylor had joined the group to complement the magnificent tenor of Tony Williams – and for five years they reigned supreme. In June 1960, however, Williams left the group to go solo and neither he nor the Platters have been able to recapture their proven magic.

The term 'rock'n'roll' was, he claimed, the invention of the era's most prominent and influential disc-jockey, Alan Freed. After moving north from Akron in 1950, Freed made his name hosting *Moondog's Rock'n'Roll Party*, a radio show broadcast from Cleveland Ohio. Inevitably he was offered, and accepted, a job in New York (at Station WINS), where his shows were even more popular with an audience which he was surprised to find mainly white – even though the music he played was still predominantly black. Several of the early rock movies featured Freed, always playing himself, and he also branched out into promoting spectacular all-star stage shows, but towards the end of the decade his career was ruined when he was made principal scapegoat in 'the payola scandal', where

D.J.s were charged with accepting bribes to push certain singles. That he was guilty has never been denied – his name appears in the writer's credits of several songs including Chuck Berry's *Maybelline*, but in his defence, Freed would never play a record he didn't like and he was very supportive of black artists whose material was covered by less-deserving whites. He died in 1965, a much maligned and broken man.

In America, 1955 also saw a flare in popularity for the mambo, novelty smashes in the shape of *The Ballad Of Davy Crockett* by Bill Hayes and *The Yellow Rose Of Texas* by Mitch Miller, and the emergence of Stan Freberg, a comedian specialising in mocking satires of current hits, whose version of *The Yellow Rose Of Texas* is still played.

In Britain, it was business as usual: Dickie Valentine, Ruby Murray, Jimmy Young, David Whitfield, Alma Cogan, Winifred Atwell, Eddie Calvert – but as the year neared its end Bill Haley's *Rock Around The Clock* sat squarely at the top of the charts . . . a taste of things to come.

A nightclub scene from *Rock Around The Clock* spotlights the Platters, arguably the most successful black vocal group of the rock'n'roll era. Left to right: Herb Reed, Dave Lynch, Tony Williams, Zola Taylor and Paul Robi.

'56

'Be Bop A Lula'

Harry Belafonte · Freddie Bell and the Bell Boys · James Brown · Johnny Cash
Sanford Clark · Lonnie Donegan · The Five Satins · Ivory Joe Hunter
Sonny James · Frankie Laine · Little Richard · Jim Lowe · Frankie Lymon
and the Teenagers · Clyde McPhatter · Guy Mitchell · Nervous Norvus
Patience and Prudence · Carl Perkins · Elvis Presley · Johnny Ray
Screaming Jay Hawkins · Shirley and Lee · Tommy Steele · Gene Vincent
and the Blue Caps · Andy Williams

If the British had remained largely unimpressed by the first uncertain screams of rock'n'roll, they were due for a rude awakening in 1956.

The floodgates opened with the arrival of the first real rock film, *Rock Around The Clock* starring Bill Haley and the Comets, Alan Freed, the Platters, and Freddie Bell and the Bell Boys. It was an unsubtle potboiler whose storyline was almost irrelevant; the film was merely a vehicle for the bands and the music. In America, it seems to have caused little commotion (aside from assisting the title song to eventual sales of over 20 million), but in Britain it was a revelation. Loud rock'n'roll thundered around Odeons and Gaumonts all over the country as fans watched Haley and his Comets cavorting and whooping in the face of parental disgust.

The generation gap widened overnight.

By this time, hard core rock'n'rollers had evolved their own anti-establishment garb. In America, teenage rebels merely duplicated the T-shirt and jeans of Brando and Dean, but in Britain they wore a unique 'uniform' which (because of its tenuous connection with Edwardian fashions) inspired the collective term 'Teddy Boys'.

The Ted's appearance was characterised by greasy hair – arranged in the shape of an elephant's trunk at the front and a d.a. (duck's aft, in polite terminology) at the back – with side whiskers, if possible; extremely tight trousers known as 'drainpipes'; bootlace tie; bright socks, luminous if possible; thick crepe-soled shoes with suede uppers (popularly described as 'brothel creepers'); and a long drape jacket with velvet collar and trimmings. A Teddy boy's girlfriend wore a flared skirt, sufficiently loose to reveal suspenders and stocking-tops when jiving; a tight sweater displaying maximum uplift and cleavage; stiletto heels; black seamed stockings; and an overall posture as close to indecency as the times would allow.

When *Rock Around The Clock* was first shown in Britain, the Teddy boys and girls impulsively left their seats to dance in the aisles – much to the horror of cinema managers previously used to no greater activity than gentle stampedes towards the ice-cream salesperson – and disciplinary action by the staff provoked the Teds to vent their spleen on the seats, which they either smashed or slashed with their favoured weapon, the cut-throat razor.

After the first spontaneous skirmishes, reported in the usual exaggeratedly lurid detail by the press, it became de rigeur to dance and slash seats during the film, which was widely banned as a result. The popular music scene immediately divided into two camps: for rock'n'roll and against rock'n'roll – with a number of fence-sitters trying to keep the peace.

The backlash induced a surge in popularity for many waning stars of the old school, though for most of them it was to be a short-lived revival.

Guy Mitchell's career had been very cold for three years, but it revived with *Singing The Blues* (a number one in America and Britain) and *Knee Deep In The Blues*. Other hits followed including the British number one *Rock-a-Billy* in 1957 and the American number one *Heartaches By The Number* in 1959, but after this he faded away into cabaret.

Johnnie Ray also made an apparently strong comeback in 1956. Ray, the most intense and histrionic white singer before Presley, came to prominence when his first single, the highly emotional, sob-filled *Cry/The Little White Cloud That Cried*, sold over two million copies in 1951. The hits continued and Ray (now dubbed 'The Cry Guy') attracted a vast female audience motivated by material instincts (he was partly deaf and said to be unhappy).

After dwindling sales, *Just Walking In The Rain* (a cover of the Prisonaires' original on Sun) returned him to the top of the charts in 1956 and further singles, including another U.K. number one in *Yes Tonight Josephine*, kept him buoyant for another year. By early 1958, however, 'The Prince of Wails' was out of vogue and en route for Las Vegas to become a secondary attraction to roulette wheels.

Francis LoVecchio, better known as Frankie

Guy Mitchell, a major hit-maker in the early fifties, revived his flagging fortunes by adding a rock beat to *Singing The Blues*, originally an American country hit for Marty Robbins.

Laine, also returned to chart prominence in 1956 when *Moonlight Gambler* became his ninth million-seller. Laine, practically unknown until he was 36, was a consistent hitmaker from 1947 until 1953 – often singing romantic cowboy ballads like *Mule Train* and *The Cry Of The Wild Goose*.

In America, he began to slip from his throne in 1954, though in Britain he was probably the most prolific hitmaker of 1955, achieving no less than six top twenty entries. When *Moonlight Gambler* reached number three in America, Laine must have thought his comeback was assured, but it was not to be: the man said to be able to fill even the largest auditorium without the aid of amplification was in the out-tray – though he continues to tour and perform even today.

A close contemporary of Laine's (they were born within a year of each other), Perry Como, was one of the few ballad singers of the old school apparently unaffected by rock'n'roll – as his score of over ninety hits between 1944 and today confirms. After a relatively poor year in 1955, Como bounced back with two million-sellers the following year – *Hot Diggity* and *More* – and since then his durability has been a constant source of admiration to his fans.

However, much as the old guard fought on, they had no defences against the new wave; leading the attack, and now backed by the powerful resources of R.C.A., was Elvis Presley. His first single for the label, *Heartbreak Hotel*, was the fastest seller they'd ever released, and by March 1956 was topping all U.S. charts. In a pattern to be repeated many times over the years, his immediate acceptance by the young was scorned by the older critics who called him 'an unspeakably untalented and vulgar young entertainer' and compared his movements, rather pathetically, to 'an aborigine's mating dance'.

Elvis walked over them, however, as his success escalated furiously during the following weeks – to the point where television companies were falling over themselves to secure his appearance. Even the staid Ed Sullivan got in on the act – and Presley's appearance on his show in September 1956 rivetted an incredible 80% of America's T.V. audience. R.C.A., almost half of whose total sales were attributable to Elvis, saturated the market in an attempt to meet the insatiable demand for Presley

Right: Johnny Ray demonstrates his famous emotion-charged delivery.

Top: Frankie Laine woos starlet Jill Day on a promotional visit to Britain.

Far right: Perry Como's popularity was boosted by his long-running weekly T.V. show, which showcased rising stars of the day.

With acoustic guitar and necktie he looks more like a country musician than the undisputed King of Rock'n' roll, yet in 1956 Elvis obliterated all opposition to become the biggest ever phenomenon in popular music.

As well as being an interesting and much copied songwriter, Perkins was a fine guitarist but his career was nipped in the bud when a car crash laid him up for most of the year. He never managed to repeat his initial feat, achieving only four entries in the lower half of the top hundred during the later fifties, and although he has now resumed a solo career, he spent many years playing guitar in Johnny Cash's group.

Cash, an Arkansas farm boy who found himself in Memphis when discharged from the Air Force the previous year, also started out on Sun Records in 1956. His weather-beaten voice combined with the sparse backing of his group, the Tennessee Two, to produce a unique, melancholy sound which appealed to both country and rock fans. Most of his early hits portrayed him as the jilted lover, though the lyrics were usually set to a jaunty rockabilly rhythm. After three top twenty singles (*I Walk The Line* in 1958, *Ballad Of A Teenage Queen* and *Guess Things Happen That Way* in 1958), he left Sun for Columbia where he has remained ever since.

During the sixties and seventies, Cash, possibly country music's most illustrious superstar, associated himself with such romantic causes as prison entertaining and the preservation of Red Indian heritage, as well as establishing strong Christian beliefs after a period off the straight and narrow.

As Elvis broke through, other major labels sought their own equivalent – but only Capitol had the fortune to stumble across an immediate winner.

Gene Vincent, on extended leave from the U.S. Navy because of a severe leg injury incurred during a spell as a motorcycle despatch rider on the base at his home town of Norfolk Virginia, began singing with the local radio station housebound during early 1956. A prominent local D.J., the self-styled 'Sheriff' Tex Davis, put together the cream of the local musicians to back Gene on a demo tape, which he sent to a friend at Capitol, who duly signed him. The subsequent single, *Be Bop A Lula*, reached number nine in Summer 56 – establishing Gene and his group, the Blue Caps, as a major attraction.

Gene's outstanding guitarist, Cliff Gallup, who played on *Be Bop A Lula* and his biggest U.K. hit, *Blue Jean Bop*, was a source of inspiration to many sixties guitarists including George Harrison and Jeff Beck – and when he left the group at the end of the year, Gene was lucky enough to find a dynamic replacement in Johnny Meeks who sparkled on the 1957 hit, *Lotta Lovin'*.

After folding the Blue Caps, Vincent moved to England where he enjoyed a new lease of life during the early sixties. Problems caused by his leg (which he'd never allowed to heal), his desperate financial condition and his dwindling career led him to alcohol, which was a contributory cause of his early death in 1971.

Probably the most tragic of all rock'n'roll casualties, Vincent has remained a lasting influence.

The most impressive black newcomer was Little Richard. Born in Macon Georgia in 1932, Richard Penniman sang in his church choir and was, at 19, signed to R.C.A. as a gospel singer. By 1955, he was considered a 'has been' in record company terms and was working as a dish-washer at the Greyhound bus station in Macon – but a demo tape convinced

product and sales totalling over ten million resulted in eight sides reaching the U.S. top 40 (including three number ones) and seven reaching the U.K. top twenty. Apart from *Heartbreak Hotel*, his greatest successes were *I Want You, I Need You, I Love You*; *Hound Dog*; *Don't Be Cruel* and *Love Me Tender*.

Little had changed in Presley's approach to recording: he still used Scotty Moore and Bill Black, though he now employed a drummer (D. J. Fontana), often a pianist (usually Floyd Cramer or Shorty Long) and a vocal backing group (the Jordanaires). The studio location moved from Memphis to Nashville to New York and later in the year to Hollywood, where Elvis was making his first film, *Love Me Tender*.

Compared with some of his subsequent forays onto celluloid, *Love Me Tender* is a fairly reasonable film – allowing Presley to try his acting wings as well as singing a few songs, all of which give him a co-writing credit (a move probably instigated by Colonel Tom Parker, since Elvis was not a natural songsmith).

Meanwhile, his 'discoverer', Sam Phillips, was seeking another Presley figure – and though his next signing had little of Elvis's charisma, he did achieve immediate success with his first single. Carl Perkins, formerly a country and western artist, reached the U.S. top five early in 1956 with a song which was to become a rock'n'roll standard, *Blue Suede Shoes*.

boards. His subsequent recordings were far from spectacular, though his shows still contained much of the magic that had made him famous.

Also working in Macon Georgia was James Brown, who, with his band the famous Flames, had his first million seller, *Please Please Please*, in 1956. One of the first of the great soul singers, his influence on black (and white) music has been considerable – as his string of almost 100 U.S. hit singles testifies.

It was perhaps his stage antics rather than his dramatic singing style which eventually acquired for Brown his huge audience. While his band wore uniform suits and were very neatly turned out, Brown would wail, scream and expend so much energy that he collapsed in mid performance – as if suffering a cardiac arrest. A heartbroken musician would examine the body, make it obvious that there was little chance of survival, and assist in his removal from the stage. Brown would then make a miraculous recovery and return to the song – which his band, very conveniently, had continued to play. Contrived and close to vaudeville maybe, but his was (and is) one of the most successful stage acts in rock'n'roll. Without ever reaching a white audience to the degree achieved by Little Richard and Chuck

Carl Perkins (*top left*) continues to command a strong cult following today, and like Johnny Cash (*below left*) was a country singer discovered by Sam Phillips.

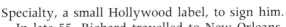

Specialty, a small Hollywood label, to sign him.

In late 55, Richard travelled to New Orleans to record the first of a string of smash hits including seven million-sellers: *Tutti-Frutti, Long Tall Sally, Rip It Up, Lucille, Jenny Jenny, Keep A-Knockin'* and *Good Golly Miss Molly*. His wild vocals and frantic piano playing made him one of the most exciting performers of all time – but in 1957 his gospel background got the better of him when a Specialty colleague, Joe Lutcher, influenced him to dedicate himself to God.

He quit rock'n'roll in favour of bible study, preaching, and releasing the occasional gospel recording.

The lure of the greasepaint prevailed, however, and in the early sixties Little Richard returned to the

Above: A memorable sequence from *The Girl Can't Help It* featured Gene Vincent and the Blue Caps recreating their smash hit *Be Bop A Lula*. Left to right: Russell Willaford (who briefly replaced original guitarist Cliff Gallup), Dickie Harrel, Gene Vincent, Jack Neal and Willie Williams.

Little Richard brought both exuberance and a sense of style to the music, and is one of the few creators of rock music still performing.

Above: Frankie Lymon and the Teenagers rehearse a routine in the foyer of the London Palladium, where their performances drew hysterical acclaim.

Above right: The Five Satins, who will always be remembered for their classic *In The Still Of The Night.*

Wild Man of Rock: Screaming Jay Hawkins.

Berry, Brown managed to sustain consistent success – and many of his records, notably *I'll Go Crazy, Night Train, Out Of Sight, Papa's Got A Brand New Bag* and *It's A Man's Man's Man's World*, were widely copied during the British R&B boom of the sixties.

Of the many black vocal groups to reach the charts during 1956, two are worthy of special mention. In February, Frankie Lymon and the Teenagers made a strong impact with *Why Do Fools Fall In Love?* Lymon was only 13 when the record was made and his dynamic, as yet unbroken voice gave it considerable appeal. After several less successful follow-ups, Lymon left the group for a solo career but received scant attention after his voice broke. In 1961, his drug problems came to the attention of the media and his failure to make any commercial headway gave him little impetus to kick the habit. In February 1968, 12 years after his dramatic entrance, an overdose of heroin took his life.

It is interesting to note that for some years after Lymon's departure, the Teenagers continued with a girl singer whose voice bore an uncanny resemblance to that of Frankie.

The other group whose innovation has stood the test of time is the Five Satins. Though their chart career was erratic, their single of *In The Still Of The Night* is regarded as the finest of all 'doo wop' records. Allegedly written by their lead singer, Fred Parris, during a long night of army guard duty, and cut in the basement of a New Haven church, it was picked up by the nationally distributed Ember label and eventually sold a million.

Among other singers to achieve national fame in 1956 were the demented Nervous Norvus who took automobile-accident-rock into the U.S. top twenty with *Transfusion*; country turned rockabilly singer Sanford Clark who made the top ten with *The Fool*; Shirley and Lee who recorded a classic in *Let The Good Times Roll*; Patience and Prudence who had two smash hits with *Tonight You Belong To Me* and *Gonna Get Along Without You Now*; ex-Drifter Clyde McPhatter, who began his solo career with *Seven Days* and *Treasure Of Love*; Jim Lowe who reached number one with *The Green Door*; Sonny James who made number two with *Young Love* – a song successfully covered by actor Tab Hunter whose version reached number one; R&B singer Ivory Joe *Hunter* who scored his only top twenty hit with *Since I Met You Baby*; and Harry Belafonte whose *Jamaica Farewell* was about to precipitate a short-lived calypso craze.

Another big name to emerge in 1956 was Andy Williams, who began his chart career with *Walk Hand In Hand*, *Canadian Sunset* and *Baby Doll* – while at the other end of the spectrum was ex-teenage boxing champion Screaming Jay Hawkins.

Rumour has it that his very influential hit, *I Put A Spell On You*, was recorded whilst Hawkins was in a state of extreme inebriation – which would account for the wildly abandoned vocal. Hawkins, who would emerge from a coffin to begin his stage act, had all the makings of a bizarre star. Never to be seen without a zebra-striped tuxedo, a skull or two, and a selection of miniature flashing devices, he unaccountably faded into obscurity – though his image was later successfully recreated in England by Screaming Lord Sutch.

The England of 1956 had little to offer in the way of homegrown rock talent until the coffee bar 'discovery' of Tommy Hicks in September. Hicks (immediately renamed Steele), the first British born rock'n'roller, soon deteriorated into an 'all round entertainer' but his rise to fame was to be the pattern for literally hundreds of lesser talents hoping to follow in his footsteps. An occasional member of the Vipers Skiffle Group, who worked at the 2Is coffee bar in Old Compton Street Soho, Steele had just escaped the Merchant Navy when spotted by his subsequent managers, the enterprising John Kennedy and Larry Parnes.

With a hastily assembled backing group, inventively dubbed the Steelmen, the former cabin boy recorded *Rock With The Caveman,* a song written by two of his mates, Mike Pratt (later an actor) and Lionel Bart (later a musical playwright). In October, it reached number 11 in the U.K. chart despite its overall shoddiness – a characteristic which hampered most British records until the arrival of Cliff Richard. Most homegrown attempts at rock'n'roll were thin, weedy confections rendered even less digestible by the total lack of understanding and interest displayed by almost every musician involved – most of whom were refugees from the jazz or big band worlds grudgingly earning a little extra cash by playing music they despised.

With his face plastered over every publication, the unchallenged Londoner soon shot to number one with his cover of Guy Mitchell's American hit *Singin' The Blues* – though his third single (a cover of Mitchell's *Knee Deep In The Blues*) was less successful. By this time, Steele was being taken very seriously by the British entertainment industry, who decided that his meteoric rise to fame should be documented on film – the result being that only nine months after his plucking from the 21s, he was the subject of a major film, *The Tommy Steele Story.* It was all but the end of his rock'n'roll career; his style softened and most of his later singles contained about as much fire as an ice cube. He quickly became acceptable to parents and eventually found cinematic fame with the Walt Disney Studios for whom he starred in 'family films' like *Half A Sixpence.*

Steele's only serious rival was a skiffler rather than a rocker: Lonnie Donegan.

Donegan's rise to fame was bizarre in the extreme. A Scotsman by birth, he had played in various traditional jazz bands, the first major group being led by trumpeter Ken Colyer, who was regarded as the most authentic Dixieland player around as he had actually been to New Orleans, the home of his chosen music.

During 1954, Colyer's entire band left their leader and reformed as the Chris Barber Band, with Donegan on guitar and banjo. To break up the set, Donegan was allowed to feature his particular interest – skiffle music, which was an off-shoot of jazz played on improvised musical instruments such as kazoos, tea-chest and broomhandle basses and empty cider jugs. Accompanied simply by bass and washboard, his nasal intonation of American folk and blues songs, freely adapted from the recorded works of Woody Guthrie and Huddie Leadbetter, were a marked contrast to Barber's pumping jazz – and Donegan soon gathered a solid following.

His first recordings were token tracks on Barber albums but one song, a version of Leadbelly's *Rock Island Line* was deemed suitable for single release. In 1956, it stormed into both the American and British top ten, influencing Donegan to leave Barber and launch a career of his own. Accompanied by his Skiffle Group, Donegan became a consistent hit-maker, registering over 30 U.K. chart entries between 1956 and 1962 – though his success extended to America only once more, when his music hall novelty *Does Your Chewing Gum Lose Its Flavour On The Bedpost Overnight* reached number five in 1961.

Donegan's influence on British music in the late fifties is incalculable. His basic three chord style was demonstrably very easy to copy and apart from anything else resulted in the sale of many thousands of guitars to aspiring skifflers (included among whom were the authors of this book).

Left: The tunes of Tommy Steele were slightly less monotonous than those of his sweater, but had little more to do with rock'n'roll. He soon stopped rocking to become an all-round entertainer and film star.

Below: Lonnie Donegan renounced his jazz career to concentrate on 'skiffle', and with a group of similarly dissatisfied jazzers he created a new musical fad in the U.K.

'56 the year

Events

11 Feb. Soviet spies Guy Burgess and Don Maclean appear in Moscow, having escaped from the U.K.

25 Feb. Kruschev attacks Stalin in a secret speech at the Communist Party Congress.

9 Mar. Archbishop Makarios is deported from Cyprus.

18 Apr. Prince Rainier of Monaco marries Hollywood star Grace Kelly.

6 June The Miami Board of Review campaigns against 'this worm wiggle' after 10,000 dance in the aisles at a local Bill Haley concert.

26 July President Nasser announces the nationalisation of the Suez Canal.

25 Oct. Adolf Hitler officially declared dead by West Germany.

31 Oct. British planes bomb Egyptian airfields in preparation for an Anglo-French invasion.

4 Nov. Soviet forces attack and bomb Budapest, Hungary.

6 Nov. President Eisenhower re-elected over Democrat candidate Adlai Stevenson.

Films of 56

Anastasia · Around The World In 80 Days · East Of Eden · The King And I · Moby Dick · Rock Around The Clock · The Searchers · The Ten Commandments

Right: Grace Kelly and Prince Rainier.

Opposite left: a Teddy Boy.

Opposite right: Yul Brynner and Deborah Kerr in *The King And I.*

U.S. CHART TOPPERS – WEEKS AT TOP

Sixteen Tons	Tennessee Ernie Ford	1
Memories Are Made Of This	Dean Martin	5
The Great Pretender	Platters	2
Rock And Roll Waltz	Kay Starr	3
Poor People Of Paris	Les Baxter	6
Heartbreak Hotel	Elvis Presley	6
The Wayward Wind	Cogi Grant	7
I Almost Lost My Mind	Pat Boone	2
My Prayer	Platters	4
Don't Be Cruel	Elvis Presley	7
The Green Door	Jim Lowe	2
Love Me Tender	Elvis Presley	4
Singing The Blues	Guy Mitchell	3

U.K. CHART TOPPERS – WEEKS AT TOP

Rock Around The Clock	Bill Haley and the Comets	2
Sixteen Tons	Tennessee Ernie Ford	4
Memories Are Made Of This	Dean Martin	4
It's Almost Tomorrow	Dream Weavers	3
Rock And Roll Waltz	Kay Starr	1
Poor People Of Paris	Winifred Atwell	3
No Other Love	Ronnie Hilton	6
I'll Be Home	Pat Boone	5
Why Do Fools Fall In Love?	Frankie Lymon and the Teenagers	3
Que Sera Sera	Doris Day	6
Lay Down Your Arms	Anne Shelton	4
Woman In Love	Frankie Laine	4
Just Walkin' In The Rain	Johnnie Ray	7

SIXTEEN TONS
By MERLE TRAVIS

Recorded by
"Tennessee" Ernie Ford
on Capitol Records

Glad Rag Doll

RECORDED BY
JOHNNIE RAY
ON PHILIPS RECORD P.B. 123
Price
2/6

Laurence Wright

You are my First Love

Words by PADDY ROBERTS • music by LESTER POWELL
as sung by RUBY MURRAY on Columbia Records
FROM THE ASSOCIATED BRITISH FILM

IT'S
GREAT
TO
BE
YOUNG

A MARBLE ARCH PRODUCTION

Starring
JOHN MILLS
AND
CECIL PARKER

'57

'That'll Be The Day'

Paul Anka · Jimmy Bowen · Ruth Brown · Dick Clark · The Coasters
Sam Cooke · Jim Dale · The Del Vikings · Terry Dene · The Diamonds
The Everly Brothers · Adam Faith · Charlie Gracie · Wee Willie Harris
Buddy Holly and the Crickets · Buddy Knox · Jerry Lee Lewis
The Johnny Otis Show · Jim Reeves · Jimmie Rodgers · Tommy Sands
The Vipers · Larry Williams · Jackie Wilson

Whilst 1957 saw the arrival of several major new rock artists, it also saw the fall of the first hero.

Bill Haley had actually faltered badly in America during 1956, though his British chart success continued happily with seven hits. 1957 also began with promise but by March, his reign was over. Coincidentally, this was around the time that Haley became the first U.S. rock star to tour Britain. Wild enthusiasm greeted his arrival but soon dwindled as it became apparent he was not quite what had been expected. He was, indeed, quite plump and quite old – and the youth of Britain, seeing more resemblance to their fathers than to Elvis, concluded he was one of 'them' rather than one of 'us'.

His career experienced a rather abrupt decline, though he did manage to star in his second Non-Academy Award movie, *Don't Knock The Rock*, which was little different from its predecessor save for some cast substitutions (the excellent Little Richard for the weak Freddie Bell and the inferior Treniers for the superb Platters).

Here today and gone tomorrow: the story of popular music. Bill Haley was the first rocker to find out.

Meanwhile, Presley's dramatic escalation had inspired fevered activity in recording studios around America, and a small independent studio in Clovis New Mexico, owned and operated by one Norman Petty, was doing particularly well in producing two top twenty hits, *Party Doll* by Buddy Knox and *I'm Sticking With You* by Jimmy Bowen

Buddy Holly, an aspiring rock star from Lubbock Texas, decided to travel to Clovis in order to make the best possible tape with which to try for a record contract. He'd started out, with little success, as a country singer, but turned to rock on hearing Elvis – assembling his own group, the Crickets: Holly on guitar and vocals, Niki Sullivan on rhythm guitar, Joe B. Mauldin on bass, and Jerry Allison on drums. Petty was not slow to recognise Holly's potential and a business alliance was formed, leading to simultaneous recording contracts under the name of the Crickets and Buddy Holly.

The Cricket's first release, in Summer 57, was a Holly/Allison song *That'll Be The Day*, which scorched to number three in the U.S. charts and number one in Britain. It was followed later in the year, by another top tenner *Oh Boy* and the equally successful *Peggy Sue*, the latter issued under Holly's name. It was the start of a little under two years of concentrated success, which saw the prolific Holly write and record a stream of much-copied classics, including *Not Fade Away*, *True Love Ways*, *Words Of Love*, *Rave On* and many more.

His major appeal was the quality of his songs and the imagination behind their recording; a combination whose consistence was unique in the rock 'n'roll field: his 'boy next door' looks, highlighted by the horn-rimmed glasses (later adopted by Elton John and Elvis Costello for similar reasons), compensated for his lack of Presleyan animality and secured a fanatical following.

As well as singing his hits on the Ed Sullivan T.V. Show, Holly toured the states with a typical package show of the day: *The Biggest Show Of Stars For 57*, also featuring Fats Domino, the Drifters, Frankie Lymon and the Teenagers, LaVern Baker, Chuck Berry, Clyde McPhatter, Paul Anka and a duo whose *Wake Up Little Susie* was currently topping the charts... the Everly Brothers.

Don and Phil Everly, the sons of successful country musicians, had appeared on their parents' Kentucky radio show since 1945 – when Don was eight and Phil six – so, despite their youth, they were relative veterans when they signed with Cadence Records in 1957. Their first success, *Bye Bye Love*, was a landslide hit and precipitated a career which over the next five years would bring them no less than 15 top ten singles including *All I Have To Do Is Dream*, *Bird Dog*, *Problems*, *Cathy's Clown* and *Walk Right Back*.

Among other country singers to beef up their sound and approach to succeed in 1957's rock market were Patsy Cline, whose *Walkin' After Midnight* made the top twenty; Ferlin Husky, a top fiver with *Gone*; Marty Robbins, whose *White Sport Coat* hung at number three; George Hamilton IV,

Opposite top: Early and late shots of Buddy Holly and the Crickets.

Bill Haley (with kiss curl) and the Comets in a scene from *Don't Knock The Rock*. They were the first white stars of rock'n'roll, but were being superseded by 57.

Above left: Phil (left) and Don were the Everly Brothers – inventive on vinyl and stylish on stage; the Everlys remained impressive until their split in 1973.

Above centre: Korean War veteran Jimmie Rodgers succeeded with a blend of folk, country and rock. His biggest British hit, *English Country Garden*, never made the American charts.

Above right: Jim Reeves (right) was a country music star with a wide appeal.

whose *Why Don't They Understand* was a generation gap winner; and Jimmie Rodgers, a chart topper with *Honeycomb*.

Rodgers, the son of country star Hank Snow, was christened Jimmie Rodgers Snow because of his father's huge admiration for the legendary *Singing Brakeman*, who died from tuberculosis in 1933 – the year his namesake was born. Following *Honeycomb*, he scored three further top twenty hits within a year – after which he returned to the chart intermittently until 1967 when he was found in his car in Los Angeles with a fractured skull, the cause of which he was unable to explain. He was forced to stop performing and appears not to have been mentioned in despatches since then.

Destined to become the biggest country star of the sixties was Jim Reeves. Already an avuncular 33 years old, the soft-voiced Texan reached number 12 with *Four Walls*, named best country and western song of 1957. His chart career continued even after his plane crash death in 1964, especially in Britain, where two-thirds of his 24 hits were posthumous – including his only number one, *Distant Drums*.

The most spectacular convert from country music to rock'n'roll was the great Jerry Lee Lewis – a brilliant musician and singer, and a 22 carat rebel. He burst onto the scene with two of the year's most

dramatic singles: *Whole Lotta Shakin' Goin' On* and *Great Balls Of Fire*, both top ten smashes on each side of the Atlantic.

Lewis, the most influential pianist of the era, was another of Sam Phillips' trump cards (his early Sun records were billed as 'Jerry Lee Lewis and his pumping piano'), and he was on course for superstardom until he married his cousin, Myra Brown, in 1958. When the world learned that Myra, ten years his junior, was only 13 years old, they crucified him. Despite a string of excellent singles, his chart showings were poor and in 1963 he returned to the country field where he managed to work up a new reputation. From time to time, he can still be convinced to perform his rock'n'roll repertoire and he remains the most charismatic of all fifties rockers.

Of all black groups to emerge during the year, by far the most interesting and important were the Coasters, whose triumphs were engineered by those backroom boys Leiber and Stoller (mentioned under 1955 in connection with the Drifters). After a hesitant start as the Robins, whose only degree of success was the minor hit *Smokey Joe's Cafe*, they switched personnel and changed their name . . . and in the summer of 1957 both sides of their single *Searchin'/Young Blood*, reached the U.S. top ten.

A break with Leiber and Stoller and numerous line-up changes meant the Coasters declined and finally dispersed in the sixties, but their achievements will never be forgotten.

were all top ten smashes in 1958 and 1959 – years when no other group could approach them for invention and originality.

Other groups to make an impact included the Diamonds (with *Little Darlin'*, *The Stroll* and *She Say* in 1959) a white quartet specialising in cover versions, and an integrated crew (three blacks and two whites) of Air Force buddies called the Del Vikings who made two classics in 1957: *Come Go With Me* and *Whispering Bells*.

Sam Cooke, Jackie Wilson, Larry Williams and Harry Belafonte were the most influential black singers to establish themselves.

Cooke, originally a member of a gospel group called the Soul Stirrers, moved into the rock arena with *You Send Me*, an American chart topper in late 57. From then until 1966, he was rarely out of the charts – even though he died (in an unsatisfactorily explained hotel shooting) in December 1964. His run of over 40 hits included *Only Sixteen*, *Wonderful World*, *Chain Gang*, *Twisting The Night Away*, *Another Saturday Night* and many other historic milestones.

Jackie Wilson, a more dynamic vocalist than the smooth-voiced Cooke, replaced Clyde McPhatter as lead singer in Billy Ward and the Dominoes, with whom he stayed until launching a solo career in 1957. Strangly enough, his first single, *Reet Petite*, written by Berry Gordy (then a struggling Detroit songwriter, later the founder of Tamla–Motown), made a greater impact in Britain – although he subsequently became one of the biggest soul artists in America, scoring over 60 hits. A true original, Wilson had top ten hits with *Lonely Teardrops*, *Night Alone At Last*, *My Empty Arms*, *Baby Workout* and *Higher And Higher*, and he was enjoying a new lease of life (due to his rediscovery by a new generation of soul afficionados) when a heart attack, suffered on stage in New Jersey in 1975, resulted in a coma from which he has not yet recovered.

Van Morrison has cited Wilson as his major influence, and many artists including the Beatles and Rolling Stones fell under the spell of Larry Williams.

Short Fat Fannie opened his run of powerful hits which included *Bony Maronie* and *Dizzy Miss*

Their subsequent stream of over a dozen hits, all written by their perceptive producers, were characterised by a snappy tune and rhythm, a humorous lyric involving the social or parental problems of a repressed teenager, and a solo by the best of fifties saxplayers, King Curtis. *Yakety Yak*, *Charlie Brown*, *Along Came Jones* and *Poison Ivy*

Lizzie, but his success was relatively short-lived and he ultimately quit performing in favour of producing.

Though anything but a rocker, Jamaican born Harry Belafonte was instrumental in shaping one of popular music's periodic trends – this one being the 'calypso' craze which ran through 1957. A folk group, the Tarriers, who'd secured a hit with *Cindy Oh Cindy* the previous year, introduced the vogue with the *The Banana Boat Song*, but Belafonte reaped the rewards with his own *Banana Boat* and five further hits within a six month period.

Few other 57 newcomers have survived – indeed, some had disappeared by 1958, although many of the year's flash-in-the-pan hits were excellent. They included *So Rare* by Jimmy Dorsey, *A Thousand Miles Away* by the Heartbeats, *Over The Mountain* by Johnnie and Joe, *Stardust* and *Deep Purple* by Billy Ward and the Dominoes, *Teenage Crush* by Tommy Sands, *Mr. Lee* by the Bobettes, *Happy Happy Birthday Baby* by the Tune Weavers, *Little Bitty Pretty One* by Thurston Harris, *Silhouettes* by the Rays, *At The Hop* by Danny and the Juniors, *Buzz Buzz Buzz* by the Hollywood Flames, *Oh Julie* by the Crescendos, and *Raunchy* by Bill Justis.

Displaying somewhat greater longevity were Dale Hawkins, Lec Andrew and the Hearts, Huey Smith and the Clowns, and two particularly interesting young chartcrashers, Paul Anka and Charlie Gracie.

Anka, a 16 year old Canadian, exploded into the headlines with the imaginatively produced *Diana* on which he pleaded for the love of an older girl. The song topped the British charts for over two months and eventually sold more than nine million copies.

After a run of best selling but rather less frenetic follow-ups (including the chart topping *Lonely Boy* and several heavily emotional ballads like *You Are My Destiny*, *Put Your Head On My Shoulder* and *Puppy Love*), he left the rock circuit for a more 'respectable' career as an 'all round entertainer' – pausing en route to write several songs including Frank Sinatra's *My Way* and his own seventies comeback *You're Having My Baby*.

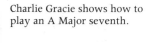

Charlie Gracie shows how to play an A Major seventh.

A national T.V. show, *American Bandstand*, hosted by Dick Clark and broadcast from Philadelphia, became the cement of a generation, setting its dress, dances, heroes and modes of behaviour. Naturally, much of the talent was of local extraction, and one of the first to benefit from this countrywide T.V. exposure was Charlie Gracie.

'57 the year

Events

9 Jan. Harold Macmillan becomes Prime Minister.

24 Sept. Federal troops are sent to Little Rock, Arkansas to enforce school integration.

4 Oct. Russia launches Sputnik I, the first satellite.

19 Oct. Little Richard throws rings worth $8,000 into the Hunter River, Australia to renounce the devil and show his faith in God.

18 Dec. The first atomic power plant, at Shippingport, Pennsylvania, begins to produce electricity.

Films of 57

The Bridge On The River Kwai · Funny Face · The Girl Can't Help It · Gunfight At The OK Corral · Jailhouse Rock · Paths Of Glory · Peyton Place · Twelve Angry Men

Below: an Alan Freed rock'n'roll show.

Opposite: Gunfight At The O.K. Corral.

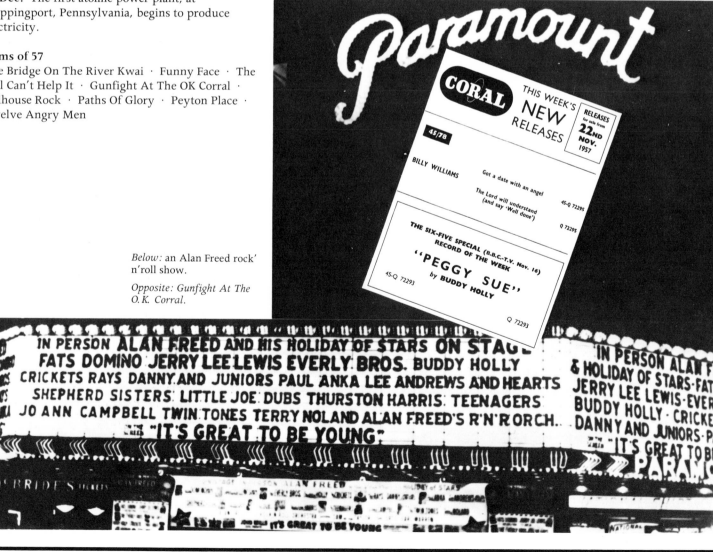

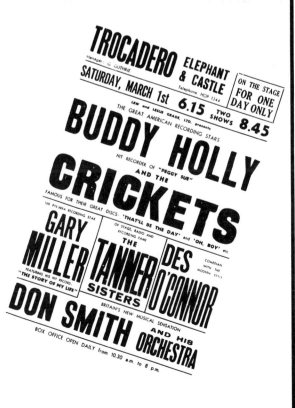

Although it only came to light during the sub-sequent payola scandal, a slice of Gracie's royalties was going to the show's producer – so it was in his interest to plug Gracie's single, *Butterfly*, which soon entered the top ten. A very Presleyish follow-up, *Fabulous*, showcasing Gracie's excellent guitar playing, made some impact but he was already fading in 1958 – despite further appearances on *Bandstand* (which was soon to launch the careers of Frankie Avalon and Fabian among others) and a cameo role in another low-budget rock movie, *Disc Jockey Jamboree*.

Notwithstanding aesthetic shortcomings, *Jamboree* featured an impressive cast and gave audiences the opportunities to see Jerry Lee Lewis, Fats Domino, Buddy Knox and Carl Perkins strut-ting their stuff. Oblivious to ridiculously thin story lines, rock fans also flocked to see their idols in two other hastily knocked out rock films, *Rock Rock Rock* with Chuck Berry, LaVern Baker and Frankie Lymon and the Teenagers, and *The Big Beat* with Fats Domino, the Diamonds and the Del Vikings. Elvis also furthered his screen career with two of his best films: *Loving You* and *Jailhouse Rock*. The plots were lightweight (he played a truck driver turned rock star in the former, a jailbird turned rock star in the latter), but the songs were substantial enough to provide several more huge hits including *Teddy Bear*, *Let's Have A Party*, *Got A Lot Of Living To Do*, *Treat Me Nice* and *Jailhouse Rock* – his sixth American number one.

This was also the year when the B.B.C. transmit-ted its first weekly television show called *The Six Five Special* and produced by Jack Good. The artists he presented on this particularly diverse pro-gramme were mainly weak copyists of the American greats, but Terry Dene, Jim Dale, Marty Wilde, Tommy Steele, Adam Faith, Wee Willie Harris and the Vipers all received tremendous boosts to their careers.

The Vipers were the only group to challenge 'skiffle king' Lonnie Donegan. They achieved three British top twenty entries during 1957 but found it

impossible to make the transition to rock'n'roll when the skiffle fad died.

Still in its infancy in Britain, rock'n'roll was constantly under fire. 'Rock'n'roll is a revival of devil dancing. The effect will be to turn young people into devil worshippers, to stimulate self-expression through sex, to provoke lawlessness and impair nervous stability' declared one noted clergyman. Undeterred, a young credit control clerk at Ferguson's T.V. factory in Enfield sat dreaming about his chances of getting somewhere in the music business. His name was Harry Webb.

It wouldn't be until May 1958 that one of his friends would convince him to change it to Cliff Richard.

Top: Presley jives in *Jail-house Rock.*

Above: The Vipers, leading skifflers, celebrate their first night of their headlining national tour. Frontman Wally Whyton (centre) later became a children's T.V. personality and is now a res-pected country music artist and disc-jockey.

'58

'Three Steps To Heaven'

Frankie Avalon · The Champs · The Chantels · Jimmy Clanton · Eddie Cochran
Bobby Darin · Dion and the Belmonts · Duane Eddy · Fabian · The Four Preps
Connie Francis · Annette Funicello · Don Gibson · The Kalin Twins
The Kingston Trio · Ricky Nelson · The Poni-tails · Cliff Richard · Jack Scott
The Silhouettes · The Teddy Bears · Conway Twitty · Marty Wilde · Link Wray

'Each successive pop music explosion has come roaring out of the clubs in which it was born like an angry bull. Watching from the other side of the gate, the current establishment has proclaimed it dangerous, subversive, a menace to youth, and demanded something be done about it. Something is. Commercial exploitation advances towards it holding out a bucketful of recording contracts, television appearances and world-wide fame. Then, once the muzzle is safely buried in the golden mash, the cunning butcher nips deftly along the flank and castrates the animal. After this painless operation, the establishment realises it is safe to advance into the field and gingerly pats the now docile creature which can then be safely relied on to grow fatter and stupider until the moment when fashion decides it is ready for the slaughterhouse.'

So noted the perceptive commentator George Melly... and in the case of rock'n'roll this castration took place in 1958 – on 24th March to be precise – when Elvis Presley was sheared and drafted into the U.S. Army for his national service.

Presley's induction received maximum publicity, of course, but to his credit he asked for no special treatment – despite bizarre offers from various units

When Uncle Sam called up Elvis, the entire rock'n'roll scene changed for ever.

of the military. His fourth film *King Creole* was in the can, as were a stockpile of recordings ready for periodic release throughout his absence – and in commercial terms his progress was unaffected.

During 1958, six sides made the U.S. top ten: *Don't*, *I Beg Of You*, *Wear My Ring Around Your Neck*, *Hard Headed Woman*, *One Night* and *I Got Stung*.

It wasn't such a happy year for some other established rock stars, who mostly experienced only sporadic success. Fats Domino, Little Richard, Jerry Lee Lewis, and the Coasters, for instance, had only one top twenty entry apiece – whilst in comparison the Everly Brothers and Chuck Berry fared only a little better with four and three hits respectively.

With Elvis out of sight, there was a fresh deluge of pretenders to his throne, though few made any real impact.

One of the most consistent and interesting of the newcomers was Ricky Nelson, who was already familiar to American teenagers through his parents' television show, *The Adventures Of Ozzie And Harriet*, in which he'd starred since the age of nine. His transition to vinyl was smooth: a cover of Fats Domino's *I'm Walkin'*, which he was able (in common with his subsequent hits) to perform on the show, purred effortlessly up the charts. Switching from Verve to the Imperial label, he enjoyed an almost constant occupation of the charts until 1964, when his popularity diminished dramatically – although he did return to the top ten with *Garden Party* in 1972.

Nelson was probably the first really successful rock'n'roller with little obvious musical ability. His appeal rested squarely on his looks, but whereas previous screen converts like Tab Hunter and Sal Mineo had foundered after brief chart flurries, Nelson was fortunate enough to be provided with excellent material and brilliant backing musicians. His guitarist, James Burton, was particularly impressive and his work on such singles as *Poor Little Fool*, *Believe What You Say*, *Just A Little Too Much*, *Travellin' Man* and *Hello Many Lou* transformed them into classics.

As the seventies approached, Rick (as he now called himself) moved into the country rock field where he currently meanders.

Frankie Avalon and Fabian were in much the same mould. Good-looking Italianate youths, they never professed to be great singers – but cleverly contrived songs and production jobs coupled with unlimited exposure on *American Bandstand* (they were, of course, from Philadelphia) ensured fame and fortune.

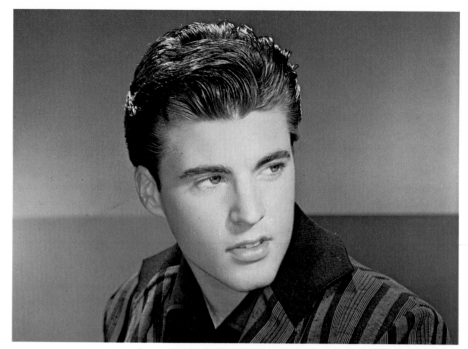

With Elvis (*right*) in the Army, the way was open for a series of younger teen idols, whose appearance echoed the successful Presley blueprint, although, as in the case of Ricky Nelson (*above*), with an emphasis on respectability rather than sexuality. Ricky was even married – how could parents of teenagers possibly consider him a threat?

Despite his restricted talents, Avalon managed to rack up 24 hits, including two number ones in *Venus* and *Why*, between 1958 and 1962 – by which time he had become the screen-idol star of innumerable beach movies, not to mention the sole survivor at *The Alamo*. His partner in crime, Fabian, was responsible for some extraordinarily dire releases although both *Tiger* and *Hound Dog Man* displayed redeeming features. The last of his 10 hits was titled *Kissin' And Twistin'*, which more or less tells the tale. Fabian also turned to a Hollywood career.

The widespread dilution of rock prevented many unusual talents from gaining much momentum, but among interesting 'one-hit-wonders' were *The Walk* by Jimmy McCracklin, *Book Of Love* by the Monotones, *Endless Sleep* by Jody Reynolds (an early 'death disc'), *Do You Want To Dance?* by Bobby Freeman, *Willy And The Hand Jive* by

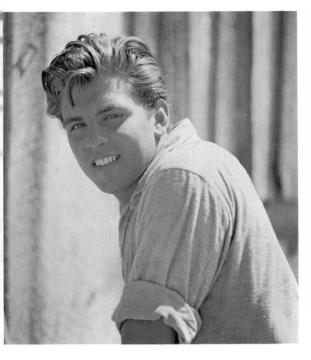

Johnny Otis and *To Know Him Is To Love Him* by the Teddy Bears (who included a newcomer to the record business, Phil Spector).

Among girl singers making an impression were Ruth Brown with *This Little Girl's Gone Rockin'*, the Poni-tails with *Born Too Late*, the Storey Sisters with *Bad Motorcycle*, and the Chantels (discovered and nurtured by George Goldner) with *Maybe...* but none scored as dramatically as Connie Francis, who became the most significant girl singer of the fifties.

After discovery on the *Arthur Godfrey Talent Show* in 1949 at the age of 11, she signed with M.G.M. Records but met only local success until the beginning of 1958 when her slightly rocked-up version of the twenties standard *Who's Sorry Now?* burst into the top five on both sides of the Atlantic to make her an 'overnight star'. For the next four and a half years, Connie was a chart fixture, notching up another nine million-sellers, the best remembered being *Stupid Cupid*, *My Happiness* and *Lipstick On Your Collar* – the last of which features one of the era's most succinct guitar solos.

Sometimes chirpy, sometimes tearful, Connie's voice was most distinctive but it was, of course, inevitable that once her teen-appeal began to dwindle she would turn to more family-oriented music. Recent comeback attempts have not been entirely successful but do not detract from her reign as the Rock'n'roll Queen 20 years ago.

Invariably, the new male singers were clean-cut and only marginally musical: Jimmy Clanton, the Kalin Twins, Robin Luke and Johnny Tillotson all basked in the spotlight to deliver fairly insipid love ballads... but there were exceptions to the rule. Conway Twitty, Don Gibson, Jack Scott, Bobby Darin, and Dion and the Belmonts all emerged as substantial talents.

Conway Twitty (who had changed his name from the unprepossessing Harold Jenkins) and Don Gibson were both country singers who modified their music to impress the rock market.

Twitty's change was the more dramatic; in the last quarter of 1958 his own composition *It's Only Make Believe*, featuring a very creditable Presley

Fabian (*above left*) and Frankie Avalon (*above*) were clean-cut youths from Philadelphia who both came to fame on *American Bandstand*. Fashion change, though, and after 1959 the hits stopped coming. Connie Francis, however (*below*), in the absence of outstanding female competition, was able to enjoy a longer reign as the unchallenged Queen of rock'n' roll before she too inevitably fell by the wayside, swept aside as the Beatles spearheaded a new revolution in music. The year also saw the first emergence of Phil Spector, although in the comparatively humble position of a group member, one of the Teddy Bears (*left*). Left to right: Phil Spector, Annette Kleinbard, Marshall Lieb.

Conway Twitty had only himself to blame for his name, which he had changed from Harold Jenkins. *It's Only Make Believe* reached number one on both sides of the Atlantic in 1958, but he never repeated this and switched to country music.

fast rocker – resulting in several double-sided classics, the best of which was his first big hit *My True Love/Leroy*, in summer 1958. By 1960, he was concentrating almost entirely on emotional ballads like his last top five appearances *What In The World's Come Over You* and *Burning Bridges*. Soon afterwards, his writing lost its currency and his popularity tapered off.

Bobby Darin, born Walden Robert Cassotto in New York's tough Bronx district, made several flops for Atlantic after leaving college in 1956. On the point of being dropped by the label, he recorded *Early In The Morning/Now We're One* under the name of his backing group the Rinky Dinks, and sold the tapes to another company, Brunswick. Meanwhile, a last-ditch Atlantic effort, *Splish Splash* captured the public's imagination and stormed to number three on the chart. Atlantic then demanded the contracted Darin's tapes back from Brunswick who, deprived of a surefire hit, had Buddy Holly record the song to produce a British top twenty hit.

Darin, now assured of Atlantic's support, followed *Splish Splash* with his greatest rocker *Queen Of The Hop* – after which he began to soften his approach to find a wider audience. He succeeded, as his subsequent run of 37 top hundred entries reveals, and though he quickly moved into a cabaret career he'll be remembered with affection for such million sellers as *Mack The Knife*, *Dream Lover*, *Beyond The Sea* and *Things*. In 1973, following a decade of varying fortune, Darin died of a heart attack at the age of 37.

Dion and the Belmonts, also from the Bronx, were a white vocal group following in the footsteps of the fading 'doo wop' pioneers. In 1958, they became Laurie Records' first signing and released a top thirty hit in *I Wonder Why* (covered by Showaddywaddy during the seventies). A year later, *A Teenager In Love*, a song written for them by Doc Pomus and Mart Schuman who were later to write hits for Elvis Presley and the Drifters, became their most memorable success – although a 1960 single, *Where Or When*, achieved a higher chart position, peaking at number three. At the end of that year, the Belmonts and Dion parted company – to reunite only for brief recording sessions in 1967 and 1972. Dion, as shall be seen, went on to great solo success.

The year produced several novelty hits including *The Purple People Eater* by Sheb Wooley, *No Chemise Please* by Gerry Granahan, *Short Shorts* by the Royal Teens, and *Chantilly Lace* by the Big Bopper. On the instrumental front, Link Wray began his lengthy career with *Rumble*, the Royaltones had a sax-dominated hit in *Poor Boy*, and the Champs had their first and biggest single, *Tequila* . . . but none magnetised the teen-world like Duane Eddy, who became an instant favourite with hard-core rockers.

With a guitar style based almost exclusively on the lower strings, Eddy, from Phoenix Arizona, soon established himself as 'the King of the Twangy Guitar' – and having evolved a seemingly infallible formula of guitar twanging peppered with sax breaks and whoops from his backing group the Rebels, proceeded to record a succession of 26 top hundred hits between 1958 and 1963, among which

impersonation, reached the top on both sides of the Atlantic. Subsequent singles, usually excellent, fared less well although *Lonely Blue Boy* (originally, as *Danny*, to have been the title song of the Elvis film *King Creole* – based on Harold Robbins' *A Stone For Danny Fisher*) achieved sales in excess of a million. As his rock audience diminished, Twitty returned to the country field where his progress has been unbounded. Between 1968 and 1977, he hit the vein with no less than 33 number one hits on the U.S. country chart.

Don Gibson's self-confessed drug dabblings probably contributed to his inability to sustain his success during the sixties. After coming to the public's notice with *Oh Lonesome Me* in spring 1958, he made another 13 U.S. top hundred appearances before the end of 1961. One of these songs, *Sea Of Heartbreak*, was a fair-sized British hit and another, *I Can't Stop Loving You*, provided Ray Charles with his finest hour.

Early singles by Jack Scott, a gifted Canadian singer and songwriter, coupled a slow ballad with a were *Rebel Rouser* in 1958, *Forty Miles Of Bad Road* in 1959, and *Because They're Young* in 1960.

After a final chart showing in 1964 with the desperate *Son Of Rebel Rouser,* Eddy rapidly fell from glory, but later guitar heroes all acknowledged his importance.

As Eddy's first hit *Movin'n'Groovin',* was creeping up the U.S. chart R&B singer Chuck Willis lay on an operating table in his home town of Atlanta Goergia. His own single, *What Am I Living For/Hang Up My Rock'n'Roll Shoes,* was about to enter the top twenty, but Willis died during the operation.

In England, the rock scene was yet to blossom: Steele and Donegan held sway over an army of surrogate Presleys... but during the year, two worthy rockers began their ascendancy.

The first of these was Reg Smith, who was launched in typical Larry Parnes style as Marty Wilde. (Parnes invariably renamed his stars, often to suggest their sexual potential... thus he subsequently delivered Billy Fury, Johnny Gentle, Vince Eager, Duffy Power and a host of others.) Wilde, much in the Presley mould visually, built a career in the Pat Boone/Tommy Steele tradition from cover versions – in his case, of American winners – and T.V. exposure assisted his passage to the charts. Two Jimmie Rodgers songs *Honeycomb* and *Oh Oh, I'm Falling In Love Again* failed but his copy of Jody Reynolds' *Endless Sleep* was a top five British hit in summer 58.

He subsequently enjoyed similar chart action with somewhat inferior duplications of Ritchie Valens' *Donna,* Dion and the Belmonts' *Teenager In Love* and Phillips' *Sea Of Love,* though his fifth hit was his own composition, *Bad Boy* – which also reached the U.S. top fifty to bring him his sole Stateside success.

His real breakthrough was certainly the weekly T.V. show *Oh Boy,* another Jack Good brainchild. Good appointed Wilde ringmaster over a gamut of diverse talents, few of whom saw little more than a flicker of fame. Lord Rockingham's XI, Cherry Wainer, Red Price, Vince Taylor, Tony Sheridan, the Vernon Girls, Cuddly Dudley, Vince Eager, and the John Barry Seven all relished moments of glory . . . but *Oh Boy*'s major revelation made his debut on the show on 15th September 1958. His name was Cliff Richard.

Richard had only turned professional the previous month, quitting his job to work a four week residency at Butlins in Clacton with his backing group, the Drifters. Before leaving, he'd cut a single for E.M.I. – a cover of *Schoolboy Crush* by Bobby Helms, a song his producer Norrie Paramor thought had chart potential. As was par for the course with the hundreds of hopefuls who turned E.M.I.'s treadmill, Cliff was allowed to slap any old song on the B-side . . . and he chose to record *Move It,* written by his guitarist Ian Samwell.

Whilst Cliff was luxuriating at Butlin's holiday camp, Jack Good was played an advance copy of the single and found it relatively unimpressive. The B-side, however, took him out of his chair. He couldn't believe that an English record could sound so good, and promptly booked Cliff for a series of appearances which would lift him to national stardom. In fact, *Move It* was on the ball in every respect. The lyric rang with teenage defiance, Cliff

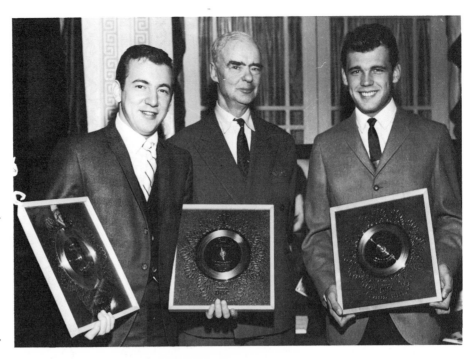

Above: Duane Eddy (right), one of the first guitarists to be widely copied, receives a gold disc for *Some Kinda Earthquake.* Not to be outdone, Bobby Darin (left) gets two for *Dream Lover* and *Mack The Knife.*

Left: Marty Wilde was one of the earliest and best of the English rockers, although he seemed to fall from grace after marrying, thus breaking the hearts of thousands of teenage girls.

sang with an intuitive authority, the guitar work was stunning and original, and the overall sound was magnificent. It was the first British rock record with any intrinsic merit. Needless to say, it rushed into the top three to become the first of many hits.

Heavily modelled on Presley's blueprint, Cliff immediately attracted criticism for his 'overt sexuality' and 'crude exhibitionism' (which only magnified his attraction) but, as the weeks rolled by, he evolved a distinct style of his own. By 1960 (when his consequent career will be reviewed), Cliff had marked up 10 top tenners, including three number ones: *Living Doll, Travelling Light* and *Please Don't Tease.* He had also become the most popular British entertainer since the Second World War.

Back in America, the overall deterioration of rock 'n'roll was having repercussions, as fans began to look elsewhere for musical stimulation . . . and *Tom*

Dooley, a fluke hit by a folk group called the Kingston Trio, touched off a boom in folk music and acoustic guitar sales.

Rock'n'roll was on its way to being nailed into a lead-lined coffin – though not before a game rearguard action, initiated by the best rock film of the fifties, *The Girl Can't Help It*. The 'girl' in question was Jayne Mansfield, and it was the

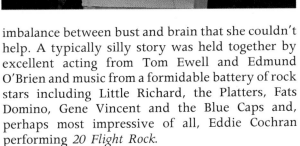

imbalance between bust and brain that she couldn't help. A typically silly story was held together by excellent acting from Tom Ewell and Edmund O'Brien and music from a formidable battery of rock stars including Little Richard, the Platters, Fats Domino, Gene Vincent and the Blue Caps and, perhaps most impressive of all, Eddie Cochran performing *20 Flight Rock.*

After a few unsuccessful recording attempts, Cochran had signed with Liberty Records and his first single, *Sitting In The Balcony*, reached the U.S. top twenty. In late 1958 came *Summertime Blues*, his biggest American hit and his first British chart appearance.

For some reason, his popularity declined in the States but increased in Britain, where he toured (with Gene Vincent) to fanatical response in spring 1960. On 17th April 1960, the car in which he was travelling spun off the road in Chippenham Wiltshire, and Cochran died from multiple head injuries.

Three Steps To Heaven, released just after his death, topped the U.K. charts to be followed by several smaller hits until 1963.

The appeal of classics like *Summertime Blues*, *C'mon Everybody*, *Weekend* and *Something Else* remains undiminished and over the years many artists, from Rod Stewart to the Sex Pistols, have recorded their (thoroughly inferior) versions of his songs.

As 1958 closed, several new stars hovered on the horizon . . . the Crests, Neil Sedaka, Ritchie Valens. Among those who had disappeared were Tom and Jerry, whose single *Hey Schoolgirl* was staggering around the lower half of the top hundred at the beginning of the year. It wasn't until 1965 that they returned to the charts . . . as Simon and Garfunkel.

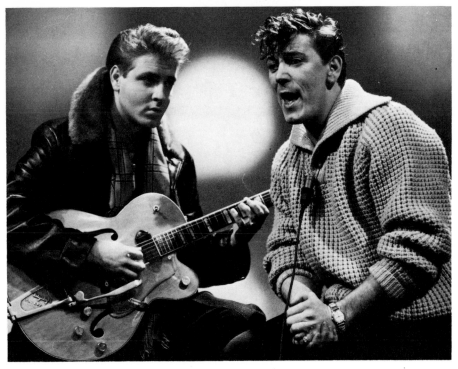

'58 the year

Events

1 Jan. The European Economic Community is inaugurated.

3 Jan. The West Indies becomes independent.

6 Feb. A B.E.A. aircraft crashes on take-off in Munich killing 23 passengers including 8 Manchester United footballers.

27 Mar. Kruschev replaces Bulganin as Soviet Premier.

29 May General De Gaulle accepts an invitation to form a new French government.

1 Sept. Serious race riots in Notting Hill Gate, London.

4 Oct. The first transatlantic commercial jet service begins, using the Comet IV.

Films of 58

The Big Country · Carve Her Name With Pride · Cat On A Hot Tin Roof · Gigi · King Creole · Separate Tables · Some Came Running · South Pacific

U.S. CHART TOPPERS – WEEKS AT TOP

At The Hop	Danny and the Juniors	
Get A Job	Silhouettes	2
Don't	Elvis Presley	
Tequila	Champs	
Twilight Time	Platters	
Witch Doctor	David Seville	
All I Have To Do Is Dream	Everly Brothers	
The Purple People Eater	Sheb Wooley	6
Yakety Yak	Coasters	
Patricia	Perez Prado	
Poor Little Fool	Ricky Nelson	2
Volare	Domenico Modugno	5
Little Star	Elegants	
It's All In The Game	Tommy Edwards	6
It's Only Make Believe	Conway Twitty	2
Tom Dooley	Kingston Trio	
To Know Him Is To Love Him	Teddy Bears	3
The Chipmunk Song	Chipmunks	2

U.K. CHART TOPPERS – WEEKS AT TOP

Mary's Boy Child	Harry Belafonte	1
Great Balls Of Fire	Jerry Lee Lewis	2
Jailhouse Rock	Elvis Presley	3
The Story Of My Life	Michael Holliday	2
Magic Moments	Perry Como	8
Whole Lotta Woman	Marvin Rainwater	3
Who's Sorry Now?	Connie Francis	6
On The Street Where You Live	Vic Damone	1
All I Have To Do Is Dream	Everly Brothers	7
When	Kalin Twins	5
Stupid Cupid	Connie Francis	6
It's All In The Game	Tommy Edwards	3
Hoots Mon	Lord Rockingham's XI	3
It's Only Make Believe	Conway Twitty	2

Right: Elizabeth Taylor and Paul Newman in *Cat On A Hot Tin Roof.*

Opposite top: a Comet IV.

Opposite centre: Cliff Richard.

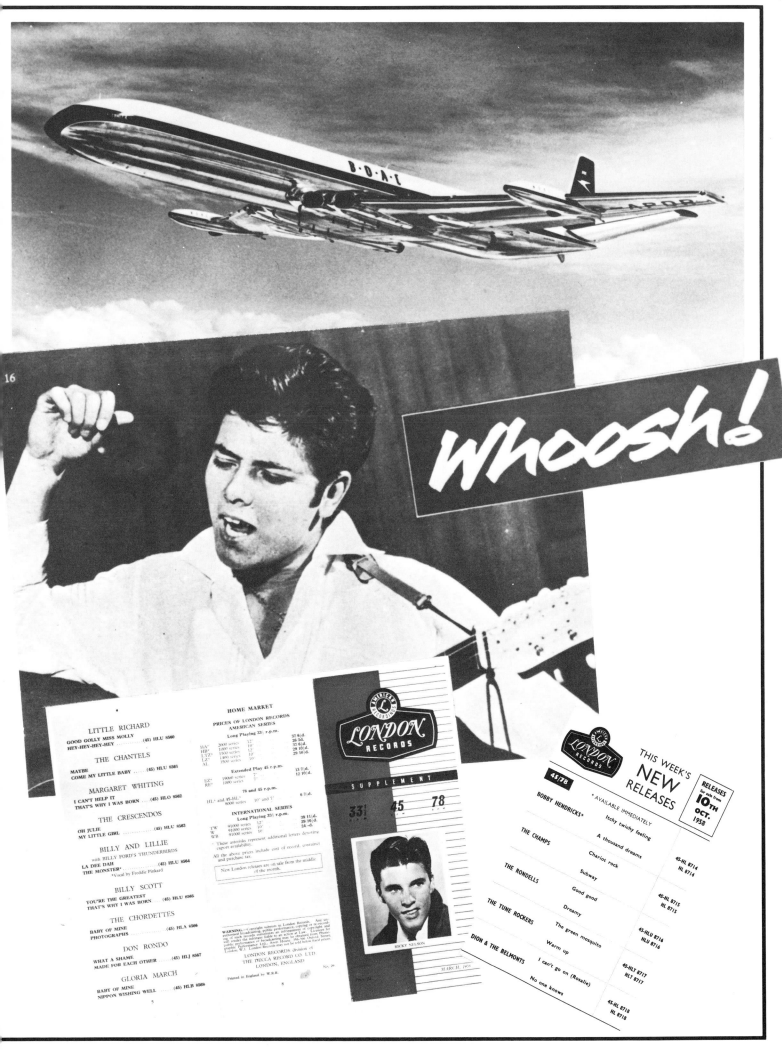

'59

'Livin' Doll'

The Browns · Freddy Cannon · The Chipmunks · Dee Clark · The Crests
Adam Faith · The Flamingos · The Fleetwoods · Emile Ford and the Checkmates
Billy Fury · The Isley Brothers · Jan and Dean · Johnny and the Hurricanes
Lloyd Price · Bobby Rydell · Neil Sedaka · Ritchie Valens

The day the music died: 3rd February 1959 when a light plane transporting Buddy Holly, Ritchie Valens and Big Bopper to the next gig of a gruelling tour crashed in bad weather, killing all on board. For many, this incident, coupled with the 'payola' scandal which closed the year, signified the death of early rock'n'roll.

Holly had agreed to headline the tour only to improve his immediate financial condition. Not long married, he had moved to New York with his wife after severing business ties with Norman Petty, who, quite legally, was holding income pending a court ruling on their contractual situation. The tour, lurching through the mid-west in the height of winter, had already become a relative disaster: coach breakdowns, bad weather, excessive travelling and a concentrated gig schedule had drained the participants – and it was only Holly's desire to snatch some sleep and attend to his dirty washing which induced him to hire a plane.

Originally, two of his backing musicians, guitarist Tommy Allsup and bassist Waylon Jennings (the other founding Crickets had decided to remain with Petty), were to accompany Holly – but Valens and the Big Bopper separately persuaded them to relinquish their places. Only minutes after take-off, the plane went out of control and crashed into a ploughed field eight miles north-west of Mason City, Iowa. The pilot and the three passengers were thought to have died at the moment of impact.

Only 17 at the time of his death, Ritchie Valens had already achieved a gold record with a song he'd written for his girlfriend, *Donna* (covered in Britain by Marty Wilde). Coupled with the much-copied Latin rocker *La Bamba*, *Donna* was high on the American charts when the tragic news was received. His previous single *Come On Let's Go* and the succeeding *That's My Little Suzie* were lesser hits but a core of devoted fans have always maintained that Valens would have become a major talent.

The Big Bopper (real name Jaye P. Richardson) was actually a disc-jockey cum songwriter/singer. He would never know that *Running Bear*, a song he wrote for his protégé Johnny Preston, would become a worldwide number one – but he did have success on his own account when *Chantilly Lace* reached the U.S. top ten in late 1958. Its popularity together with encouraging sales for the follow-up, *Big Bopper's Wedding*, persuaded Richardson to take the fatal plunge into performing. A large man, he found himself unable to sleep in the cramped conditions of the tour bus and took the plane in order to rest before the next show, which was to have been in Fargo, North Dakota.

But it was Buddy Holly's loss which was most keenly felt. Following his split with the original Crickets, he had begun to experiment, recording with other musicians including King Curtis, who was specially flown from New York at Holly's expense to perform on *Reminiscing*. Holly himself recorded in New York on a couple of occasions, cutting Bobby Darin's *Early In The Morning* and three tracks which, after his death, would feature among his best known: *It Doesn't Matter Anymore* by Paul Anka, *Raining In My Heart* by Boudleaux and Felice Bryant, and his own *True Love Ways*. These tracks featured a full orchestra, indicating Holly's desire to expand his horizons now that he was free of Petty's direction, but they were to be the last he completed.

Released back to back as a single, *It Doesn't Matter Anymore/Raining In My Heart* peaked at number 13 in America on the day Holly died, whereas in England (where it wasn't released until 10 days later) it reached number one and became his biggest hit.

In his homeland, Holly was soon temporarily forgotten. Not so in Britain, however; no less than 11 singles entered the top fifty in the five years following his death, and the constant demand for Holly product has resulted in numerous compilation and reissue albums since then.

Throughout America, mainstream rock continued to soften. Paul Anka, Frankie Avalon, Pat Boone, Bobby Darin, Fabian, Johnny Mathis and

Ritchie Valens was another young rock'n'roller who died before his considerable talents could be realised. Apparently, he had only wanted to travel in the doomed aircraft because he felt that travelling on a bus with the rest of the touring party was beneath his dignity as a rock'n'roll star.

Right: An early shot of Neil Sedaka recording with Brill Building associates in New York. Sedaka is in the striped shirt.

Far right: Carole King (née Klein), who along with Sedaka was one of several highly prolific and successful Brill Building songwriters at the turn of the 60s. Carole, however, was one of the few who managed to survive professionally, achieving even greater prominence as a recording artist.

Andy Williams all enjoyed abundant chart activity and inspired a plethora of new artists in their mould. Among those to break nationally were Jerry Keller (*Here Comes Summer*), Jimmy Darren (who scored with *Gidget* although his greatest hits were *Goodbye Cruel World* and *Her Royal Majesty* in 1961 and 1962 respectively), Bobby Rydell (*Kissin' Time* and *We Got Love*) and Jerry Wallace (*Primrose Lane*).

Two interesting stars did emerge, however: Neil Sedaka, who displayed eminently more talent, and Freddy Cannon, who displayed eminently more spunk.

Sedaka, a well-mannered Jewish lad from New York, had trained as a classical pianist but after writing *Stupid Cupid* (one of Connie Francis' biggest and best singles) decided to drop academic pursuits in favour of a rock career. He joined Aldon Music, a publishing company headed by Al Nevins and Don Kirshner, operating from New York's famous Brill Building where literally hundreds of music-biz middlemen were billeted during the late fifties and early sixties. Among his conspirators were Carole King and Gerry Goffin, and Barry Mann and Cynthia Weill – songwriting teams who turned out dozens of hits during their Aldon days.

Together with his writing partner Howard Greenfield, Sedaka wrote over 500 songs – recording a large number of them himself. Between *Oh Carol* (written for Carole King) in 1959 and *Next Door To An Angel* in 1962, Sedaka had six top twenty entries including a U.S. chart topper in *Breaking Up Is Hard To Do*. There can be no doubt that Sedaka's talent and currency were enormous, but he was one of the hardest hit when the Beatles arrived and wiped the slate clean of almost all that had gone before. As a result, he went into

hibernation for almost 10 years. In 1973, Sedaka came back with a string of hits including *Laughter In The Rain*, an American number one, but by the end of the decade his popularity had waned and he was concentrating almost entirely on cabaret work.

Freddy 'BoomBoom' Cannon burst onto the scene in summer 1959 when *Tallahassee Lassie* hit the U.S. top ten. The 18 year old Cannon immediately quit his truck driving job to start a recording career

Right and far right: Freddy Cannon (né Picariello) relaxes on a British tour with the kind of magazine many of his female fans favoured. Cannon fell into obscurity during the mid-60s, but like many of his contemporaries, is still recording (albeit without much success) today.

Johnny and the Hurricanes whose recording speciality was setting well known standards to a rocking beat. Strangely, although American, he achieved greater chart success in Britain.

capitalise on his success of 20 years ago.

Among 1959's novelty hits were *Deck Of Cards* by Wink Martindale, *Kookie Kookie, Lend Me Your Comb* by Ed Byrnes (the heart-throb from the T.V. series *77 Sunset Strip*), *A Pub With No Beer* by Australian Slim Dusty, and two 'death songs': Mark Dinning's *Teen Angel* and Tommy Dee's *Three Stars* about the Holly plane crash. By far the biggest novelty item of the year, however, was *The Chipmunk Song* by the Chipmunks.

After changing his name to David Seville, Ross Bagdasarian, a Californian of Armenian extraction, began to write songs (often with his cousin, the celebrated novelist William Saroyan), some of which were recorded by Rosemary Clooney, Johnnie Ray and Sammy Davis Jr. – but Seville sought hits of his own and recorded *Witch Doctor*, a 1959 number one which included a speeded-up chorus.

Building on the idea, he invented a three-piece harmony group, the Chipmunks – each with a distinct identity and personality. Theodore, Simon and Alvin (the naughty but lovable one) were named after executives at Liberty Records, Seville's label, and their first single, *The Chipmunk Song*, was released for the 1958 Christmas market and sold over $3\frac{1}{2}$ million copies within five weeks – making it the fastest seller of all time at that point. The single re-entered the top fifty around each of the four following Christmasses and Seville, in the meantime, had created several more hits for the 'group' including *Alvin's Harmonica* and *Ragtime Cowboy Joe*. As his recording success trailed off, Seville reverted to an acting career which he pursued until his death in 1972.

The Crests and the Fleetwoods were the big new groups of 1959, though others enjoyed isolated moments of glory. The Clovers scored with *Love Potion Number Nine*, the Skyliners with *Since I Don't Have You*, the Flamingos with *I Only Have Eyes For You*, the Impalas with *Sorry (I Ran All The Way Home)* and the Isley Brothers with the song which put them on the long and winding road to fame, *Shout*.

The Crests, led by New Yorker Johnny Maestro, were in the top five with their memorable *Sixteen Candles* when the year opened and during the following 18 months recorded another six chart-bound singles including *The Angels Listened In* and *Trouble In Paradise*. After personnel shuffles, they lost their magic touch and eventually split up, and Maestro, following a disappointing solo career, joined New York harmony group Brooklyn Bridge.

The Fleetwoods, two girls and a boy from Seattle, had two of the year's smashes in *Come Softly To Me* and *Mr. Blue*. Four top thirty hits followed during the next two years but they couldn't sustain their level of inventiveness, and faded quickly after their top ten cover of Thomas Wayne's *Tragedy*. However, many consider their close harmony sound to have been the blueprint for the Mamas and the Papas in the mid-sixties.

The year's most significant new act was a duo. Jan Berry and Dean Torrence, better known as Jan and Dean, started out singing in informal groups which included L.A. schoolmates Sandy Nelson (of *Teen Beat* fame) and subsequent Beach Boy Bruce Johnston.

On leaving school, Jan and Dean determined to

which brought him a straight run of 18 hits for Swan, a Philadelphia-based label operated by Bob Crewe and Frank Slay. Slay and Crewe, who wrote many of Cannon's hits, had appropriate connections at *American Bandstand* which ensured nationwide exposure – but the show's fading credibility eventually worked to his disadvantage and after his beefy revival of *Way Down Yonder In New Orleans* in late 59, his only U.S. top five entry was *Palisades Park* in summer 62. In late 63, he moved to Warner Brothers where he cut the million selling *Abigail Beecher* and the marginally less successful *Action!* – but after 1966 little was heard of him.

Some of the year's other big hits were *I've Had It* by the Bell Notes, *Sea Cruise* by Frankie Ford, *Kansas City* by Wilbert Harrison, *It Was I* by Skip and Flip, *Sea Of Love* by Phil Phillips and *Running Bear* by Johnny Preston – though none of the artsists were able to repeat their initial success.

No girl singers surfaced to challenge Connie Francis, though Toni Fisher (*The Big Hurt*) and Dodie Stevens (*Pink Shoe Laces*) both achieved significant, albeit short-lived, sales.

On the instrumental front, there were many one-off hits, the best of which were *Guitar Boogie Shuffle* by the Virtues, *The Happy Organ* by Dave 'Baby' Cortez, *Sleep Walk* by Santo and Johnny, and *Teen Beat* by Sandy Nelson. All subsequently returned to the charts with lesser hits, but none of them had the staying power of Johnny and the Hurricanes, a blaring outfit from Toledo Ohio who crashed into the charts with three hits in 1959: *Crossfire, Red River Rock* and *Reveille Rock*. With a distinctive sax/organ combination, Johnny and the Hurricanes had six other instrumental hits during the next two years and leader Johnny Paris still leads a group of Hurricanes, touring the U.S.A. and Europe to succeed as a team – though their friend Arnie Ginsberg was indirectly responsible for their initial fame. Arnie, it appeared, had become infatuated with a stripper called Jennie Lee, whose major attributes were 'the biggest pectorals this side of Tucson'. Jan and Dean went with Arnie to view this eighth wonder of the world and were sufficiently inspired to write a celebratory song. With Dean singing lead, they recorded the piece on primitive equipment in Jan's garage – but, despite the overall muffled jumble, the resulting sound contained enough unrepeatable magic for commercial release. *Jennie Lee* was released under the name of Jan and Arnie (because Dean had begun his national service by this time) and became the first of many 'garage' hits, peaking at number eight on the U.S. chart in summer 1958.

By the middle of 1959, Dean had returned, elbowed Arnie, and was working on new ideas with Jan. An alliance with Sam Cooke's former producer and co-writer Lou Adler and his partner Herb Albert (both of whom would become millionaries during the sixties) produced a string of singles on the Dore label, but only the first, *Baby Talk*, was a real winner.

After another fairly barren period on Challenge, they signed with Liberty in late 1961 and it was here that they established themselves with a run of 18 hits, the biggest of which was *Surf City*, co-written with Brian Wilson (who at the time, summer 63, was riding high with his own group, the Beach Boys). *Ride The Wild Surf* also exalted surfing, whilst other hits celebrated hot-rod racing (*Drag City* and *Dead Man's Curve*) and skateboarding (*Sidewalk Surfin'*).

What made Jan and Dean so different and exceptional was their subject matter, vocal arrangements, production technique and abundant use of a secret ingredient, California. Very little white rock 'n'roll had emerged from Los Angeles during the fifties but as the new decade opened the music industry began to gravitate to the West Coast – and a slice of Californian sun, fun and romance became the nation's dream.

Jan and Dean's career continued until early 1966, when Jan was involved in a car accident which almost claimed his life. Dean attempted to hold things together with sporadic releases but eventually conceded that it would never be the same again and started a successful art studio called Kittyhawk Graphics, since when he has been responsible for many distinctive album sleeves.

In stark contrast to previous years, the principal black newcomers were balladeers rather than rockers. Tommy Edwards, who'd reached number one with *It's All In The Game* the previous year, continued his chart run with eight entries in 1959; Sammy Turner scored with *Lavender Blue* and *Always* – both produced by the ubiquitous Leiber and Stoller; Brook Benton had eight charts entries, including a number three in *It's Just A Matter Of Time*; Jesse Belvin, who'd written *Earth Angel*, had two solo hits for R.C.A. (and was killed the following year in yet another car accident); and Dee Clark reached the top twenty with *Just Keep It Up* and *Hey Little Girl.*

The odd man out was Lloyd Price, whose raucous rocker *Stagger Lee* was shooting to number one as the year began. Price, from New Orleans, had

Jan (left) and Dean, an initial inspiration for the Beach Boys, documented the Californian teen scene. Their original partners, Lou Adler and Herb Alpert would both go on to launch their own record companies.

Lloyd Price emerged from a rhythm & blues background in New Orleans to score briefly in the pop charts, after which he retreated to comparative obscurity.

enjoyed a massive R&B hit in 1952 when his original version of *Lawdy Miss Clawdy* was certified as a million seller – but then major success eluded him until 1959 when *Stagger Lee*, *Personality* and *I'm Gonna Get Married* all made the top three. These, however, were to be his swan songs; after a succession of lesser hits he returned to his first love, R&B.

In Britain, Cliff Richard still led the field by a considerable distance, but new challengers were at least making their presence felt. Adam Faith, who'd returned to his day job at the Rank Studios following the failure of his first solo attempt in 1957, suddenly attracted the spotlight when he landed the position of resident anchorman on a new T.V. show, *Drumbeat*. The man who suggested he apply for it, John Barry, was instrumental, both literally and figuratively, in Faith's instant popularity – having orchestrated the distinctive *What Do You Want?* which reached number one at the end of the year.

Faith's gimmick-laden nasal delivery, combined with Barry's thoughtful string arrangements, took

Above: Adam Faith's whining voice made him one of Britain's biggest early teen idols. But would he and his mohair sweater have become so famous if he hadn't changed his name from Terence Nelhams?

Above right: Emile Ford, perhaps the first black rock star to come to prominence in Britain, scored heavily for a few months before inevitably disappearing in the wake of the preponderance of new talent constantly appearing at the start of the new decade.

several more singles into the top five – and by the middle of 1965, he had logged a total of 23 chart entries. Like Marty Wilde and Cliff Richard before him, he found American audiences impossible to crack – but when his chart run ended he turned to acting and capped a fluctuating career with impressive performances in the David Essex film *Stardust* and the British T.V. drama series *Budgie* in which he played the title role.

After an ill-advised comeback attempt, Faith started anew as a manager and producer, showing considerable prowess as the guiding light behind Leo Sayer's spectacular rise.

Hot on Faith's trail at the end of 1959 were Emile Ford and the Checkmates, who specialised in beaty revivals of popular oldies. Ford, a Bahaman immigrant, started out in the flourishing London coffee bar scene and made an immediate impact with *What Do You Want To Make Those Eyes At Me For?*, which was soon occupying the number one slot. Its almost goes without saying that he never repeated this achievement – although *Slow Boat To China* made number four and *Counting Teardrops* number six – and like so many artists of the era, Ford simply

faded away during the early sixties.

Billy Fury displayed more tenacity. Originally Ronald Wycherley from Liverpool, Fury wrote his own songs and benefitted from unusually skilful and sympathetic production. His discovery (by Larry Parnes, of course) had come after he'd inveigled his way into Marty Wilde's dressing room when a package show visited Liverpool, and very soon he was appearing on the same bill as Wilde. In spring 1959, *Maybe Tomorrow* reached the top twenty, but his chart run didn't really get underway until the following year when *Colette* preceded 23 top forty entries, including *That's Love*, *Halfway To Paradise* and *Like I've Never Been Gone*.

Fury's were among the very best early British rock'n'roll recordings (his singles meant nothing in the States – in common with more than 99% of pre-Beatle British releases), but by the mid-sixties, his menace had evaporated and he was making increasingly softer singles to appeal to the housewives who constituted the more vociferous part of his cabaret audiences. He had a cameo role in the David Essex film *That'll Be The Day*, but his persistent ill health has kept him fairly inactive.

As the fifties drew to a close, details of 'payola' – a system whereby American disc-jockeys were paid to plug certain records – were coming to light and the resultant scandal more or less finished rock 'n'roll and many of its propagators. On the face of it, payola appeared iniquitous but it did bring many small labels, excellent artists and great records to the public's attention – and it broke the stranglehold of the major companies which had previously monopolised the record business.

Added to that, the average salary of a fifties disc-jockey was far less than might be supposed: in many cases his greatest reward was ego gratification. Nevertheless, tribunals, witch-hunters and tax-inspectors moved in and heads began to roll; after all, there was an election due in 1960 and America's silent majority, feeling that rock'n'roll was a bad thing anyway, would no doubt be impressed by the authorities' much-publicised attempts to eradicate such un-American activities as corruption in the entertainment industry.

The resulting furore resulted in many disc-jockeys testifying before agents of the Federal Trade Commission, prior to a law prohibiting payola being passed in September 1960. Numerous suspected culprits were indicted although many of them apparently gave their testimony in exchange for immunity. Dick Clark, after relinquishing his music publishing interest, escaped unscathed and continued his career unimpeded . . . but Alan Freed, one of rock'n'roll's most sincere and important popularisers, was washed up.

On 21st November 1959, whilst playing *Shimmy Shimmy Koko Bop* by Little Anthony and the Imperials, a sobbing Freed told W.A.B.C. listeners of his 'resignation' – although the station had dismissed him as a result of payola allegations. After refusing to testify in the hearings, he appeared before a grand jury on charges of bribery, to which he pleaded guilty. A nominal fine and suspended prison sentence ensured that he would never regain his prominence.

It was a sour note on which to end the decade.

Above: Billy Fury, a member of the Larry Parnes' rock'n'roll stable. started promisingly as an innovative rocker but soon deteriorated into a wispy balladeer. One person who probably wasn't too concerned, though, was his bank manager, and hopefully Billy made enough money to support himself through a later period of prolonged ill health.

Left: Alan Freed (right) with Chuck Berry (looking very young) and starlet Sandy Stewart. This shot was used as publicity material for the film *Go, Johnny Go!*, which also featured Jimmy Clanton, Eddie Cochran and posthumous-footage of Ritchie Valens. Freed's pre-eminence among rock'n'roll disc jockeys was the major factor behind his being hounded out of the business during the celebrated payola investigations.

'59 the year

Events

1 Jan. Fidel Castro becomes Cuban head of state after overthrowing the previous government.

3 Jan. Alaska becomes the 49th state of the U.S.A.

18 Mar. EMI discontinues the production of 78 r.p.m. records.

30 Mar. 10,000 members of the Campaign for Nuclear Disarmament march from Aldermaston to Trafalgar Square, London.

7 Apr. Oklahoma repeals prohibition, leaving Mississippi the only 'dry' state.

25 Apr. The St. Lawrence Seaway, linking the Great Lakes and the Atlantic, is formally opened by Queen Elizabeth and President Eisenhower.

26 June Ingmar Johansson defeats Floyd Patterson to become world heavyweight boxing champion.

21 Aug. Hawaii becomes the 50th state of the U.S.A.

2 Nov. The M1 motorway is opened in Britain.

Films of 59

Anatomy Of A Murder · Ben Hur · The Diary Of Anne Frank · Inn Of The Sixth Happiness · Look Back In Anger · North By Northwest · Some Like It Hot · Wild Strawberries

Right: Charlton Heston in *Ben Hur*.

Opposite top: Elizabeth Taylor and Eddie Fisher marry.

Opposite bottom: Fidel Castro.

U.S. CHART TOPPERS – WEEKS AT TOP

The Chipmunk Song	Chipmunks	2
Smoke Gets In Your Eyes	Platters	3
Stagger Lee	Lloyd Price	4
Venus	Frankie Avalon	5
Come Softly To Me	Fleetwoods	4
The Happy Organ	Dave 'Baby' Cortez	1
Kansas City	Wilbert Harrison	2
The Battle Of New Orleans	Johnny Horton	6
Lonely Boy	Paul Anka	4
A Big Hunk Of Love	Elvis Presley	2
The Three Bells	The Browns	4
Sleep Walk	Santo and Johnny	2
Mack The Knife	Bobby Darin	9
Mr. Blue	Fleetwoods	1
Heartaches By The Number	Guy Mitchell	2
Why?	Frankie Avalon	1

U.K. CHART TOPPERS – WEEKS AT TOP

It's Only Make Believe	Conway Twitty	3
I Got Stung/One Night	Elvis Presley	5
Smoke Gets In Your Eyes	Platters	5
Side Saddle	Russ Conway	2
It Doesn't Matter Anymore	Buddy Holly	2
A Fool Such As I	Elvis Presley	7
Roulette	Russ Conway	1
Dream Lover	Bobby Darin	5
Living Doll	Cliff Richard	4
Only Sixteen	Craig Douglas	7
Travellin' Light	Cliff Richard	7
What Do You Want?	Adam Faith	4

The '50s

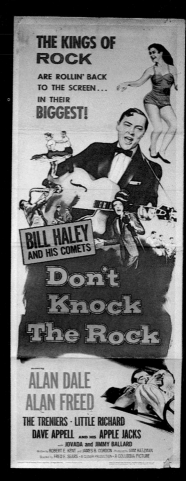

'60

'Itsy Bitsy Teenie Weenie Yellow Polka Dot Bikini'

Bill Black's Combo · Gary U.S. Bonds · Johnny Burnette · Jerry Butler
Chubby Checker · Brian Hyland · Johnny Kidd and the Pirates · Brenda Lee
Roy Orbison · Charlie Rich · Rosie and the Originals · The Shadows
The Shirelles · Ike and Tina Turner · Bobby Vee · The Ventures
Maurice Williams and the Zodiacs · Kathy Young and the Innocents

The sixties started without a bang. If rock'n'roll fans had expected the new decade to bring fresh excitement they were in for a big disappointment because it was business as usual . . . and it would be until the arrival of the Beatles, who at this point were just about to visit Hamburg for the first time.

In America, Elvis was still King. His two year absence from active rock'n'roll service had not impaired his popularity, as his chart score of three number ones out of three releases proved most conclusively. Even two of the B-sides made the top twenty on their own account, and the demobbed Presley's comeback was equally dramatic in Britain where *It's Now Or Never* and *Are You Lonesome Tonight?* made number one and *Girl Of My Best Friend* and *Stuck On You* number two.

Colonel Tom Parker's managerial strategies had obviously paid off but around this time he made a decision which would deny the world's countless millions of Elvis fans the chance of ever seeing him in the flesh. From now on, Elvis would undertake no live concerts but would instead concentrate all his activities in the recording and movie studios of Hollywood.

This might have been a good idea, but it soon became painfully obvious that Presley's advisers were unable to distinguish a good script from the football results. Nevertheless, 1960's pair of Hollywood epics, *G.I. Blues* (vaguely based on Elvis' army exploits) and *Flaming Star* (a western), were decidedly superior to much of what was to follow.

Of the other rock giants, many were still turning out great hit records. Fats Domino, Hank Ballard, Dion and the Belmonts, and the Everly Brothers were as prolific as ever, and the Drifters, Ray Charles, Duane Eddy and Sam Cooke were about to enter their most productive periods. Certainly their only serious new rivals in 1960 were in the unlikely shapes of Roy Orbison and Chubby Checker.

Another Sam Philips protégé, Orbison had left Sun Records some years earlier – seemingly losing his rocking capabilities in the process, but thereby becoming a major star during this fallow period. He had originally been encouraged to try his luck as a recording artist by his college friend Pat Boone and during the fifties had made a brief impression with his sole hit for Sun, *Ooby Dooby*. After that, however, he devoted most of his time to writing songs, two of which appeared on the Crickets' first album, and a third on the B-side of *All I Have To Do Is Dream* by the Everly Brothers. (The song in question, *Claudette*, reached the U.S. top thirty on its own account and was written for his wife, who was subsequently killed in a motorcycle accident.)

By 1960, he was again a performer, but his former uninhibited style had softened towards the moody introspection of the dramatic beat-ballad. In the execution of these, the high-pitched Orbison had few peers. His songs were mostly desolate and doomy, but obviously fulfilled a need in the hearts of crossed lovers – for Orbison accumulated the remarkable total of 12 million-selling singles in four years. Self-pitying classics like *Only The Lonely*, *Crying*, *It's Over* and *Running Scared* were interspersed with relatively unconvincing rockers like *Dream Baby* and *Mean Woman Blues* to

While quite obviously lacking the youthful good looks of many of his rivals, Roy Orbison's mournful vocal delivery seemed to appeal to those whose personal lives were tinged with sadness. Orbison had a right to sing in his distinctive style – his own life was punctuated by family tragedies during the 60s and 70s.

maintain a variety of styles which prolonged his active life. By the end of 1966, however, his well had more or less run dry and since then he has slipped towards a wealthy retirement.

Chubby Checker's main attribute was luck: he happened to be on hand when a cover version of Hank Ballard's single *The Twist* was required. It is said that Ballard was given a chance to perform the song on Dick Clark's famous *American Bandstand* but he refused to rehearse – whereupon Clark suggested that Checker record the song and appear on his show. On such foibles are careers made and destroyed! It was soon humming its way to number one and Checker, who as Ernest Evans had been working in a Philadelphia chicken market until recently, couldn't believe his good fortune.

With the decline of rock'n'roll, jiving had become passé, and the Twist, a new dance based around the single, was just the very thing to keep the cash registers active. Soon America was full of gyrating people – from Jackie Kennedy on down – as the Twist spread like forest fire to become the biggest dance craze since the Charleston. The steps of the Twist were so easy that anyone could master the dance – which they did – whereas efforts to introduce the Madison earlier in the year had foundered due to the relative virtuosity involved. Nevertheless, *The Madison* by Al Brown's Tunetoppers had reached number 23 and *Madison Time* by Ray Bryant number 30.

A succession of further dance-oriented hits including *The Hucklebuck, Pony Time, Let's Twist Again, The Fly, Limbo Rock* and a re-released *The Twist* (which flew straight back to number one), made Checker one of the early sixties' biggest stars ... but he inevitably ran out of new steps (as his 1965 effort *Let's Do The Freddie* attests). By this time, however, he had married a former Miss World and had possibly devised more interesting ways to stay in shape.

Checker wasn't the only artist to capitalise on the Twist craze. Sam Cooke made perhaps the best Twist single in *Twisting The Night Away* before reverting to less fashion-linked songs, thus extending his career. The Isley Brothers also got into the act with their seminal *Twist And Shout*, as did Danny and the Juniors, the Marcels, Santo and Johnny, Jimmy Soul and scores of others with uniformly dreadful efforts.

Joey Dee and the Starlighters, however, had more success. They were the house band at an ultra-fashionable New York night club, The Peppermint Lounge, where wealthy groovers displayed their twisting skills. Dee's song about the club, *Peppermint Twist,* became a number one and his cover of the Isley Brothers' *Shout* reached number six (making it the best-selling version), but follow-ups fared less well and by the end of 1963 the group had reverted to local status. Nevertheless, Dee can truthfully claim that the Ronettes and three of the Young Rascals passed through the Starlighters on their way to fame.

The only other artist to get the better of the Twist was Gary U. S. Bonds, who had been singing in groups around Norfolk Virginia since 1952, when he was 13. Progress eluded him until he met a local record shop owner who was about to start his own label and had written a song titled *New Orleans,*

which he invited Bonds to record. *New Orleans* became the first of five top ten smashes, including *Quarter To Three* (a number one – allegedly recorded by accident during a jam session), *School Is Out,* and his two Twisters, *Dear Lady Twist* and *Twist Twist Senora.* On all of these hits, Bonds' distinctive vocals were almost shrouded by the babble of excited background whoopers and the most muffled 'garage' sound since Jan and Dean's *Jennie Lee.*

By late 62 the Twist was hanging on, but Bonds had gone. So too had a host of fly-by-nights whose careers peaked with superb hit singles in 1960: Rod Holden *(Love You So),* Jessie Hill *(Ooh Poo Pah Doo),* Jimmy Jones *(Handy Man* and *Good Timing),* Maurice Williams and the Zodiacs *(Stay),* the Fendermen *(Mule Skinner Blues),* Barret Strong *(Money),* Billy Bland *(Let The Little Girl Dance),* Joe Jones *(You Talk Too Much),* and Jimmy Charles *(A Million To One).*

Exhibiting considerably more resilience were Johnny Burnette, Jerry Butler, and Ike and Tina Turner.

Burnette, who attended the same school as Elvis Presley, began his career during the mid-fifties as one of the wildest rockers around, and records by the Burnette Rock'n'Roll Trio remain highly prized items today. However, their true worth was barely recognised when they were released and Johnny and his brother Dorsey turned to songwriting to pay their bills.

Between them they penned three million-sellers for Ricky Nelson, *Believe What You Say, Just A Little Too Much* and *It's Late,* before Johnny decided to return to performing in 1960. Stowing his untamed youth, he plugged into the Frankie Avalon market, though he was far more talented than most of his competitors in that field, and scored two immediate winners in *Dreamin'* and *You're Sixteen.* After a third top twenty entry, *Little Boy Sad,* which like the excellent but unsuccessful *Cincinatti Fireball,* was closer to his earlier records, Burnette fell into artistic decline from which he had not recovered when a boating accident took his life in 1964.

His brother Dorsey also made the charts twice in 1960 – with *Tall Oak Tree* and *Hey Little One* – after which he turned to a singing/songwriting career in the country field.

With Curtis Mayfield, Jerry Butler formed the Impressions but after reaching number 11 with *For Your Precious Love* in 1958, he left for a solo career. *He Will Break Your Heart,* a top ten entry in 1960 provided the first of over 30 hits – though he only returned to the top ten twice with *Let It Be Me* (with Betty Everett in 1964) and *Only The Strong Survive* in 1969. After varying fortunes during the seventies, he assumed a back-seat role, grooming potential stars from his Chicago offices.

Ike and Tina Turner, the most enduring of all American acts to emerge during the year, had their first chart success in 1960 with *A Fool In Love.* Ike was a respected R&B pianist, having played on records by B. B. King and Howlin Wolf during the fifties, when he met Annie Mae Bullock for the first time. She asked to sing with his band and, after some hesitation, he agreed – discovering to his surprise, that this 16 year old was one of the most powerful and sensuous vocalists he had ever heard. When another girl failed to appear for a recording session, he allowed Annie Mae to duet with him on

Above: Chubby Checker (né Ernest Evans) demonstrates the Twist to British audiences. Performing the new dance, he claimed, had led to his losing far more weight than any medical diet had achieved – even so, he retained his original corpulent epithet. *Right:* Gary 'U.S.' Bonds (he claimed the U.S. was short for Ulysses Samuel) also scored a few twist hits, even though most of his records sounded as though they were recorded at a fairground.

what would be the first of many hits – after which they married and Annie Mae became Tina Turner.

During the sixties, Tina fronted one of the raunchiest stage acts ever seen, with Ike leading the band behind her. The British invasion put them into temporary decline but unlike most American recording stars of the early sixties, the Turners were able to make an astonishing recovery – as will be seen.

At the other end of the musical spectrum were two Bobbys and a Brian.

Bobby Rydell was a Frankie Avalon clone and had even played in a teenage band with Avalon before graduating to stardom in late 59 via the *American Bandstand* finishing school. As a singer, he was somewhat superior to Avalon (not too difficult a task) and managed to stroke the hearts of a million impressionable teenage girls, amassing 14 top twenty hits by 1963 when he retired to comfortable obscurity as an early casualty of Beatlemania.

Bobby Vee's career also began in earnest during 1960. His first big break came as a result of the death of his favourite singer, Buddy Holly. Vee, who was 15 years old at the time, lived in Fargo, North Dakota, where the Holly package played the night after the crash – and in the best traditions of the show going on was asked to make up the depleted bill. A Liberty Records talent scout saw the show, and by the end of 1959 Vee's first single, the Holly-slanted *Suzie Baby*, had become a minor hit.

In 1960, *Devil Or Angel* and *Rubber Ball* were the first of five million sellers within three years and Vee found himself a teen idol. His fan following was particularly solid in Britain, which he visited on several occasions during the early sixties, and this to some extent insulated him against the 'British Invasion' of 1964-65 which sealed the fate of so many of his peers.

His run of American hits continued until 1970, when he reconsidered his future and began to record, less frequently, under his real name of Robert T. Velline.

Brian Hyland's success also ran into the seventies, which is surprising for one who began his recording career with such a lightweight novelty as *Itsy Bitsy Teenie Weenie Yellow Polka Dot Bikini* – a number one smash in summer 1960. He had to wait two years for his next substantial hits which were *Ginny Come Lately* and *Sealed With A Kiss* – after which his name appeared in the charts periodically until late 1970 when *Gypsy Woman* entered the U.S. top three.

Hyland's *Bikini* wasn't the only peculiarity to prosper in 1960's charts. Also achieving high placings were *Ally Oop* by the Hollywood Argyles, *Mr. Custer* by Larry Verne, *Yogi* by the Ivy Three, and *Tell Laura I Love Her* – the year's big 'death-disc' by Ray Peterson (who followed it with the top tenner *Corinna Corinna,* produced by Phil Spector).

Brenda Lee was the only girl to hold a candle to Connie Francis' female supremacy during 1960. A child prodigy whose age, diminutive stature and powerpack voice earned her the nickname *Little Miss Dynamite*, Brenda was already a seasoned television performer when she signed her first recording contract in 1956, aged 11.

Her pop chart successes in the early sixties, sandwiched between her main career in country

music, were rarely of interest to rock'n'rollers – although two definite exceptions were *Sweet Nothins* and *Let's Jump The Broomstick,* which flared like beacons among her three dozen hits between 1960 and 1965. Brenda's family life now takes precedence over her musical activities although she still performs from time to time.

Four black teenagers from New Jersey, the Shirelles were one of the earliest and best of the sixties girl groups, working a vein which had been opened by the Chantels in the fifties and would be mined most productively in a couple of years when Phil Spector got to work.

Frequently under-rated in the glow of their successors, the Shirelles, powered by the emotional voice of Shirley Alston (from whom they'd taken their name), were responsible for a string of magnificient and much-copied singles stretching from *Tonight's The Night* (1960) to *Soldier Boy* (1962), and taking in such classics as *Will You Love Me Tomorrow* (1960) and *Dedicated To The One I Love* (1961).

They continued to record for several years, achieving minor hits until 1967, but their success rate declined when the Beatles and their cohorts turned America's record buying habits upside down. This was particularly ironic because the Beatles had been inspired by the Shirelles to the extent that two of their songs, *Boys* and *Baby, It's You*, had appeared on their first album.

Another song beloved of the Liverpudlian groups was *Lonely Weekends,* which Charlie Rich recorded at Sun Records and it took him into the charts for the first time in Spring 1960. Like Hank Locklin (*Please Help Me I'm Falling*) and Bob Luman (*Let's Think About Living*), Rich was a country singer who achieved a fluke national hit – but unlike the others, he returned to the charts in a big way some years later.

In 1965, several labels later, he returned to prominence with *Mohair Sam* before retreating into country and western music where he remained obscurely ensconced until the mid-seventies when he stumbled into superstardom in the wake of two massive hits, *Behind Closed Doors* and *The Most*

Brenda Lee (*above left*) achieved more than 20 pop hits before leaving her teens, but marriage subsequently curtailed her recorded output. Bobby Vee (*above*), like Brenda Lee, was rarely photographed in a manner which would betray his lack of stature, and his frequent visits to Britain helped him withstand the British beat boom for a few years longer than most of his American contemporaries. The Shirelles (*left*) were also affected by the emergence of the Beatles, who ironically worshipped the girl quartet to the extent of covering two of their recordings. Any belated recognition failed to prevent the girls from vanishing into obscurity, although leader Shirley Alston made a brief comeback at the end of the 70s.

'60

the year

Events

13 Feb. France becomes the fourth nation to explode an atomic bomb.

19 Feb. Prince Andrew is born.

21 Mar. South African police open fire on crowds at Sharpeville and Langa, killing over 70.

1 May U.S. pilot Gary Powers, flying a U-2 reconnaissance plane, is shot down by a Soviet missile near Sverdlovsk.

6 May Princess Margaret marries Anthony Armstrong Jones in Westminster Abbey.

9 May The first birth control pills are sold.

30 June Belgium grants independence to the Congo, leading to civil war.

25 Aug. The 17th Olympic Games opens in Rome. Cassius Clay wins the light-heavyweight boxing gold medal.

12 Oct. The 25th anniversary meeting of the United Nations is adjourned in pandemonium after Kruschev pounds his shoe on the table and makes a dramatic exit.

8 Nov. John F. Kennedy is elected President, narrowly defeating Richard M. Nixon.

Films of 60
The Alamo · The Apartment · Elmer Gantry · I'm All Right Jack · Never On Sunday · Psycho · Sons And Lovers · Spartacus

U.S. CHART TOPPERS – WEEKS AT TOP

El Paso	Marty Robbins	2
Running Bear	Johnny Preston	3
Teen Angel	Mark Dinning	2
A Summer Place	Percy Faith	9
Stuck On You	Elvis Presley	4
Cathy's Clown	Everly Brothers	5
Everybody's Somebody's Fool	Connie Francis	2
Alley Oop	Hollywood Argyles	1
I'm Sorry	Brenda Lee	3
Itsy Bitsy Teenie Weenie Yellow Polka Dot Bikini		
	Brian Hyland	1
It's Now Or Never	Elvis Presley	5
The Twist	Chubby Checker	1
My Heart Has A Mind Of Its Own	Connie Francis	2
Mr. Custer	Larry Verne	1
Save The Last Dance For Me	Drifters	3
I Want To Be Wanted	Brenda Lee	1
Georgia On My Mind	Ray Charles	1
Stay	Maurice Williams and the Zodiacs	1
Are You Lonesome Tonight?	Elvis Presley	5

U.K. CHART TOPPERS – WEEKS AT TOP

What Do You Want?	Adam Faith	1
What Do You Want To Make Those Eyes At Me For?		
	Emile Ford	1
Why?	Anthony Newley	6
Poor Me	Adam Faith	1
Running Bear	Johnny Preston	2
My Old Man's A Dustman	Lonnie Donegan	5
Cathy's Clown	Everly Brothers	9
Good Timing	Jimmy Jones	4
Please Don't Tease	Cliff Richard	3
Apache	Shadows	6
Tell Laura I Love Her	Ricky Valance	2
Only The Lonely	Roy Orbison	3
It's Now Or Never	Elvis Presley	8
Poetry In Motion	Johnny Tillotson	1

Right: Melina Mercouri (right) in *Never On Sunday.*

Opposite: Congolese troops.

THE BEATNIKS

Who? | What? | Where? | Why?

There are settlements of Beatniks in most of the major cities throughout the U. S., and the colony in New York's colorful Greenwich Village is one of the most publicized.

Most of the male Beats live in furnished rooms, paying $7-$10 in weekly rent. The girls generally share apartments—two to four teaming up to split the rent. However, about one third of the Beatchiks live with males. To conquer the housing shortage some ingenious Beats rent "living lofts" in old factory buildings. The space is partitioned to accommodate as many as seven members of a particular herd. Often the group is made up without regard to sex or race, but they live harmoniously. There is always room for one more Beat, and the temporarily unsheltered never are turned away.

About 80 per cent of the Beats are not regularly employed, and they struggle to keep it that way. They work at part-time jobs to provide just enough money to meet their meager needs. They take jobs that require little or no thinking, preferring to save the mental exercise for their artistic interests.

The subject of money seldom is discussed at a *klatsch*. "It is not a matter of serious involvement," says McDarrah. However, there is suspicion that some Beats have a source of secret income—a periodic check from home.

The Beats eat haphazardly and poorly. They ignore the breakfast-lunch-dinner routine and turn to food only when the pangs of hunger persist. Only the cheapest items on the menu are selected. Often they go in groups to Chinatown, where a big meal costs little. Some pads operate a co-op kitchen, and the occupants take turns whipping up inexpensive dishes that go a long way—meatballs and spaghetti, for example.

The Beats dress shabbily mostly because they are poor, according to Mc-Darrah. They buy their clothes in Army-Navy stores, or at second-hand clothing exchanges. The dark glasses are worn mostly for identification. The beard also is a symbol. Most Beats bathe, says Mc-Darrah, even though they appear unclean.

The "free love" brand stamped on the Beatchiks is completely erroneous, SAGA's expert reports. The girls are faithful to one guy—almost always a Beat. They shun the free-spending transients.

The Beats are largely non-drinkers—mostly because they can't afford the luxury. Beer or coffee are social drinks. Many have at one time or other experimented with some form of stimulant, but, generally speaking, they are not drug addicts.

The New York colony is made up of Beatniks from many foreign lands. The age bracket for both men and women runs between 25 and 35. About 20 per cent of the group is married; some, not many, have children. Few go to church or embrace a religion. This, in capsule, is the Beat Generation.

An early shot of Charlie Rich in his days as a rocker from the Sun Records stable. Rich returned to his biggest successes in the early 70s, when his prematurely grey hair led him to become known as 'The Silver Fox'.

The Shadows – Tony Meehan (drums), Bruce Welch (guitar), Hank B. Marvin (guitar) and Jet Harris (bass) – the longest lived instrumental group in rock'n'roll history, with nearly thirty hits to their credit – not counting another thirty on which they backed Cliff Richard.

Beautiful Girl In The World. His days of 'playing the piano as badly as Jerry Lee', as he was reportedly instructed to do during his days with Sun, were long behind him.

Another Sun alumnus, Bill Black, had played bass on Presley's early hits until he quit after a pay dispute. Forming his own band, Bill Black's Combo (with subsequent Nashville studio ace Reggie Young on guitar), he proceeded to record a stream of extraordinarily successful records for another Memphis label, Hi. Six consecutive singles, including *White Silver Sands* and a version of *Don't Be Cruel* (which he'd previously cut with Elvis), made the U.S. top twenty but Black's formula inevitably lost its potency and the success rate plummeted. The band kept going, even after Black died from a brain tumour in 1965, but session work accounted for their main income.

The only other new instrumental unit to make any headway during 1960 was the Ventures, led by a pair of construction workers, Bob Bogle and Don Wilson, who discovered a common interest in the guitar while working together on a building site in Seattle.

First appearances before an audience after working on the site all day were encouraging but tiring and led to a decision to turn professional – but attempts to convince record companies of their potential were fruitless. Finally, Wilson's mother

formed a label for them, Blue Horizon, and their first release, a version of jazz guitarist Johnny Smith's *Walk Don't Run*, took off after local enthusiasm had sparked national interest. Dolton Records, a Liberty subsidiary, took over their contract and pushed the single to number two.

The Ventures returned to the top ten only three times during the sixties, with *Perfidia*, *Walk Don't Run 64* and *Hawaii Five-0*, but although their American success was inconsistent, they somehow became a major attraction in Japan during the seventies. To date over a hundred albums have been released in the Far East, though few are issued elsewhere – and Bogle and Wilson reportedly now take a back seat, instructing studio musicians to duplicate their highly recognisable style.

The Shadows can claim to have outrun every other instrumental outfit in the world. Their mainstays, Hank B. Marvin and Bruce Welch had moved down from Newcastle in Spring 1958, and their conviction and ability soon landed them positions in the Drifters, a group hastily assembled to back the meteoric Cliff Richard on a national package tour. (Cliff's own group were unable to make the transition from local youth club work.)

Within months the Shadows (as they now called themselves to avoid confusion with the American Drifters) began to establish their own identity with a series of melodic rockers which took them into the

British top ten 12 times between 1960 and 1963. Included among these were five chart toppers: *Apache*, *Kon Tiki*, *Wonderful Land*, *Dance On* and *Foot Tapper*. Their bespectacled lead guitarist, Hank Marvin, precipitated the most widespread guitar-buying epidemic since the days of skiffle and became the most influential British guitarist of the early sixties.

The Shadows' unabated success continued until the end of 1968 when Bruce Welch left to concentrate on record production (most notably with Olivia Newton-John) and the group split up soon after. However, following the success of a hits compilation which became the second biggest selling album of 1977 in Britain, they reformed for recording sessions and concert appearances and their stylised versions of film and show tunes soon made them regular visitors to the charts once more.

Their erstwhile boss, meanwhile, had broadened his initial horizons with a series of film roles, the first of which was a small part in *Serious Charge*, which contrived to include a performance of his Lionel Bart-penned million seller *Living Doll*. This was followed, in 1960, with a starring role in *Expresso Bongo*, a film whose scenario revolved around the coffee-bar milieu from which Cliff had himself emerged. The soundtrack spawned a hit E.P. and a number two single, *A Voice In The Wilderness*, and Cliff's popularity with fans of both sexes and all ages was further consolidated by *The Young Ones* and *Summer Holiday*, in both of which the Shadows also starred.

Throughout the sixties and seventies, Cliff has continued to be amazingly successful, achieving over 60 consecutive British hits – an unapproachable record. In America, his success rate has been rather more erratic: *Living Doll* and *It's All In The Game* made the top thirty during the early sixties, but only *Miss You Nights*, which reached number six in 1976, has achieved significant sales. His unparalleled British hitmaking prowess remains undiminished, however, as evidenced by his 1979 chart topper *We Don't Talk Anymore* . . . and he still has a long way to go. One token of the widespread esteem he is held in was seen in the 1980 New Year's Honours List in which he was awarded an O.B.E. (Order of the British Empire) – a decoration one grade higher than the Beatles' M.B.E.s.

Only one new star of any note emerged in Britain . . . Johnny Kidd. After a skiffle group apprenticeship, Londoner Fred Heath changed his name and moved into rock'n'roll with a vengeance – and Johnny Kidd and the Pirates soon became the most exciting live band in the country. The Pirates, over-dressed as swashbuckling gangsters of the high seas, were an excellent hard-rocking band, and Kidd, in similar piratical garb reinforced with an eye-patch and a cutlass which he waved about on stage, was an inspired and intuitive vocalist.

Their first three singles attracted little attention, but the fourth, *Shaking All Over*, sliced its way into the top three during the summer. Ranking with Cliff Richard's *Move It* as one of the few genuinely exhilarating and authentic British rock'n'roll records, it raised Kidd to a level he couldn't maintain, though *I'll Never Get Over You* put him in the top five three years later. After losing two excellent sets

of Pirates, he quit the music business but was subsequently encouraged to try a final rally. In October 1966, during a series of dates in the north of England, he lost his life in a car crash.

Apart from Kidd, and a relatively interesting minor hit called *Jet Black Machine* by Vince Taylor and his Playboys, the British scene of 1960 was pretty dull. Unless, of course, you were amused by incredible attempts to emulate American originals, in which case you may have gone for Mark Wynter, Ricky Valance, Wee Willie Harris, Craig Douglas, Terry Dene, Michael Cox, Duffy Power, the Brook Brothers, Johnny Gentle or Dickie Pride.

All in all, 1960 was not an auspicious year . . . it seemed as if rock'n'roll had fallen into a coma and no-one was around to resuscitate it.

Top: Cliff and the Shadows discuss the possibilities presented by cloning (particularly impressive, as the concept was not popularised until ten years after this picture was taken).

Above: Johnny Kidd and the Pirates with swashbuckling backdrop and nautical clothing. Kidd (second right) was the only significant rock star to emerge from the North London suburb of Willesden until the late 70s, when one of the members of Boney M admitted to the same unlikely origins.

'61

'Walkin' Back To Happiness'

The Crystals · Dion · Ral Donner · Lee Dorsey · Berry Gordy
The Highwaymen · The Impressions · Ben E. King · Gladys Knight and the Pips
John Leyton · Barry Mann · The Marvellettes · Joe Meek · Gene Pitney
Smokey Robinson and the Miracles · Del Shannon · Helen Shapiro · Phil Spector
Mary Wells

Musically, 1961 was a fairly nondescript and bitty year. Any overall unity or growth was absent and most of the trends were short-lived – possibly because the repercussions of the payola scandal were still being felt, but certainly because top forty radio programming had arrived and tended to be very conservative. To make this black picture bleaker, America had descended into a state of extreme normalcy: political activism had yet to invade the colleges, and serious students felt that rock music was just for kids . . . certainly most of the year's pop music seemed to be aimed at the lowest common denominator.

Nevertheless, as in any year, there were plenty of great records if you took the trouble to seek them out. Some of the best were to be found on the Tamla and Motown labels. Both labels had been launched in Detroit by Berry Gordy, a sometime assembly-line worker at the city's Ford factory. Gordy had already been involved with a number of best sellers, either as producer, songwriter or both, including *You've Got What It Takes* and *Move Two Mountains* by Marv Johnson and *Reet Petite* and *Lonely Teardrops* by Jackie Wilson.

Motown (named after Detroit's nickname, 'Motor Town') and Tamla (which he'd originally wanted to call 'Tammy' after the 1957 Debbie Reynolds' hit, but had been prevented from so doing by copyright law) were intended to promote local black talent, and three of their acts were national stars within 18 months.

The first to break were the Miracles, led by the multi-faceted Smokey Robinson, who wrote practically all the group's material, including their first hit *Shop Around*, which reached number two during the opening weeks of 1961. Over the next 12 years, they scored more than 40 hits, the most memorable of which were *You've Really Got A Hold On Me*, *What's So Good About Goodbye*, *Going To A Go-Go*, *The Tracks Of My Tears*, *I Second That Emotion* and *Tears Of A Clown*, a chart-topper in 1970. By 1972, Robinson had left the group for a solo career but, as one of the chief architects behind Tamla-Motown's astonishing growth, he was made a Vice President of the company and he continues to be a creative force today. As well as possessing one of rock's finest voices, Robinson is an exceptional lyricist – Bob Dylan is reported to have described him as 'America's greatest living poet' – and his compositions have boosted the careers of most artists on the label.

Gordy's second major success, Mary Wells, reached the national charts within weeks of the Miracles. Her hit, *Bye Bye Baby,* was followed by a top tenner in *The One Who Really Loves You*, and a

brace of Smokey Robinson songs, *You Beat Me To The Punch* and *Two Lovers*, firmly established her during 1962. Two years later, Mary's career peaked when another Robinson song, the much admired *My Guy*, provided her with a number one record, but she was subsequently wooed away from Motown and her career declined rather drastically as a result.

Tamla's first chart-topper appeared just before Christmas 1961 in the shape of *Please Mr. Postman* by a girl quintette called the Marvellettes. They reappeared in the top ten the following year with *Playboy* and again in 1966 with *Don't Mess With Bill* – a song by the prolific Robinson who also furnished them with substantial hits in *The Hunter Gets Captured By The Game* and *My Baby Must Be A Magician*. When lead singer Gladys Horton left in 1968, the Marvellettes lost their distinctive sound and their hits trailed off, leaving them to rely on their stage act to see them into the seventies.

Gladys Knight, then on Fury Records but later to sign with Motown, also struck gold in 1961 when *Every Beat Of My Heart*, a song written by R&B pioneer Johnny Otis, began a chart career which has yet to fade. Gladys, 17 at the time, sang lead in front of three members of her family, collectively known as the Pips. After joining the Gordy empire in 1966, she eased into the top ten with *I Heard It Through The Grapevine* and *If I Were Your Woman*, and a further move, to Buddah, yielded the spinetingling *Midnight Train To Georgia* among several other huge hits.

By 1977, by which time they had accumulated nearly a dozen million-sellers, Gladys split from the Pips to go solo. The Pips, who had suffered only one personnel change since their inception, began a career of their own whilst Gladys signed with C.B.S. to continue her achievements as one of the all-time greats of soul music.

Soul wasn't entirely the preserve of Berry Gordy and his signings, of course. Equally significant acts could be found on other labels, though not in the same profusion. Atlantic, who had pioneered and popularised R&B and soul in the fifties, may have lost Ray Charles to A.B.C. Paramount, but they came up with two new winners in Solomon Burke and Ben E. King.

Although Burke failed to repeat the success of *Just Out Of Reach* (his 1961 chart debut) his singles, the best of which were produced by Bert Berns and Jerry Wexler, maintained a consistently high standard. Greatly respected by his many copyists, he racked up 23 top hundred entries during the sixties.

Ben E. King, formerly lead singer with the Drifters (who themselves had four hits, including

Sweets For My Sweet in 1961), cruised into the top ten with his first solo outing *Spanish Harlem*, a song written by the rare partnership of Jerry Leiber and Phil Spector. His second single, *Stand By Me*, was even more successful and the hits continued with *Don't Play That Song* and *I Who Have Nothing*.

After mellowing towards a Billy Eckstine style, King left Atlantic only to rejoin in the mid-seventies, when he regained his direction following fallow spells on other labels. Currently an infrequent hitmaker, he seems to have lost much of the fire which made him a legend.

Hanging up his boxing gloves, Kid Chocolate reverted to his real name, Lee Dorsey, and reached the top ten with *Ya Ya*, the first of several hits including *Do Re Mi*, *Ride Your Pony*, *Working In A Coalmine* and *Holy Cow* – most of which were masterminded by the New Orleans soul svengali Allan Toussaint.

Smashes emanating from localised soul /R&B scenes included: *But I Do* and *You Always Hurt The One You Love* by Clarence 'Frogman' Henry, *I Like It Like That* by Chris Kenner, *It Will Stand* by the Showmen, *You Can Have Her* by Roy Hamilton, *Tossing And Turning* by Bobby Lewis and *Mother-in-law* by Ernie K. Doe.

Gene McDaniels had three hits within a year – *A Hundred Pounds Of Clay*, *Tower Of Strength* and *Chip Chip* – only to slip into obscurity until the early seventies when he made a brief comeback.

The Impressions, who came from various parts of the country to team up in Chicago in 1957, boasted two of the finest soul singers the world has ever seen: Jerry Butler and Curtis Mayfield. After Butler had decided to go solo, Mayfield led the group through a run of classic hits, beginning with *Gypsy Woman* in 1961 and including *It's All Right*, *Keep On Pushing*, *Amen*, and *People Get Ready*. In 1968, Mayfield also left the group, who continued to record with sporadic success throughout the seventies.

Despite the preponderance of black talent, several new white stars came to the fore in 1961, notably Dion, Del Shannon and Gene Pitney.

The Impressions (*above*) were one of the more consistent American hitmakers during the early 60s, but curiously, they never achieved a British top twenty single until 1975.

Dion Di Mucci (*above left*) was one of the finest singers of the early 60s. Like Del Shannon (*left*) Dion is still highly regarded among critics, although he has achieved little commercial success during the last 15 years, despite releasing several albums, most of which contain at least one exceptional performance.

Right: Gene Pitney also remains active but relatively unsuccessful. His recording of the Jagger/Richard song, *That Girl Belongs To Yesterday*, was one of ten top tenners in a chart career spanning 14 years.

Events

13 Jan. Fighting breaks out in Katanga, Congolese Republic, between U.N. troops and forces supporting Patrice Lumumba.

12 Apr. Yuri Gagarin becomes the first man in space.

17 Apr. An abortive invasion of the Bay of Pigs, Cuba is launched by Cuban exiles.

27 Apr. Sierra Leone becomes independent.

5 May Alan B. Shepard becomes the first American in space.

16 June Soviet ballet dancer Rudolf Nureyev defects at Paris Airport.

1 Oct. New York Yankee Roger Maris hits a record-setting 61st home run – breaking Babe Ruth's 1927 total.

U.S. CHART TOPPERS – WEEKS AT TOP

Wonderland By Night	Bert Kaempfert	3
Will You Love Me Tomorrow?	Shirelles	2
Calcutta	Lawrence Welk	2
Pony Time	Chubby Checker	3
Surrender	Elvis Presley	2
Blue Moon	Marcels	3
Runaway	Del Shannon	4
Mother-In-Law	Ernie K. Doe	1
Travellin' Man	Ricky Nelson	2
Running Scared	Roy Orbison	1
Moody River	Pat Boone	1
Quarter To Three	Gary U.S. Bonds	2
Tossin' And Turnin'	Bobby Lewis	7
Wooden Heart	Joe Dowell	1
Michael	Highwaymen	2
Take Good Care Of My Baby	Bobby Vee	3
Hit The Road Jack	Ray Charles	2
Runaround Sue	Dion	2
Big Bad John	Jimmy Dean	5
Please Mr. Postman	Marvelettes	1
The Lion Sleeps Tonight	Tokens	3

U.K. CHART TOPPERS – WEEKS AT TOP

Poetry In Motion	Johnny Tillotson	1
Are You Lonesome Tonight?	Elvis Presley	4
Walk Right Back	Everly Brothers	4
Wooden Heart	Elvis Presley	4
Are You Sure?	Allisons	2
You're Driving Me Crazy	Temperance Seven	2
Blue Moon	Marcels	2
Runaway	Del Shannon	2
Surrender	Elvis Presley	5
Temptation	Everly Brothers	4
Well I Ask You	Eden Kane	1
You Don't Know	Helen Shapiro	2
Johnny Remember Me	John Leyton	5
Kon Tiki	Shadows	1
Michael	Highwaymen	1
Walkin' Back To Happiness	Helen Shapiro	4
His Latest Flame	Elvis Presley	3
Take Good Care Of My Baby	Bobby Vee	1
Tower Of Strength	Frankie Vaughan	2
Stranger On The Shore	Acker Bilk	2

19 Nov. East Germany begins erecting a concrete barrier soon known as 'the Berlin Wall'.

11 Dec. President Kennedy sends 400 helicopter crewmen to Vietnam – the first overt military support.

12 Dec. An Israeli court finds Adolph Eichmann guilty of war crimes against the Jewish people. He is sentenced to death.

Films of 61

Breakfast at Tiffany's · Fanny · The Guns of Navarone · The Hustler · Judgment At Nuremberg · La Dolce Vita · Two Women · West Side Story

Left: Yuri Gagarin, the first man in space.

Opposite top and bottom left. West Side Story.

Opposite bottom right: Anita Ekberg in *La Dolce Vita*.

Until they parted in the middle of the previous year, Dion had been leader of the Belmonts, who were never able to recover from his departure. Dion, on the other hand, became enormously successful between 1961 and 1964, when the British invasion blew him away for a few years.

Runaround Sue and *The Wanderer*, both of which won gold discs in 1961, were two of 11 top thirty entries including *Lovers Who Wander, Little Diane, Ruby Baby* and *Drip Drop*. After *Abraham, Martin And John*, a comeback hit in 1968, he continued to record with varying degrees of success. Critical acclaim greeted several of his albums, including the excellent Phil Spector-produced *Born To Be With You*, but changing tastes denied him any widespread re-acceptance.

Runaway, featuring his distinctive falsetto vocal and a memorable theremin solo, shot Del Shannon to number one on both sides of the Atlantic. It was to be his greatest achievement, even though he managed to keep the hits coming. *Hats Off To Larry* and *Keep Searchin'* both made the U.S. top ten and these, plus five more including *Swiss Maid* and *Little Town Flirt*, attained similar British placings. By 1970, Shannon had become an occasional performer but he also demonstrated his producing skill during that year when he supervised Brian Hyland's million selling re-make of the Impressions' *Gipsy Woman*.

Gene Pitney began his music business involvement as a songwriter, providing *Today's Teardrops* for Roy Orbison and *Hello Mary Lou* for Ricky Nelson among others, but after experimenting with multi-tracking effects he embarked on a spectacularly successful career as a singer, netting five million-sellers before 1965. After *Town Without Pity* had put him on the map, he scored heavily with *The Man Who Shot Liberty Valance, Only Love Can Break A Heart, It Hurts To Be In Love* and *I'm Gonna Be Strong*, but his most celebrated performance was *24 Hours From Tulsa*. His American appeal waned during the late sixties, but he remained a big star in Britain, where he still commands a fair following.

Pitney's second single, *Every Breath I Take*, had been produced by Phil Spector and although the collaboration ended there, they both guested on the Rolling Stones' first album, their presence being commemorated on *Now I've Got A Witness (Like Uncle Phil And Uncle Gene)*. Pitney also wrote a song which would carry Spector's fabulous Crystals to number one: *He's A Rebel*.

Phil Spector was born in New York but his family moved to California in 1953 after his father died. As leader of the Teddy Bears, he scored an immediate number one with *To Know Him Is To Love Him* in 1958 after which he decided to learn about record production, studying under Lee Hazlewood and Lestor Sill, who were responsible for Duane Eddy's finest moments. Spector later worked for Leiber and Stoller in New York before undertaking his first production job in late 1960. The record, *Corinna Corinna* by Ray Peterson was a top ten hit and Spector was on his way.

After two more top tenners, *I Love How You Love Me* by the Paris Sisters and *Pretty Little Angel Eyes* by Curtis Lee, Spector felt ready to form his own label, which he did in conjunction with Lester Sill in late 1961. Philles records was born . . . and seven of

the first 15 singles were by the Crystals, a group of five New York schoolgirls.

Two top twenty entries, *There's No Other* and *Uptown*, preceded the chart topping *He's A Rebel* and a couple more classics in *Da Doo Ron Ron* and *Then He Kissed Me* – but then their success rate fell away sharply as Spector began to concentrate on the Ronettes, who were more appropriate to the ' Wall of sound' he had evolved. The Crystals, however, will never be forgotten – which is more than can be said for some of the other girls who edged into the spotlight during 1961.

Cathy Jean and the Room-mates experienced five minute stardom with *Please Love Me Forever*, as did Linda Scott with *I've Told Every Little Star* and

Phil Spector looks on as the Ronettes (*left*) sign a contract with his Philles label. The Crystals (*below*) were the first major group whom Spector guided to stardom, but they returned to obscurity after less than two years at the top.

Opposite: Helen Shapiro was yet another child prodigy whose talents were less appreciated after she moved closer to adulthood. Possessor of an undeniably unique voice, Helen has regularly attempted to make comebacks during the last 15 years, but thus far has never looked like recapturing her teenage fame.

Barbara George with *I Know*. The Angels (*'Til* in 1961 and *My Boyfriend's Back* in 1963) hung on a little longer, so too did Sue Thompson (*Sad Movies* and *Norman*), Maxine Brown (*All In My Mind* in 1961 and *Oh No, Not My Baby* in 1964) and Timi Yuro (*Hurt* in 1961 and *What's A Matter Baby?* the next year).

Two film starlets also had isolated record success before returning to the silver screen: Ann Margaret with *I Just Don't Understand* and Hayley Mills with *Let's Get Together*.

Hayley wasn't the only British girl to hit the charts, however. Far more flamboyant was the rise of a 15 year old East Ender called Helen Shapiro: her first single, *Don't Treat Me Like A Child* reached number four on the British chart in Spring 1961, and her two other releases that year, *You Don't Know* and *Walkin' Back to Happiness*, made number one. Helen's hits tailed off during 1962 and two years later, at 18, she was a has-been – laid waste by the Beatles.

The same fate lay in store for John Leyton, though he was able to fall back on the acting ability he'd been nurturing before anyone told him that he might succeed as a singer. It's said that, during the late fifties, a car in which Leyton was a passenger was involved in a crash in North London, and when Leyton dragged himself out of the wreckage several teenage girls fainted, apparently thinking they had witnessed the reincarnation of James Dean.

Leyton found fame playing the part of a singer in

John Leyton was one of Joe Meek's first protegés. In the same way that Phil Spector tended to overshadow his artists, Meek's acts relied heavily on his artistry to maintain their popularity.

You was the first of five considerable hits but he too went out of style very quickly, as did quasi-country singer Karl Denver. Both outlasted the Allisons, however. After contriving to represent Britain in the Eurovision Song Contest (where they came second), the Allisons watched their Buddy Holly-influenced single *Are You Sure?* climb to the top, but it was to be their only success.

Also here today and gone tomorrow was 'the trad jazz boom', which had been sparked off by Chris Barber's *Petite Fleur* in 1959 and fed by a series of lightweight confections from Kenny Ball and Acker Bilk. Eventually, the initial quality and enthusiasm of the music which had inspired the boom in the first place was diluted and plasticised beyond all recognition and the traditional jazz revival died a rather ignoble death as a result.

Equally feeble was America's parallel fad, ' the folk boom', which saw a million clean-cut college boys trying to emulate the success of the Kingston Trio. Most commercial acceptance was found by the Highwaymen, who made number one with *Michael*, and the Tokens, who achieved similar heights with *The Lion Sleeps Tonight.* The Highwaymen returned to the charts with *Cotton Fields* and *The Gypsy Rover* before subsiding into cabaret whilst the Tokens cleverly modified their style in order to survive. They became a harmony pop group, succeeding later with *He's In Town* and *I Hear Trumpets Blow*, and after their eventual dissolution became the guiding forces behind Cross Country and Dawn.

When the aforementioned Dawn swept into the headlines in the early seventies, it marked the re-emergence of Tony Orlando, whose previous chart career had started and ended in 1961. His big hits were *Halfway To Paradise* and *Bless You.* Equally fleeting was Ral Donner's flight. After two excellent singles, *Girl Of My Best Friend* and *You Don't Know What You've Got*, he also drifted into the unknown. Others who put a temporary dent into the 1961 chart included Eddie Hodges (*I'm Gonna Knock On Your Door*), Joe Dowell (*Wooden Heart*), Dick and Dee Dee (*The Mountain's High*), Troy Shondell (*This Time*) and Barry Mann (*Who Put The Bomp*).

The lack of any dominant movement produced a superabundance of vocal groups, most of whom fell by the rock-strewn wayside after delivering one classic. Among these were the Marcels (*Blue Moon*), the Jive Five (*My True Story*), the G–Clefs (*I Understand*), the Jarmels (*A Little Bit Of Soap*), the Flares (*Foot Stompin'*), the Edsels (*Rama Lama Ding Dong*), the Marathons (*Peanut Butter*), the Regents (*Barbara Ann*), the Echoes (*Baby Blue*), the Dovelles (*Bristol Stomp*) and Little Caesar and the Romans (*Those Oldies But Goodies*).

The American instrumental scene threw up hits by the Ramrods (*Ghost Riders In The Sky*), the Stringalongs (*Wheels*), Freddy King (*Hideaway*), Floyd Cramer *(On The Rebound),* the Duals *(Stick Shift),* Kokomo (*Asia Minor*), the Fireballs (*Quite A Party*) and Ace Cannon (*Tuff*). Of these, only the Fireballs and Floyd Cramer would see the top thirty again.

As the year ended, the rock world was desperately seeking a new force to sweep out the cobwebs and clear away the dross. By the end of the following year it would have arrived, and the Americans would begin to lose their grip.

a long forgotten television soap opera in which he sang *Johnny Remember Me.* Released as a single, it topped the chart to become the biggest of nine hits between Summer 1961 and early 1964. Like *Wild Wind, Son This Is She* and the others, *Johnny Remember Me* was produced and engineered by Joe Meek – certainly the most ingenious and prolific independent producer on the early sixties British scene. While most of his contemporaries were still coming up with pale imitations of American rock, Meek originated a full, echo-laden sound which was to bring him worldwide renown the following year when he put together a session group called the Tornados to record a tune he'd just written.

Eden Kane was Leyton's only rival. *Well I Ask*

'62

'Let's Twist Again'

Arthur Alexander · Joan Baez · The Beach Boys · The Beatles · Brooker T. and the M.G.s · Joe Brown · B. Bumble and the Stingers · Bruce Channel Judy Collins · The Contours · The Cookies · Bob Dylan · Shane Fenton The Four Seasons · Marvin Gaye · Frank Ifield · Carole King Bobby 'Boris' Pickett and the Crypt Kickers · Tommy Roe · Mike Sarne Dee Dee Sharp · Bob B. Soxx and the Blue Jeans · The Tornados

The last of the static years, 1962 heralded a period of change, as many established stars faded. Already past their most productive years were Jerry Lee Lewis, the Coasters, Little Richard, Gene Vincent, the Platters, Gary Bonds, Frankie Avalon and Fabian . . . and by the end of the year Paul Anka, the Everly Brothers, Duane Eddy, Ricky Nelson, Del Shannon, Freddy Cannon, Fats Domino, Connie Francis and Pat Boone could all see the writing on the wall, even if the message wasn't yet completely clear.

However, Presley's supremacy was still unquestionable, with three U.S. top tenners and four U.K. number ones: *Can't Help Falling In Love With You, Good Luck Charm, She's Not You,* and *Return To Sender.*

Most of the other rock pioneers were either forgotten or dead.

A number of interesting new performers sprang from nowhere only to drop out of sight when their sole hits fell from the playlists. What happened to Larry Finnegan after *Dear One* reached number 11 or to Bruce Channel after *Hey Baby* reached the top? Where did the Earls go after *Remember Then,* or the Routers after *Let's Go?* Did Ernie Maresca knock himself out on *Shout Shout,* did Bunker Hill lose himself after *Hide And Go Seek?* Shall we ever know?

We do know that Gene Chandler had more luck. Nothing could stop the chart-topping *Duke Of Earl* or over 20 subsequent hits, including some as recent as 1979. And Johnny Crawford had eight hits, including *Cindy's Birthday,* before reverting to his television career as the son of *The Rifleman.* It was all over for Jimmy Clanton, however: he fell from grace very abruptly after coming off a number one in *Venus In Blue Jeans* . . . and Chris Montez had to wait four years for his next success after making the top five with *Let's Dance.*

Several girls came and went too. Ketty Lester never found the reply to her excellent *Love Letters,* and Barbara Lynn lost a good thing after *You'll Lose A Good Thing* left the top ten. Little Esther faded after *Release Me,* and Marcie Blane after *Bobby's Girl* . . . and how Claudine Clark could have failed to return after the classic single *Party Lights,* nobody knew. Shelley Fabares went back to her screen career after her surprise number one *Johnny Angel,* and the Ikettes returned to the shadows of their bosses, Ike and Tina Turner, after their solo hit *I'm Blue.*

Sixteen year old Dee Dee Sharp, another Philadelphian, had a spectacular if short chart career. In Spring 1962, she had simultaneous top three entries with *Slow Twistin',* a duet with Chubby Checker, and her own *Mashed Potato Time.*

Gravy and *Ride* returned her to the top ten in 1962, as did *Do The Bird* in 1963, but after that it was downhill all the way for the energetic Dee Dee, who was happy to pursue domesticity as the wife of noted producer Kenny Gamble, although she did restart her career in the late seventies as Dee Dee Sharp Gamble.

Carole King, however, was here to stay. With her songwriting partner and husband, Gerry Goffin, she'd hit the big time in 1961 with *Will You Love Me Tomorrow?*, the Shirelles' first number one. The same year, they wrote hits for the Drifters, Tony Orlando and Bobby Vee, who registered their second number one in *Take Good Care Of My Baby.* In 1962 the Goffin/King team was responsible for top tenners by the Drifters and James Darren, but they also launched the careers of Little Eva and of the Cookies.

Eva Boyd, a black teenager from North Carolina, had moved to New York where she earned pocket money babysitting for Goffin and King, and after hearing her singing around the apartment, they wrote a song for her. *The Locomotion,* describing yet

The Isley Brothers, one of the least consistent, but most enduring groups of all time. 1962 was the year when they released the original version of *Twist And Shout.*

another new dance, was soon the best selling single in America. Follow-ups inevitably fared less well and Eva's fame was all over after a few months. On *The Locomotion* and various other Goffin/King creations, three girls collectively known as the Cookies, provided background vocals – and the prolific songwriting team was moved to provide them with material of their own to record. Their first single, *Chains* (covered by the Beatles on their first album), reached the top twenty and a follow-up, *Don't Say Nothing Bad About My Baby*, got to number seven. Again their days of glory were numbered and within a year they had reverted to anonymity as studio singers.

Carole King had already sang on several unsuccessful records (including *Oh, Neil* in answer to Sedaka's *Oh, Carol*) when in 1962 she recorded *It Might As Well Rain Until September* for Don Kirshner's Dimension label (which also carried Little Eva and the Cookies). The single only reached number 22 in America but in Britain it hurtled to number three. It was to be a one-off success. Carole subsequently confined herself to back-seat roles and was absent from the charts until her dramatic re-emergence in the early seventies.

Besides consolidating the success of his existing acts, Berry Gordy introduced three new names to the charts: the Contours, Eddie Holland and Marvin Gaye.

The Contours didn't have the longevity of their stablemates, but their debut, *Do You Love Me?*, which reached number three during the late summer, was a classic. Eddie Holland's hit, *Jamie*, was equally powerful but he went on to achieve far greater success as part of the Holland/Dozier/Holland writing and producing team which provided the impetus behind the Supremes, the Four Tops and so many other Tamla–Motown giants.

Gordy's most substantial new find was Marvin Gaye, the son of a minister. On leaving the Air Force, Gaye had joined the Moonglows, by then well past their popularity peak, and after learning the business with them, had gone solo in 1962. A Detroit nightclub appearance led to an invitation to record for Tamla, where he has remained ever since. *Hitch Hike*, recorded at the end of 1962, was the first of 10 top thirty entries within three years – including such classics as *Can I Get A Witness?*, *How Sweet It Is* and *Ain't That Peculiar*, all of which put Gaye on the road towards becoming one of the most consistently successful soul singers of all time.

Other hit singles from the soul and R&B fields included *What's Your Name?* by Don and Juan, *Lover Please* by Clyde McPhatter (his second and last top tenner), *I Sold My Heart To The Junkman* by the Bluebelles (Patti La Belle's first taste of stardom), *Snap Your Fingers* by Joe Henderson and two influential killers from Arthur Alexander, *You'd Better Move On* and *Anna* (later recorded by the Rolling Stones and Beatles respectively).

Phil Spector continued to devote his energies to

Left: Bernard Jewry, who became Shane Fenton in the early 60s and Alvin Stardust in the early 70s. Under which name will he masquerade in the early 80s?

Below: The Beach Boys (left to right Carl Wilson, Brian Wilson, Dennis Wilson, Mike Love and Al Jardine) pose outside their British record company, who couldn't provide any surf, but at least found a dragster to remind them of home.

the Crystals, but also launched a new group, Bob B. Soxx and the Blue Jeans. Their revival of *Zip-A-Dee-Doo-Dah* reached number eight and though theirs was a flash-in-the-pan success, one of the Blue Jeans, Darlene Love, went on to make three great singles for Spector the following year.

Both Britain and America produced a significant new instrumental group in 1962. The nucleus of the Tornados had been an early line-up of Johnny Kidd's Pirates, but had been backing Billy Fury prior to their being signed by producer Joe Meek. *Telstar*, a swirling Meek melody inspired by the recently launched satellite, rocketed them to a million selling number one on both sides of the Atlantic. Unfortunately, they were never able to deliver anything as contagious again and when their bass player, Heinz Burt, left for a solo career, they lost what little visual appeal they possessed and eventually became very successful session musicians.

Their American contemporaries were a different kettle of fish altogether.

Previously studio musicians for Stax Records, organist Booker T. Jones, drummer Al Jackson, bassist Lewis Steinberg (later replaced by Donald 'Duck' Dunn) and guitarist Steve Cropper combined to form Booker T. and the M.G.s, who burst out of Memphis with the smouldering *Green Onions* to become one of the best known and most respected instrumental units of the sixties. Their impact and influence on the subsequent British R&B boom was enormous, never more so than when it was

discovered that Cropper was not, as had been widely supposed, black – a fact which heartened many an earnest white disciple.

As well as cutting their own distinctive records, the M.G.s were much in demand as backing musicians for the many soul stars breaking out of the Memphis scene. In the early seventies, however, they split up to pursue individual projects: Booker T. moved to California where he continues to record; Duck Dunn remained a Memphis-based session man, as did Al Jackson until 1975 when he was murdered by burglars whom he surprised in his house; and Steve Cropper became a producer, working with Poco, Jeff Beck, John Prine and the Temptations among others.

Other notable instrumental hits of 1962 were *Rinky Dink* by Dave 'Baby' Cortez (his second and last top tenner), *Wild Weekend* by the Rebels, *Nut Rocker* by B. Bumble and the Stingers (a scorching rape of Tchaikovsky's *Nutcracker Suite* supervised by Kim Fowley, late of the Hollywood Argyles), and *Surfer's Stomp* by the Marketts – the very first surfing hit.

'Surf music' reached a peak the following year but began in 1962 with the Marketts' disc and the first two hits by the Beach Boys, a new group from Hawthorne Los Angeles, who were to become one of the world's biggest over the next decade. With the help of his younger brothers Dennis and Carl, his cousin Mike Love, and a school friend Al Jardine, Brian Wilson drew on a wide range of influences from the Four Freshmen to Chuck Berry to create a unique soaring sound, characterised by strong lyrics and melodies, and intricate vocal arrangements. Though the subjects of his songs were not the sole prerogative of Californian teenagers, he certainly made it seem that way. The delights of cars, girls, parties, beaches, sunshine and surfing were, they discovered, a magical and long-lasting formula for hit records.

Brian, the principal songwriter, was not a surfing afficionado himself, but Dennis was an accomplished wave-rider and was able to fill him in on whatever esoteric vernacular was needed for authenticity. *Surfin'*, released on the small Candix label, became a local hit and Capitol subsequently signed the group in Summer 1962. Within weeks, their first single for the label, *Surfin' Safari,* was climbing the top twenty to set a pattern for the decade. Among their best remembered songs were *Surfin' U.S.A.*, *Fun Fun Fun, I Get Around, Help Me Rhonda, California Girls* and *Good Vibrations* – by which time, late 1966, the Beach Boys' achievements were held in reverence by the entire rock world.

1962's other idiosyncratic group hits were *The Wah Watusi* and *Don't Hang Up* by the Orlons, *Tell Him* by the Exciters, *A Wonderful Dream* by the Majors, *Let Me In* by the Sensations, *Hey Paula* by Paul and Paula (if two counts as a group), *You Belong To Me* by the Duprees, and *She Cried* by Jay and the Americans, who alone managed to survive until the seventies. Other than the Beach Boys, the brightest new American group was indisputably the Four Seasons.

As the Variatones and later the Four Lovers, the core of the group had been together since the mid-fifties, but when Bob Crewe (who had helped mastermind Freddie Cannon's career) convinced them to adopt a vocal technique similar to that used by Maurice Williams and the Zodiacs, the Four Seasons went into orbit, producing 18 top twenty singles and five million-sellers within the next five years. Of these, four reached number one: *Sherry, Big Girls Don't Cry, Walk Like A Man* and *Rag Doll.* Most of their hits were co-written by group member Bob Gaudio and producer Crewe, but it was the unique falsetto of lead singer Frankie Valli which set them apart and made them the most influential of the East Coast groups.

After the top tenner *C'mon Marianne* in summer 67, the Four Seasons became less active on the charts until 1976 when they returned with a remarkable new album *Who Loves You?* From this came three hits: *Silver Star, December 1963 (Oh What A Night)* and the title track, and their popularity was restored. In the late seventies, Frankie Valli, who had concurrently been enjoying a very fruitful solo career, considered leaving – but neither sees any reason why further success should be denied them throughout the eighties.

Country music had a thin time on the rock charts, the only newcomers being Claude King with *Wolverton Mountain*, Rex Allen with *Don't Go Near The Indians* and Bobby Bare with the first of his six hits, *Shame On Me.*

Novelty records didn't fare too well either. Ray Stevens had a top tenner in *Ahab The Arab*, whiskery actor Walter Brennan returned with a top five hit *Old Rivers,* and Dickie Lee had the year's 'death' hit with *Patches.* Biggest of all, however, was *Monster Mash* by Bobby 'Boris' Pickett and the Crypt Kickers, which zoomed straight to number one. It was Pickett's only real success, but on it he managed to build a reputation which carried him well into the seventies.

British actor Mike Sarne had two unexpected hits with *Come Outside* and *Will I What?* before heading into a movie career, and Shane Fenton had five British chart entries in 1962 – though it was only when he returned to the fore as Alvin Stardust in 1973 that he could be considered a novelty act. In the early sixties he was a soft rocker – soon to be crushed by the weight of Merseybeat.

As a hit maker, Joe Brown went under too, though his overstated cockney chirpiness has kept him in the public eye ever since his emergence as a red-hot teenage guitarist on British T.V. shows of the late fifties. As a singer, and leader of his own band, the Bruvvers, he scored seven hits including *A Picture Of You* and *That's What Love Will Do,* which he still performs in his current rock and comedy cabaret act.

The Crickets, with Sonny Curtis as their new front man, made a surprise comeback to the British chart with *Please Don't Ever Change* – and in America Tommy Roe adopted a Buddy Holly formula for his worldwide smash, *Sheila.* It was the forerunner of five more top tenners, including *Everybody, Sweet Pea* and *Dizzy,* and his career remained buoyant throughout the decade.

That Roe was the most successful white solo act to appear in 1962 was indicative of the slump in American rock music – and many aspiring young musicians were looking elsewhere. For them, the answer lay in folk music, for beneath the commercial superficiality of the current boom was a

depth and heritage to provide endless exploration and interest. In New York's Greenwich Village and in student communities across America, folk clubs and record companies were proliferating to meet the new demands – and singers had little trouble securing gigs. Inevitably, new heroes began to emerge. Pete Seeger, an established folksinger and writer, soon found himself with a new larger, younger audience eager to listen to his songs and stories – and he became the eminence grise of the movement.

Judy Collins, a clear voiced 22 year old from Denver, made an immediate impact on arriving in New York, and a barefoot contessa from the Boston/Cambridge college millieu, Joan Baez, soon captured an international audience with her intensity and charisma.

Above: Black leather rebel Gene Vincent and crewcut cockney Joe Brown get it together for British television in Jack Good's *Boy Meets Girls* show.

Left: Symptomatic of the softening face of rock was Tommy Roe.

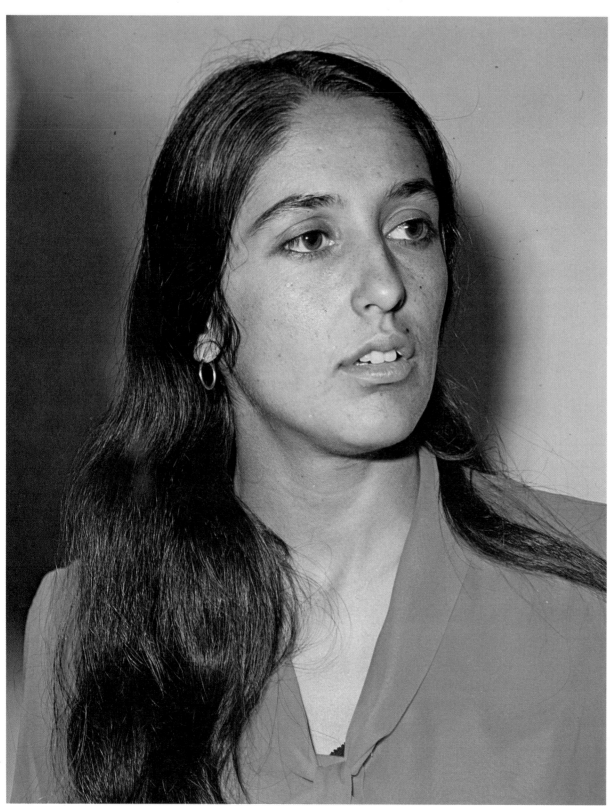

Left: Joan Baez, one of the first and most influential popularisers in the early 60s folk music renaissance in America. Later a leading light in the protest and pacifist movements, she has remained committed to her ideals.

Opposite above: A pre-electric Bob Dylan arrives in London to make his point.

Opposite below: Sometime parliamentary candidate Screaming Lord Sutch fails to oust his Tory opponent.

Below: Guitar whizz kid Joe Brown succeeded with a blend of technical virtuosity and comedy.

By 1962, a distinct subsection had manifested itself within the overall unity ... contemporary folk. Whilst most continued to sing traditional songs which had been passed down through generations, the 'contemporary' set were writing their own songs – using the conventions, instruments and very often the melodies of traditional folk to do so. The subject matter was primarily confined to such conventional themes as romance, travelling and unhappiness (rather than the sex, cars and fun of pop music) but before long a political vein began to permeate some songs and 'protest music' (to reach its commercial peak in 1965) was born . . . led by Bob Dylan.

Born in Minnesota in 1941, Robert Zimmerman

had changed his name to Bob Dylan by the time he arrived at Greenwich Village in late 1960. Early performances in local clubs were based on traditional material, old country blues and the works of his idol Woody Guthrie – and this was reflected in his first album, *Bob Dylan*, released in March 1962.

Before the year was out, however, he had become the most prolific songwriter of the genre and it was evident to all around him that his was a lasting talent. Among his first batch of songs was *Blowin' In The Wind*, which became the anthem of the Civil Rights movement and was subsequently covered by over a hundred artists ranging from Sam Cooke to Duke Ellington, and most popularly by Peter, Paul and Mary ... but it wasn't until 1965, when he put aside his acoustic guitar and moved into 'folk rock', that he really took off.

In Britain, folk music made absolutely no impact on the rock market, but the times were changing nevertheless. The scene had become limp and static. A handful of groups like Neil Christian and the Crusaders, Johnny Kidd and the Pirates, and Screaming Lord Sutch and the Savages were whipping up a bit of excitement on the club circuit, but it was mainly down to mediocre Elvis and Shadows copies. A new injection of vitality was needed – and, unknown to most of Britain, it was about to be administered.

In Liverpool, an energetic club scene was in full swing and an army of rock groups was ready to ride out and conquer the country. At the spearhead, preparing to lead the charge, was a quartet destined to become the most famous musical group in the history of the world ... the Beatles.

They were still in their formative stages at this time, despite the fact that John Lennon, George Harrison and Paul McCartney had been playing together since the late fifties. A succession of drummers and a fifth member, Stuart Sutcliffe, who had decided to concentrate on his painting career and remained in Germany following one of their extended dues-paying excursions to Hamburg, had departed and with their current drummer, Pete Best, they signed a management deal with Brian Epstein, the owner of a record shop in Liverpool. Though very popular in Liverpool and Hamburg, the only cities affording them regular gigs, the Beatles had been unable to convince record companies of their worth – despite having done sporadic recording, including session work with expatriate British rocker Tony Sheridan, in Hamburg – but Epstein's conviction and determination won them a contract with the E.M.I. label, Parlophone. Before going into the studio, however, they decided to drop Best in favour of their Liverpudlian mate Ringo Starr, then drumming with another local band, Rory Storme and the Hurricanes.

To satisfy their worship of things American, their repertoire was almost entirely made up of U.S. rock and R&B covers, but by the time they came to record they had a number of impressive songs of their own, and two of these, *Love Me Do/P.S. I Love You*, were coupled for their first single release in November 1962.

It made the charts, but only reached number 17. Nobody had any idea of what was to happen the following year.

'62 the year

Events

4 Feb. Two Swiss mountaineers make the first successful winter attempt on the north face of the Matterhorn.

10 July Telstar, the first U.S. communications satellite, is launched.

14 Aug. Tunnellers from France and Italy meet under Mont Blanc.

18 Aug. Rebuffed by U.S. doctors, Sherri Finkbine has a Swedish abortion of a foetus deformed by Thalidomide.

10 Sept. The U.S. Supreme Court upholds a ruling that James H. Meredith, a black, be admitted to Mississippi University. Two people are killed in riots on his enrolment.

9 Oct. Uganda becomes independent.

17 Nov. Dulles Airport, Chicago, the first designed for jets, is opened.

30 Nov. U Thant becomes Secretary General of the United Nations.

Films of 62

Days Of Wine And Roses · Jules Et Jim · Lawrence Of Arabia · The Longest Day · Mutiny On The Bounty · Summer Holiday · To Kill A Mockingbird · Whatever Happened To Baby Jane?

Right: Peter O'Toole in *Lawrence Of Arabia.*

Opposite top: Telstar is mated to the third stage of a Delta rocket.

Opposite bottom: Bette Davis in *Whatever Happened To Baby Jane?*

U.S. CHART TOPPERS – WEEKS AT TOP

The Lion Sleeps Tonight	Tokens
The Twist	Chubby Checker
The Peppermint Twist	Joey Dee and the Starlighters
Duke Of Earl	Gene Chandler
Hey Baby	Bruce Channel
Don't Break The Heart That Loves You	Connie Francis
Johnny Angel	Shelley Fabares
Good Luck Charm	Elvis Presley
Soldier Boy	Shirelles
Stranger On The Shore	Acker Bilk
I Can't Stop Loving You	Ray Charles
The Stripper	David Rose
Roses Are Red	Bobby Vinton
Breaking Up Is Hard To Do	Neil Sedaka
The Locomotion	Little Eva
Sheila	Tommy Roe
Sherry	Four Seasons
Monster Mash	Bobby 'Boris' Pickett
He's A Rebel	Crystals
Big Girl's Don't Cry	Four Seasons
Telstar	Tornados

U.K. CHART TOPPERS – WEEKS AT TOP

Stranger On The Shore	Acker Bilk
The Young Ones	Cliff Richard
Rock A Hula Baby	Elvis Presley
Wonderful Land	Shadows
Nut Rocker	B. Bumble and the Stingers
Good Luck Charm	Elvis Presley
Come Outside	Mike Sarne
I Can't Stop Loving You	Ray Charles
I Remember You	Frank Ifield
She's Not You	Elvis Presley
Telstar	Tornados
Lovesick Blues	Frank Ifield
Return To Sender	Elvis Presley

'63

'Please Please Me'

The Chiffons · The Dave Clark Five · Freddie and the Dreamers · Gerry and the Pacemakers · Lesley Gore · Jet Harris and Tony Meehan · The Hollies The Kingsmen · Billy J. Kramer and the Dakotas · Darlene Love · Lonnie Mack Manfred Mann · Peter, Paul and Mary · Brian Poole and the Tremeloes Martha Reeves and the Vandellas · The Rolling Stones · The Ronettes The Rooftop Singers · The Searchers · Jackie de Shannon · Rufus Thomas Bobby Vinton · Stevie Wonder

Until now, almost everything of any artistic value in the rock'n'roll world had been American. Of the handful of British records to go gold, most were novelties and few had any intrinsic merit. 1963 was the transitional year: it was definitely spring-cleaning time at the American hit factory.

Not that the Americans didn't come up with some winners: one couldn't argue about the quality of Stevie Wonder, for instance, or the Ronettes, or the Chiffons ... but the British rock scene was fired with tremendous enthusiasm and energy and during the year, a surprising number of groups came to national prominence.

Out in front were the Beatles. Their second single *Please Please Me*, shot to number two and their three other 1963 releases, *From Me To You, She Loves You* and *I Want To Hold Your Hand*, all moved swiftly to number one. Moreover, their first album, *Please Please Me*, topped the album charts for 30 weeks – only to be dislodged, in early December, by their second album, *With The Beatles*. Their success, however, was confined to Britain; the Americans stuck their heads in the sand and hoped they'd go away ... but they didn't, of course.

A hubbub of activity followed the Beatles' emergence: record company talent scouts flocked to Liverpool and Liverpudlian groups were gripped with fresh determination. Cheque books were produced, signatures scrawled, hands shaken, and the floodgates were opened.

Tripping along behind the Beatles came two other Brian Epstein-managed groups: Gerry and the Pacemakers and Billy J. Kramer and the Dakotas.

Gerry Marsden's pedigree was similar to that of his mentors: he'd worked up a local reputation in the Liverpool clubs, notably the Cavern, and slogged through weeks of all-nighters in Hamburg before being signed by Epstein. The group's first three singles, *How Do You Do It?, I Like It* and *You'll Never Walk Alone* all skipped to the top of the chart in double quick time. Never before had any act achieved such results with its first three releases. Gerry and the Pacemakers were on their way.

The first two songs had been specially written for the group by London songwriter Mitch Murray, whilst *You'll Never Walk Alone* was from the score of Rodgers and Hammerstein's *Carousel*. The last was an unlikely choice but became one of the year's biggest sellers and was subsequently adopted by Liverpool Football Club's supporters, who sang it earnestly from the terraces at every match. After further convincing hits like *I'm The One* and the title song from the film *Ferry Cross The Mersey*, Gerry decided to widen his scope and embarked on an acting career.

Like Gerry, Billy J. Kramer had left school to become a discontented British Rail employee. Epstein, seeing star potential, drafted in the Dakotas, a crack instrumental unit from Manchester, and persuaded Lennon and McCartney to give him one of their new songs to get his career off to a flying start. The ploy worked: by June 1963, *Do You Want To Know A Secret?* stood at number two. Its successor, another Lennon and McCartney song, *Bad To Me*, reached the top as did one of two top tenners the following year, *Little Children*. In common with most of the Mersey groups, however, Billy J. Kramer and the Dakotas fell from the charts rather abruptly during 1965, never to return.

Epstein had other strings to his bow during the early Merseybeat era – like the fairly successful Fourmost and Tommy Quickly and the Remo Four – but there was still talent to spare in Liverpool. As the Searchers (who took their name from the John Wayne film) were to demonstrate.

Yet another group who had tightened up their act in Germany, the Searchers were snapped up by Pye, and their first single, a reworking of the Drifters' 1961 American hit *Sweets For My Sweet* carried them

Below: Liverpool's first chart toppers, Gerry Marsden (left) and the Pacemakers.

Above: The Beatles with some of their less successful contemporaries, including Billy J. Kramer and the Dakotas, Cilla Black, Rolf Harris and the Barron Knights.

Right: Play It Cool, a non-Academy Award winning low budget British rock movie which furthered the careers of none of its stars.

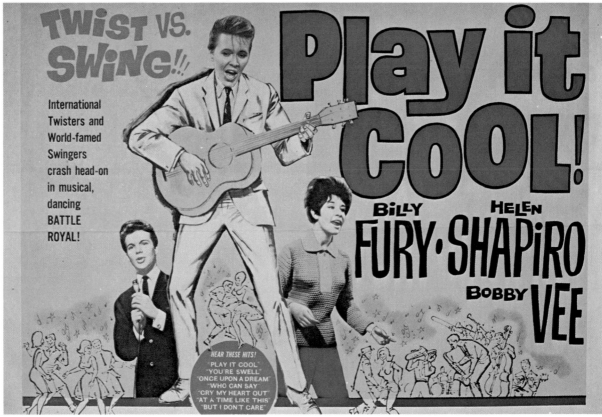

TWIST VS. SWING!!!

International Twisters and World-famed Swingers crash head-on in musical, dancing BATTLE ROYAL!

Play it CooL!

BILLY FURY · HELEN SHAPIRO · BOBBY VEE

HEAR THESE HITS!
"PLAY IT COOL" "YOU'RE SWELL"
"ONCE UPON A DREAM" "WHO CAN SAY"
"CRY MY HEART OUT"
"AT A TIME LIKE THIS"
"BUT I DON'T CARE"

A slightly more successful cinematic enterprise, *What A Crazy World* starred Joe Brown, Marty Wilde and Freddie and the Dreamers, seen here making fools of themselves as usual.

to the top. *Sugar And Spice* was almost as successful and during 1964 they scored five top twenty entries including two number ones in *Needles And Pins* and *Don't Throw Your Love Away*. Despite a couple of personnel changes, the group continued to visit the chart regularly through 1965 and 1966, after which they concentrated on live work. During the last months of the seventies, however, they completed a comeback album for the American company Sire and their distinctive 12-string jangle may well return to the airwaves during the eighties.

Freddie and the Dreamers, from Manchester not Liverpool, were fronted by the faintly amusing Freddie Garrity and were best-known for their live comedy routines as their music was at best average. However, the demand for Merseybeat had reached epidemic proportions and their version of James Ray's U.S. hit *If You Gotta Make A Fool Of Somebody* reached the top three. Freddie was able to give up his job as a milkman and enjoyed a couple of years as a big star, making three more top ten entries. Inevitably, his popularity declined, but his stage act enabled him to make a smooth transition to pantomine celebrity and children's television entertainer.

On the other hand the Hollies, also from Manchester, have become almost an institution. During the first 10 years of their career they achieved 22 top twenty hits in Britain and their number of million sellers is exceeded only by two other groups, the Beatles and the Stones. After starting out as 'cover version' specialists, they developed their own songwriting skills and came up with a string of winners including *We're Through*, *Stop Stop Stop*, *Carrie Anne*, *Jennifer Eccles* and *Long Cool Woman In A Black Dress*. Personnel changes didn't destroy their overall unity or distinctive sound and they continue to perform around the world with undiminished enthusiasm. Founder member Graham Nash, who left the group in 1968,

subsequently rose to superstardom with Crosby, Stills and Nash.

The first wave of Merseybeat washed away much of what had gone before, although Mike Berry and the Outlaws had a big hit with *Don't You Think It's Time?* and Bille Davis made the top ten with her cover of *Tell Him*. Ex-Tornado bassist Heinz was able to launch a short chart career with his Eddie Cochran tribute *Just Like Eddie* and two refugees from the Shadows, Jet Harris and Tony Meehan, established themselves as the year's most successful new instrumental unit with three top five entries *Diamonds*, *Scarlett O'Hara* and *Applejack*.

Practically everything else, however, was Beatle-shaped or at least Beatle-influenced. The Essex-based Brian Poole and the Tremeloes watched their version of the Isley Brothers' *Twist And Shout* rise to number four. Their revival of the Contours' *Do You Love Me?* was even more successful, reaching number one towards the end of the year. After a couple more top tenners, the group fell on bad times and split up – Poole eventually returning to the family business and the Tremeloes going on to carve a career of their own. Relying almost exclusively on American material, Poole had been unable to duplicate his British success in America whereas his contemporaries the Dave Clark Five were to become second only to the Beatles during the heady days of 1964.

The Dave Clark Five had sought to start their chart career with yet another cover of *Do You Love Me?* but, after losing the chart battle to Poole, had realised the error of their ways and began coming up with original material. Their next single, *Glad All Over*, made number one and the subsequent *Bits And Pieces* number two. By this time, Spring 1964, they were also huge in America and concentrated their activities there. As a result, their British success rate deteriorated whilst in America they zoomed to spectacular heights. During 1964-65, the group had no less than 12 top twenty singles, an astonishing nine of them becoming million sellers.

Over the next two years their radiance faded in the States but they picked up again in Britain where the hits continued until 1970 – after which they broke up, no doubt to enjoy a comfortable retirement.

Musically, the two most important new bands from the London area were the Rolling Stones and Manfred Mann. During the first half of 1962, most of the few rhythm'n'blues fans in London gravitated towards Alexis Korner's club in Ealing where his group Blues Incorporated played. Inspired by his pioneering work, several of Alexis' devotees set about forming their own blues group and, after many incubation problems, the Rolling Stones emerged in Summer 1962.

By the beginning of 1963, the line-up had resolved itself into a sextet comprising Mick Jagger, Keith Richard, Brian Jones, Bill Wyman, Charlie Watts and Ian Stewart, and within weeks they had secured a Sunday afternoon residency at the Crawdaddy Club, Richmond, London. It was here that ex-public schoolboy Andrew Loog Oldham saw

Left: Renegade Shadows Jet Harris (left) and Tony Meehan seemed to lack the staying power of their former colleagues.

Below: The Rolling Stones (left to right Mick Jagger, Brian Jones, Bill Wyman, Keith Richard and Charlie Watts). Their first tentative steps, but their characters already clearly defined.

them and convinced them to work under his managerial wing – even though it meant axing Stewart, whose image was at odds with the overall picture he had in mind.

Their musical outlook broadened considerably over the next few months and increasingly commercial singles (covers of songs by Chuck Berry, Lennon/McCartney and Buddy Holly) culminated in their fourth, *It's All Over Now*, reaching number one. It was the first of eight number ones during the sixties, and they weathered many storms to enter the seventies as the most popular album group in the world – with five consecutive chart toppers in Britain and six in America. They enter the eighties as the world's biggest and, incidentally, most enduring rock group.

After working up a club reputation, the Mann Hugg Blues Brothers realised the expediency of a more commercial approach and changed their name to the less restrictive Manfred Mann as well as introducing more instantly accessible music into their repertoire. *5–4–3–2–1* took them to number five as the theme tune to *Ready, Steady, Go!*, and they stayed in the charts throughout the sixties.

Particularly successful were *Doo Wah Diddy Diddy, Pretty Flamingo* and *The Mighty Quinn* – all of which reached number one in Britain.

When the group eventually disbanded, keyboard player Manfred Mann led a series of bands through various ups and downs but periodically came up with another winner to boost his considerable live following.

In America, there were some excellent new black girl groups and some interesting developments in the field of soul and R&B, but little else had any staying power.

Most of the real folk talent was still fighting to get out of the clubs, although the year's big folk breakthrough group: Peter, Paul and Mary, were doing their best to publicise up and coming writers, especially Bob Dylan. Their three 1963 top tenners included two Dylan songs, *Blowin' In The Wind* and *Don't Think Twice*, as well as the children's song *Puff The Magic Dragon*.

The surf scene was at full crest too, with the Beach Boys and Jan and Dean spearheading the attack and everybody from Bo Diddley to the Four Seasons riding the wave. There were also several successful surf-oriented instrumental hits, notably *Pipeline* by the Chantays, *Wipe Out* by the Surfaris, *The Lonely Surfer* by Jack Nitzsche and *Out Of Limits* by the Marketts.

Instrumentally, the most interesting new act was Lonnie Mack, who began his chequered chart career with a wordless interpretation of Chuck Berry's *Memphis*. Herb Alpert and the Tijuana Brass made the top ten with *The Lonely Bull*, and Boots Randolph scored with his timeless *Yakety Sax*. Other novelty and one-off hits included *Six Days On The Road* by Dave Dudley, *Hot Pastrami* by the Dartells, *Martian Hop* by the Ran-Dells, *Surfing Bird* by the Trashmen, *Hey Little Cobra* by the Rip Chords and *Dominique* by the Singing Nun, which was the year's surprise smash.

Many other ladies, mostly of a less ecclesiastical disposition, visited the charts during 1963. For Jan

Bradley (*Mama Didn't Lie*), Doris Troy (*Just One Look*), Betty Harris (*Cry To Me*) and Darlene Love (*Today I Met The Boy I'm Gonna Marry* and *Wait Til My Bobby Gets Home*) it was a fleeting affair, but for Shirley Ellis, Barbara Lewis and Lesley Gore it was the start of a longer romance,

Shirley Ellis had three top ten hits between 1963 and 1965: *The Nitty Gritty*, *The Name Game* and *The Clapping Song* – all soul-flavoured nursery rhyme novelty numbers written by her husband Lincoln Chase. *Hello Stranger*, Barbara Lewis' debut, reached number three and was her only hit until 1965, when she got back to the top twenty twice, with *Baby I'm Yours* and *Make Me Your Baby* – songs which again had crossed over from the soul charts.

Lesley Gore, on the other hand, was pure pop. Strong songs, clever productions and impassioned vocals were the secrets behind her healthy chart career which began with *It's My Party*, a number one hit recorded when she was only 16. She returned to the top five three times the same year, with *Judy's Turn To Cry*, *She's A Fool* and *You Don't Own Me*, and her run continued until the end of 1967 when she disappeared after almost 20 hits.

The principal girl groups were the Ronettes, the Chiffons, and Martha and the Vandellas. Three New York Puerto Ricans led by Veronica (Ronnie) Bennett, the Ronettes were Phil Spector's latest investment. Spectacularly visual, with slit skirts, high heels and high-piled hair, they began as back-up singers and dancers with Joey Dee's revue at the Peppermint Lounge, but attempts to establish themselves as a solo singing trio came to little avail. Following the failure of early singles, they reverted to background studio work – appearing on hits by Del Shannon and James Darren – and it was in this capacity that Spector first hired them.

Instantly recognising their potential, Spector signed them as artists and together with Ellie Greenwich and Jeff Barry wrote the classic *Be My Baby* for their debut. It zoomed to number two and sold over a million. Follow-ups were less successful commercially but are nevertheless some of the finest girl-group records ever made. Ronnie's plaintive lead vocals perfectly complemented Spector's 'wall of sound' – produced by over-dubbing four guitars, three pianos, two basses, a drummer, three other percussionists and four horn players. Apart from *Be My Baby*, four other Ronettes singles are unfor-gettable: *Baby I Love You*, *The Best Part Of Breaking Up*, *Walkin' In The Rain* and *Born To Be Together*.

By then the most respected producer in the world, Spector (who later married Ronnie) set the seal on his achievements by gathering all his artists for a dazzling Christmas album, lavishing on it more care than on any previous recording – but its release coincided with the assassination of President Kennedy and it was lost in the subsequent con-fusion.

The Chiffons weren't a Spector group, but might have been. Four girls from New York, they were produced by moonlighting members of the Tokens. *He's So Fine*, later acknowledged as George Harrison's source for *My Sweet Lord*, reached number one and was followed into the top five by the marginally less successful *One Fine Day*. Subsequent releases failed until *Sweet Talking Guy* returned them to the top ten in 1966.

'63 the year

Events

1 Mar. Revelations of the Profumo scandal begin, severely damaging the British Government.

21 Mar. Alcatraz Prison, California is closed.

5 Apr. A telephone 'hot line' is established between the White House and the Kremlin.

3 June Pope John XXIII dies at the age of 81.

26 June President Kennedy asserts 'Ich bin ein Berliner' at the Berlin Wall.

26 July Over 1,000 die in an earthquake which destroys Skopje, Yugoslavia.

8 Aug. Over two million pounds is stolen in the Great Train Robbery.

28 Aug. Reverend Martin Luther King makes his 'I have a dream' speech.

22 Nov. President Kennedy is assassinated in Dallas, Texas.

12 Dec. Kenya becomes independent.

Films of 63

The Cardinal · Cleopatra · Hud · Irma La Douce · The L-Shaped Room · Lilies Of The Field · This Sporting Life · Tom Jones

U.S. CHART TOPPERS – WEEKS AT TOP

Telstar	Tornados	2
Go Away Little Girl	Steve Lawrence	2
Walk Right In	Rooftop Singers	2
Hey Paula	Paul and Paula	3
Walk Like A Man	Four Seasons	3
Our Day Will Come	Ruby and the Romantics	1
He's So Fine	Chiffons	4
I Will Follow Him	Little Peggy March	3
If You Wanna Be Happy	Jimmy Soul	2
It's My Party	Lesley Gore	2
Sukiyaki	Kyu Sakamoto	3
Easier Said Than Done	Essex	2
Surf City	Jan and Dean	2
So Much In Love	Tymes	1
Fingertips Part Two	Little Stevie Wonder	3
My Boyfriend's Back	Angels	3
Blue Velvet	Bobby Vinton	3
Sugar Shack	Jimmy Gilmer and the Fireballs	5
Deep Purple	Nino Tempo and April Stevens	1
I'm Leaving It Up To You	Dale and Grace	2
Dominique	The Singing Nun	3

U.K. CHART TOPPERS – WEEKS AT TOP

The Next Time	Cliff Richard	3
Dance On	Shadows	1
Diamonds	Jet Harris and Tony Meehan	
The Wayward Wind	Frank Ifield	3
Summer Holiday	Cliff Richard	2
Foot Tapper	Shadows	1
How Do You Do It	Gerry and the Pacemakers	4
From Me To You	Beatles	7
I Like It	Gerry and the Pacemakers	4
Confessin'	Frank Ifield	2
Devil In Disguise	Elvis Presley	1
Sweets For My Sweet	Searchers	2
Bad To Me	Billy J. Kramer and the Dakotas	3
She Loves You	Beatles	6
Do You Love Me?	Brian Poole and the Tremeloes	3
You'll Never Walk Alone	Gerry and the Pacemakers	4
I Want To Hold Your Hand	Beatles	3

Right: President Kennedy in Dallas.

Opposite clockwise from top left: Richard Burton and Elizabeth Taylor in *Cleopatra*; President De Gaulle; Albert Finney in *Tom Jones*; Pope John XXIII.

Martha and the Vandellas were one of two major new acts launched by Tamla Motown, and for Martha Reeves, it was a storybook rise to fame. She first worked for the company as a secretary, occasionally helping out as a backing singer on recordings by Marvin Gaye and Mary Wells. When Wells failed to arrive for a session, Martha and two of her friends were allowed to use the studio time – and so promising were the results that they were signed as artists.

After an apprenticeship as Marvin Gaye's regular back-up group, they began to record under their own name and in 1963 scored with two top tenners, *Heat Wave* and *Quicksand*, both written by the Holland/Dozier/Lamont team (who would later furnish the Supremes with dozens of hits). This trio wrote most of Martha's subsequent hits, including three more top tenners in *Nowhere To Run*, *I'm Ready For Love* and *Jimmy Mack* – although her biggest hit, *Dancing In The Street*, was by Marvin Gaye.

Following several years in the shadows of the Supremes, Martha and the Vandellas broke up in 1971 and neither party managed to recapture the former magic.

Motown's other newcomer, Stevie Wonder, goes from strength to strength and advances into the eighties as one of the rock world's true superstars. Blind from birth, Wonder was only 11 when Ronnie White of the Miracles, impressed by his harmonica playing and intuitive singing, introduced him to the powers-that-be at Motown. He had just turned 13 when his recording of *Fingertips Part 2* spun its way

Top: Martha Reeves (right) and the Vandellas. Despite their excellence, they were to languish in the shadow of the more sophisticated Supremes.

Right: Little Stevie Wonder (centre) with Frankie Avalon and child-star/singer Annette Funicello.

to the top of the charts in the summer of 1963.

Whilst still a teenager, he scored another eight top tenners including *Uptight*, *I Was Made To Love Her*, *For Once In My Life* and *Yester-me, Yester-you, Yesterday*, and during the seventies he recorded a trio of number ones in *Superstition*, *You Are The Sunshine Of My Life* and *You Haven't Done Nothin'*.

A series of exceedingly personal but equally commercial albums firmly established Wonder as a genius whose talents as a singer, songwriter and multi-instrumentalist are admired by all who hear him.

Other soul acts to come to the fore in 1963 included Inez Foxx, who hit the big time with *Mocking Bird*; Garnett Mimms and the Enchanters, who reached the top five with *Cry Baby*; Freddie Scott with *Hey Girl* (he returned three years later to turn out some excellent singles for Bert Burns' Shout label), Bob and Earl, who recorded the influential *Harlem Shuffle*; and Jimmy Soul, who reached number one with *If You Wanna Be Happy*.

Rufus Thomas also hit the charts for the first time. A middle-aged ex-disc jockey from Tennessee, he made several R&B styled singles during the forties and fifties for Chess and Sun but a series of novelty dance songs brought him his first national success. *Walking The Dog*, subsequently covered by the Rolling Stones, was his biggest hit, reaching the top ten at the end of the year, but he continued to record throughout the sixties – often with his daughter Carla. In 1970 he returned to the U.S. top thirty and the British top twenty with *Do The Funky Chicken*.

Few American groups were able to move beyond a significant debut and less impressive follow-ups, but there were nevertheless the usual crop of noteworthy hits, which included *Denise* by Randy and the Rainbows, *So Much In Love* by the Tymes (who hung on to make periodic returns with such classics as *People* and *Ms Grace*), *I'm Leaving It Up To You* by Dale and Grace, *The Kind Of Boy You Can't Forget* by the Raindrops (who included songwriters Ellie Greenwich and Jeff Barry), *Easier Said Than Done* by the Essex, *Sugar Shack* by Jimmy Gilmer and the Fireballs (whom Norman Petty had used to doctor Buddy Holly's unfinished demos into a commercially palatable form), and *Deep Purple* by Nino Tempo and April Stevens. Special mention should also be made of *Louie Louie* by the Kingsmen, a great 'garage' rocker which was immediately added to the repertoire of just about every beat group in Britain, and was subsequently covered by artists as diverse as the Sandpipers and Frank Zappa. It reached number two in America and earned the Kingsmen a permanent place in the Rock Hall of Fame.

Bobby Vinton, a Pennsylvanian balladeer, was the biggest thing white America had to offer. Following his previous year's chart topper, *Roses Are Red*, he made number one twice in 1963, with *Blue Velvet* and *There I've Said It Again* – but he and his ilk were no match for what was to come.

Tommy Roe, Roy Orbison and Christ Montez, who all had toured Britain with the Beatles, knew what was in store . . . and as the year closed, the Americans, armed with outmoded equipment, prepared to repel the British invasion, which was to begin with the Beatles' first visit in February 1964.

The Yanks didn't stand a chance.

'64

'I'm Into Something Good'

The Animals · The Applejacks · Cilla Black · The Dixie Cups
Marianne Faithfull · Georgie Fame · Wayne Fontana and the Mindbenders
The Four Pennies · The Four Tops · The Honeycombs · The Kinks
The Merseybeats · The Mojos · The Moody Blues · The Nashville Teens
Peter and Gordon · The Pretty Things · P. J. Proby · Johnny Rivers
The Shangri-Las · Sandie Shaw · Dusty Springfield · The Supremes
The Swinging Blue Jeans · Twinkle · Dionne Warwick · The Zombies

In 1963, only one of America's 50 best-selling singles was British (*Telstar* by the Tornados). In 1964, 12 were British – including the top two, *I Want To Hold Your Hand* and *She Loves You* by the Beatles.

Thinking they were just another localised flash in the pan, E.M.I.'s American arm, Capitol, had failed to pick up their option on the Beatles, whose early singles had been issued, to little acclaim, on Tollie, Vee Jay and Swan. By the time the Beatles arrived for their first U.S. tour in the early weeks of 1964, however, Capitol had realised their mistake and now had the group securely under contract.

They were just in time. Beatlemania gripped America even more ferociously than it had Britain – to the extent that by early April all five best-selling singles were by the Beatles – and in its wake came the adulation of all things British. The major British groups, wasted no time exploiting the lucrative

Left: American hairdressers for tonsorial revolution as Beatlemania spreads across the States.

Below: The lovable Mop tops, left to right Paul McCartney, George Harrison, Ringo Starr and John Lennon.

The Kinks get in on the act as the British Invasion of America gets under way.

market. Leading the attack were the Beatles, who managed no less than 15 top twenty entries during the year, and the Dave Clark Five with seven. Close behind were Billy J. Kramer and the Dakotas, Gerry and the Pacemakers, Manfred Mann, and the Searchers, who all enjoyed huge hits and consistent sales; bringing up the rear were the Rolling Stones, who were just beginning to make an impression by the end of the year.

There was also plenty of chart activity on both sides of the Atlantic for a second wave of groups who emerged during 1964. The most exciting and successful of these were the Kinks, the Zombies, the Animals and the Moody Blues.

Led by brilliant songwriter Ray Davies, the Kinks, from the suburbs of North London, started hesitantly. However, the total failure of their first two singles was completely eradicated by the success of their third: *You Really Got Me*, loosely based on the sprung rhythms of *Louie Louie* by the Kingsmen, hit the top of the charts and the Kinks were here to stay.

Tired Of Waiting For You and *Sunny Afternoon* provided them with further number ones in a run of 11 top tenners over the next four years, and though their chart appearances were rarer and briefer during the late sixties they made a spectacular return with *Lola* and *Ape Man* in 1970.

Although written off by critics several times during the seventies, the Kinks demonstrated their consistency with *Low Budget*, which saw them riding the crest of the American album charts once more as the decade closed.

After winning a talent competition, the Zombies,

from St. Albans, were signed by Decca Records, who promoted them as 'the group with more than 50 "O" Levels'. Their first single, *She's Not There*, was only a moderate hit in Britain but became a million seller as a result of huge sales in America. Only their follow-up, *Tell Her No*, enjoyed significant sales and despite several enthusiastically received American tours the group had ground to a dejected halt by 1968.

Their last C.B.S. album, *Odyssey And Oracle*, had evoked little initial response but a track singled out for American release, *Time Of The Season*, rose steadily to reach the top three. By this time, however, the group was no more: Colin Blunstone was about to begin a solo career, keyboard player Rod Argent had formed his own group, and the other three were working as record company executives and producers.

The Animals and the Moody Blues, from Newcastle and Birmingham respectively, took the cream of local musicians to form dedicated super-groups playing rhythm'n'blues and had no difficulty impressing the business and the media.

By the time the Animals came to record, they had broadened their horizons somewhat and were now experimenting with electrified versions of American folk songs. In fact, adaptations of two songs from Dylan's debut album, *Baby Let Me Take You Home* and *House Of The Rising Sun*, were released as the Animals' first singles, and though the former was only a minor U.K. hit, the latter was one of the year's great chartbusters, reaching number one on both sides of the Atlantic.

Following various personnel changes, including

The Moody Blues (left to right) Ray Thomas, Clint Warwick, Graeme Edge, Denny Laine and Mike Pinder. This shot was taken before the group became the ultimate cosmic philosophers.

the departure of founder/organist Alan Price, who suffered from an insurmountable fear of flying, the group fell apart in 1966 after a run of several excellent hits – and though lead singer Eric Burdon subsequently fronted a new group of the same name (which at one point included Andy Summers, later of the Police), that too broke up after a handful of sporadic hits including *San Franciscan Nights* and *Monterey*. Burden, suffering from ill-health and over-indulgence, later appeared as vocalist with War (who, after breaking with him, became one of the biggest acts in America), since when his achievements have been somewhat below his impressive mid-sixties peaks.

The Moody Blues broke through with their classic version of an obscure American single by Bessie Banks, *Go Now*, which took them to the top of the U.K. charts and into the U.S. top ten, accumulating sales of a million along the way. After progressively smaller hits, they entered a three year slump during which two of the founders, including front man Denny Laine – later guitarist with Wings, left the remaining three to pick up the pieces.

In 1968, they did just that. With a new line-up and a new sound based on the mellotron, which keyboard player Mike Pinder had helped to develop, they returned to resurrect themselves as one of the most influential groups of the seventies by turning out a succession of astonishingly successful albums.

Above: The Kinks (left to right Ray Davies, Pete Quaife, Mick Avory and Dave Davies). The red hunting jackets became their early trademark.

Right: The Animals (left to right John Steel, Alan Price, Eric Burdon, Chas Chandler and Hilton Valentine). Earthy Geordies, they were the North East's major contribution to the British beat boom.

Several new groups emerged from the Mersey training grounds but most faded quickly. The Mojos never found another song to equal their stunning *Everything's Alright* and the Four Pennies experienced similar difficulties after their chart-topping *Juliet*. The Merseybeats showed initial promise with *It's Love That Really Counts* and *I Think Of You*, but their interesting efforts were generally underrated thereafter. The Swinging Blue Jeans revived a couple of old rockers to good effect, but their inability to write their own material soon led them into cabaret.

Wayne Fontana and the Mindbenders, from Manchester, lasted a little longer. Their version of Major Lance's *Um Um Um Um Um Um* took them into the top five and they managed four other top twenty entries including the worldwide hit, *Game Of Love*, before disappearing from sight in 1967 – by which time the Mindbenders were working independently of Fontana and had a huge hit of their own, *Groovy Kind Of Love*. Lead guitarist Eric Stewart subsequently returned to prominence with 10cc.

As well as the Moody Blues, Birmingham produced two chart acts in the Rockin' Berries and the Applejacks. The Berries, a smooth harmony vocal group, achieved a string of hits including *He's In Town* and *Poor Man's Son*, before returning to the night clubs, where, even today, they specialise in musical parody; the Applejacks sank without trace after making waves with three singles including the top tenner *Tell Me When*.

If the Applejacks' predominant publicity angle was their girl bassplayer, the Honeycombs' gimmick was their girl drummer, who drove the group to number one in Britain and number five in America with the foot-stomping *Have I The Right?* – the last of Joe Meek's many smash-hit productions.

A group from Glasgow, Lulu and the Luvvers, boasted such a raunchy R&B vocalist that one had difficulty in believing it was the same girl who later came across so sweetly and innocently in *To Sir With Love*. Not long after their top ten debut, *Shout* (the old Isley Brothers' song), Lulu went solo and, as noted, mellowed her approach considerably to provide the impetus for a lifelong career.

The Barron Knights began their parody series with *Call Up The Groups*, the Nashville Teens had their first and biggest hit, *Tobacco Road,* and Cliff Bennett and the Rebel Rousers, a very exciting club act, made their first chart appearance with *One Way Love*. It wasn't until Paul McCartney offered them *Got To Get You Into My Life* two years later that they managed to get back to the top ten.

The Beatles' seal of approval was undoubtedly the secret ingredient behind the instant success of the pleasantly melodic duo known as Peter and Gordon. At the time of their launch, Paul McCartney was enjoying a widely publicised romance with Peter's sister, Jane Asher, and when he presented the boys with an unreleased Lennon/McCartney song *World Without Love* there was no other place for it to go but the top of the charts – on both sides of the Atlantic.

They never made it quite that high again, despite more Beatles songs, but nevertheless accumulated ten hits by 1967, many appealing much more to the American market, which they exploited to the full until parting in 1968. While Gordon Waller took a fast train to obscurity, Peter Asher used his show-biz experience to become one of the best and most respected managers and producers of the seventies, his most notable successes being with James Taylor and Linda Ronstadt.

If Peter and Gordon were all that was clean-cut and nice, the Pretty Things were exactly the opposite. Rougher, dirtier and more uncouth than the Rolling Stones (with whom their guitarist Dick Taylor had originally played), the Things specialised in Bo Diddley-inspired R&B peppered with the odd original like *Don't Bring Me Down*, which took them into the top ten at the end of the year. After *Honey I Need*, the hits trailed off and the group went underground to produce some excellent albums during the late sixties, before frustration eventually precipitated their dissolution.

Gathering momentum in the closing months of the seventies was another cult intent on reviving 'bluebeat' – music of West Indian origin which was pioneered in London by Georgie Fame and the Blue Flames during 1964. After serving in Larry Parnes' stable, Fame (real name Clive Powell) spearheaded a

Above: Marianne Faithfull, whose love affair with Mick Jagger became the romance of the 60s.

Left: In pensive mood, Peter Asher (right) and his partner Gordon Waller reflect on the benefits of friendship with the Beatles.

jazz-slanted, sophisticated R&B movement which pivoted around a Soho, London club called the Flamingo, where he and similar groups like Herbie Goins and the Night Timers and Ronnie Jones and the Blue Jays would draw capacity crowds split equally between young white mods and young West Indian immigrants. Though their music was seldom adequately represented on vinyl, their influence was great and started a distinct boom in Caribbean music which enabled the early Jamaican stars to tour Britain to enthusiastic response.

By the time Fame started making the charts, he had graduated to jazzy ballads like *Yeh Yeh* and *Get Away*, both of which reached number one; his most frequent appearances during the seventies were on television extolling the wonder of Woolworths and the value of Maxwell House coffee.

The only real hit to emerge from the early British bluebeat/ska scene (from which reggae was to develop) was *My Boy Lollipop* by a 15 year old Jamaican girl, Millie Small, which reached number two in Britain and America, eventually selling over three million copies worldwide. Millie had been brought to England by Chris Blackwell, subsequently the founder of Island Records.

Although her success was a flash in the pan, 1964 was, overall, a very good year for British girls with Cilla Black, Marianne Faithfull, Sandie Shaw, Dusty Springfield and Twinkle all getting off to a flying start.

There was no way Twinkle could follow her dramatic death hit *Terry* and she wisely retired into domestic bliss, as did Sandie Shaw when her long British chart career ended with the sixties. Aided by appearances on the ultra-popular television programme *Ready Steady Go*, the barefoot Sandie hit the top with her second single *There Is Always Something There To Remind Me* – which was followed by four more top tenners over the next year. Her career reached its apex when 50 million viewers watched *Puppet On A String* sweep the board at the 1967 Eurovision Song Contest – although many saw it as her nadir.

Cilla Black and Marianne Faithfull came to light as a result of associations with the Beatles and the Stones. The Beatles knew Cilla for her stalwart work as cloakroom attendant at the Cavern and, after Brian Epstein had signed her up and changed her name from Priscilla White, provided her with the unheard Lennon/McCartney song *Love Of The Loved*. The ruse had worked for Billy J. Kramer, as it would for Peter and Gordon, but Cilla's debut rose no higher than number 35. However, her next single, a cover of Dionne Warwick's *Anyone Who Had A Heart*, leapt to number one as did the follow-up, *You're My World* – and by the end of the sixties, with a dozen top twenty hits to her credit, she had moved into 'middle of the road' entertainment with her own television series.

Marianne Faithfull gained notoriety through her affair with Mick Jagger, who with guitarist Keith Richard wrote her first single, *As Tears Go By*, a top ten hit in Summer 1964 and next year *Come And Stay With Me* and *This Little Bird* were even bigger hits ... but life as a pop star and especially Mick Jagger's sweetheart presented pressures which induced her to give up singing for acting. After several well-received film and theatre roles, Marianne re-emerged in the late seventies as an unlikely adjunct of the punk rock scene.

Undoubtedly the most interesting of the flock was Dusty Springfield, who had originally come to notice as a member of the Springfields trio with her brother Tom and Mike Hurst, who subsequently became a record producer. The Springfields' singalong friendliness endeared them to a wide audience and provided them with five hits including *Island Of Dreams* and *Say I Won't Be There*. The group also achieved the rare accolade of being invited to record in Nashville, the American country music capital, and one of the subsequent releases, *Silver Threads And Golden Needles*, reached the U.S. top twenty in 1963.

That year, Dusty decided to work as a solo artist to explore her new-found passion for more soulful material, and her first single, *I Only Want To Be With You*, took her high into the British and American charts, winning a gold disc along the way.

Right: An early shot of the Supremes, with Diana Ross (left), Motown's biggest ever act.

Far right: Dionne Warwick drops her sophisticated front.

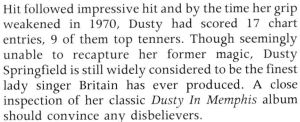

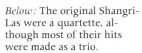

Hit followed impressive hit and by the time her grip weakened in 1970, Dusty had scored 17 chart entries, 9 of them top tenners. Though seemingly unable to recapture her former magic, Dusty Springfield is still widely considered to be the finest lady singer Britain has ever produced. A close inspection of her classic *Dusty In Memphis* album should convince any disbelievers.

America was too busy contending with the British influx to originate many worthwhile new acts – though for the unruffled Tamla Motown conglomerate business progressed as usual. They reaffirmed their dominance in the soul sphere by coming up with yet another brace of winners in the Four Tops and the Supremes.

The Four Tops, all from Detroit, had worked in local clubs since the mid-fifties and had recorded for Chess in 1956, but when they signed with Motown in 1964 their status improved immeasurably. Under the wing of the Holland/Dozier/Holland team they had turned out a dozen big American hits by the end of 1967, including such epics as *I Can't Help Myself, It's The Same Old Song, Reach Out I'll Be There* and *Bernadette*, but at that point the producers had a disagreement and left to start their own labels, Invictus and Hot Wax.

The Four Tops never recovered: unable to find suitable new material they began reviving oldies with varying success until they left Motown for Dunhill in 1972. Since then they have done relatively little to restore their chart reputation, though they remain an immensely popular live act.

The Supremes were also the fortunate recipients of songs from the Holland/Dozier/Holland hit factory, although they struggled for several years before finally clicking in 1964 with the first of five consecutive American number ones, *Where Did Our Love Go?* Diana Ross, Mary Wilson and Florence

Ballard, who had grown up on the same Detroit housing estate, were originally known as the Primettes, and made several inconsequential singles while still at school. Their triumph in a local talent contest brought them to the attention of Berry Gordy, and though their first six singles with him saw only disappointing chart action, they enjoyed an incredible run of success once they had broken through.

Of the 13 singles released between July 1964 and April 1967, no less than 10 reached number one. Their success rate wilted somewhat when Florence Ballard, closely followed by Diana Ross (now Mrs. Berry Gordy) left but Mary Wilson, aided by new cohorts, carried their flag until the late seventies when they appeared to revert to local work. With over 30 hits to their credit, the Supremes remain unchallenged as the most successful female group in rock history even though Mary Wilson began a solo career in 1979.

Rather less tenacious, but equally impressive, were the Shangri-Las. Two pairs of white sisters from New York, they were introduced to record producer George 'Shadow' Morton by a local disc jockey. Morton used them to produce a series of brilliant pop vignettes, somewhat in the style of the Coasters' hits of the fifties, but with romance, drama and sophistication instead of humour.

After dubbing seagulls and breaking waves over the teenage heartbreaker *Remember (Walking In The Sand)*, a single quite unlike anything which had gone before, he took the tape to Red Bird Records, which had recently been set up by the ubiquitous Leiber and Stoller. It reached number five and sold a million, as did the even more melodramatic follow-up *Leader Of The Pack*, which was an American number one and a top twenty hit in Britain on three separate occasions!

By the end of 1966, Red Bird had folded and the Shangri-Las had disappeared. Despite constant

rumours of a major comeback attempt, they reformed only for periodic revival concerts at the turn of the seventies. Their flight was short but spectacular.

The Dixie Cups, also on Red Bird, made their debut with the chart-topping *Chapel Of Love*, but were subsequently lost in the British invasion. Similarly, the careers of several other new acts were terminated rather abruptly after brief chart forays. Terry Stafford had a smash with *Suspicion*, the Newbeats with *Bread And Butter*, Ronnie and the Daytonas with *G.T.O.*, the Rivieras with *California Sun*, Betty Everett with *The Shoop Shoop Song*, Tommy Tucker with *Hi-Heel Sneakers*, and Brenda Holloway with *Every Little Bit Hurts*, but none achieved a significant follow-up.

The Vibrations came back with *My Girl Sloopy*, Little Anthony and the Imperials with *Goin' Out Of My Head*, and Chuck Berry, riding a resurgence created by his British imitators, with five U.S. hits – his first since 1960 – including *No Particular Place To Go* and *You Never Can Tell*. The big novelty hits were *Ringo*, a monologue by Bonanza star Lorne Greene, and the inevitable death song, *Last Kiss* by J. Frank Wilson and the Cavaliers.

There were only two major new American solo stars in 1964: Dionne Warwick and Johnny Rivers.

Dionne worked as a backing singer on records by the likes of the Drifters and Garnett Mimms before Burt Bacharach (then almost unknown) recommended her to the president of Scepter Records. That was in 1962, and after several small hits and near misses, she finally cracked the American top twenty in 1964 with the first of many Bacharach/ Hal David songs which established her as an enduring star. Among the 30 hits she amassed during the sixties were such classics as *Walk On By*, *I Say A Little Prayer* and *Do You Know The Way To San José* – though, strangely, she failed to achieve a number one until *Then Came You* with the Detroit Spinners in 1974, by which time the relationship with Bacharach and David had been severed.

New Yorker John Ramistella allegedly changed his name to Johnny Rivers on the recommendation

of Alan Freed in the late fifties, though success didn't come until 1964 when his update of Chuck Berry's *Memphis* took him to number two. Nearly all of his two dozen U.S. hits were revivals of previous winners, the notable exceptions being *Secret Agent Man*, written by folk rocker P. F. Sloan, and his only number one, *Poor Side Of Town*, which he himself wrote in conjunction with Lou Adler.

Above left: Sandie Shaw with some of the shoes she never seemed to wear in public, and (*above*) in classic pose, belying her Dagenham origins.

Below: P. J. Proby's trousers give way in the wrong place.

Right: Marianne Faithfull
prepares for a cold spell – in
chart terms at least.

Below: Johnny Rivers, a
superstar in America, but a
nonenity in Britain.

By the late sixties, he had formed his own label, Soul City, to which he signed the highly successful vocal group the Fifth Dimension, but his own successes centred around his live performances rather than his records during the seventies.

Another American, P. J. Proby, was imported to England by T.V. producer Jack Good, who was impressed by his exaggerated vocal mannerisms. His appearance in a Beatles special was so well received that Proby decided to remain and, after years of struggling in Los Angeles, established himself in Britain overnight. His tortured remakes of two thirties show tunes (*Hold Me* and *Together*) followed by selections from *West Side Story* (*Somewhere* and *Maria*) all put Proby into the top ten but he was unable to survive the puritanical backlash which followed the onstage disintegration of his velvet trousers. He descended into ignominy and bankruptcy which many years of toil could not redress.

However, though Proby's trousers were in poor shape, the world of rock'n'roll was healthy again, and the horizon sparkled with promise as the year drew to a close.

'64

the year

Events

25 Feb. Cassius Clay defeats Sonny Liston to become world heavyweight boxing champion and changes his name to Muhammad Ali.

10 Mar. Prince Edward is born.

27 May The Indian Prime Minister Jawaharlal Nehru dies.

5 June The British Blue Streak rocket makes its first test flight from Woomera, Australia.

21 June In baseball, Jim Bunning pitches the first perfect game in the American National League since 1880.

15 Sept. *The Sun* newspaper begins publication.

10 Oct. In Tokyo, the 18th Olympic Games begins.

15 Oct. The Labour Party wins the General Election with a majority of five. Harold Wilson becomes Prime Minister.

15 Oct. Martin Luther King is awarded the Nobel Peace Prize.

3 Nov. Lyndon B. Johnson heavily defeats Republican Candidate Barry Goldwater for the Presidency.

Films of 64

Becket · Dr. Strangelove · Goldfinger · A Hard Day's Night · Mary Poppins · My Fair Lady · Topkapi · Zorba The Greek

Below right: the Beatles.

Opposite top left: Peter O'Toole and Richard Burton in *Becket*.

Opposite top right: Peter Sellers in *Dr. Strangelove*.

Opposite below: Dr. Martin Luther King.

U.S. CHART TOPPERS – WEEKS AT TOP

There I've Said It Again	Bobby Vinton
I Want To Hold Your Hand	Beatles
She Loves You	Beatles
Can't Buy Me Love	Beatles
Hello Dolly	Louis Armstrong
My Guy	Mary Wells
Love Me Do	Beatles
Chapel Of Love	Dixie Cups
A World Without Love	Peter and Gordon
I Get Around	Beach Boys
Rag Doll	Four Seasons
A Hard Day's Night	Beatles
Everybody Loves Somebody	Dean Martin
Where Did Our Love Go?	Supremes
House Of The Rising Sun	Animals
Oh Pretty Woman	Roy Orbison
Do Wah Diddy Diddy	Manfred Mann
Baby Love	Supremes
Leader Of The Pack	Shangri-Las
Ringo	Lorne Greene
Mr. Lonely	Bobby Vinton
Come See About Me	Supremes

U.K. CHART TOPPERS – WEEKS AT TOP

I Want To Hold Your Hand	Beatles
Glad All Over	Dave Clark Five
Needles And Pins	Searchers
Diane	Bachelors
Anyone Who Had A Heart	Cilla Black
Little Children	Billy J. Kramer and the Dakotas
Can't Buy Me Love	Beatles
A World Without Love	Peter and Gordon
Don't Throw Your Love Away	Searchers
Juliet	Four Pennies
You're My World	Cilla Black
It's Over	Roy Orbison
House Of The Rising Sun	Animals
It's All Over Now	Rolling Stones
Hard Day's Night	Beatles
Do Wah Diddy Diddy	Manfred Mann
Have I The Right?	Honeycombs
You Really Got Me	Kinks
I'm Into Something Good	Herman's Hermits
Oh Pretty Woman	Roy Orbison
Always Something There To Remind Me	Sandie Shaw
Baby Love	Supremes
Little Red Rooster	Rolling Stones
I Feel Fine	Beatles

The Official Elvis Presley Fan Club

OF GREAT BRITAIN AND THE COMMONWEALTH

★ ★

You are Official Fan Club Member —

N° 411

until December 31st, 1964.

Honorary President

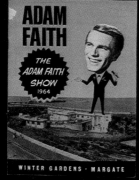

THE ADAM FAITH SHOW 1964
WINTER GARDENS · MARGATE

ELVIS PRESLEY
G·I· BLUES
A HAL WALLIS PRODUCTION · JULIET PROWSE · TECHNICOLOR

MEET BILLY FURY

MEET BILLY.J KRAMER

Boyfriend 63 BOOK

MOVIELAND AND TV TIME

DONT WORRY

Boyfriend BOOK

"HEY, LET'S TWIST!"

PEPPERMINT Lounge

MR. TWIST HIMSELF
CHUBBY CHECKER
SINGIN' AND DANCIN' IN A BIG NEW ROLE!
DON'T KNOCK THE TWIST
LANG JEFFRIES · MARI BLANCHARD · GEORGINE DARCY

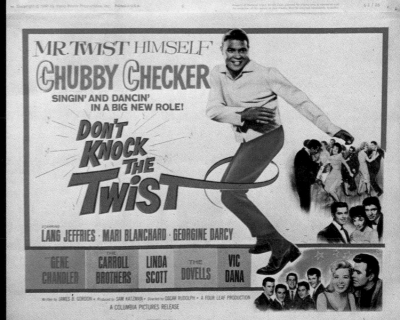

'My Generation'

The Byrds · Petula Clark · Spencer Davis Group · Donovan
Sir Douglas Quintet · The Fortunes · Herman's Hermits · Tom Jones
Jonathan King · The Lovin' Spoonful · Barry McGuire · Roger Miller
Wilson Pickett · The Righteous Brothers · Sam the Sham · The Small Faces
Sonny and Cher · The Temptations · Joe Tex · Them · The Turtles
The Walker Brothers · Junior Walker · The Who · The Yardbirds

'England swings!' proclaimed country star Roger Miller in his American top tenner – and it was true. Britannia ruled the radio waves in 1965, and though American groups began to retaliate, most acknowledged the Beatles as the inspiration behind their new musical directions.

The most successful American groups to surface were the Byrds from Los Angeles and the Lovin' Spoonful from New York.

The Byrds were all disgruntled folk musicians, itching to experiment with electric music – which they did for six months before coming up with their distinctive jangling smash hit, *Mr. Tambourine Man*, in Spring 1965. Having been written by Bob Dylan, the song qualified as the first popular American 'folk-rock' hit, and unlocked the door for a spate of similar hybrids, but the Byrds always kept ahead of trends and became one of the most innovative groups of the sixties.

As well as folk-rock, they pioneered 'drug rock' and 'country rock' and achieved a colourful run of hit singles, including *Eight Miles High, So You Want To Be A Rock'n'Roll Star* and *Chestnut Mare*. By the time the group split up in the early seventies, their charismatic leader Roger McGuinn was the only remaining founder. The others had left for various group ventures, though the only one to land on his feet was David Crosby of Crosby, Stills and Nash.

The Lovin' Spoonful's folk-rock sound was based on blues and jug band music rather than the current Dylan vogue. The Spoonful's leader, John Sebastian, soon revealed himself to be one of the classier American rock songwriters and the group's finest works came from his pen: *Do You Believe In Magic, You Didn't Have To Be So Nice, Daydream* and their chart-topping *Summer In The City*.

At the end of 1967, after a run of 10 exceptional hits, their magic dissipated and they broke up a year or so later.

Another group to use folk-rock as a launch pad were the Turtles. Like the Byrds, they were a Los Angelean group who reached the top ten with a souped-up Dylan song – in their case *It Ain't Me Babe* – but greater success came two years later when their classic *Happy Together* reached number one. Further hits, including *She'd Rather Be With Me* and *Elenore*, followed until their dissolution at the turn of the seventies.

Their immensely likeable frontmen, Mark Volman and Howard Kaylan, subsequently joined Frank Zappa's Mothers of Invention before forming their own act as Flo and Eddie, under which names they recorded some interesting but obscure L.P.s.

The We Five also had a folk-rock smash hit with *You Were On My Mind* (covered in Britain by Crispian St. Peters), and Barry McGuire had his one and only hit with *Eve Of Destruction* – a protest song specially concocted for him by Californian mini-Dylan P. F. Sloan.

I Got You Babe, a worldwide number one, got Sonny and Cher's spectacular career off to a flying start after they'd fluffed an earlier attempt as Caesar and Cleo. Their success prompted solo attempts and though Sonny burned out after his first hit, Cher, a

Opposite: A Beatles connection with a product apparently increased its value by 100% or more, as well as reputedly decreasing its quality in many cases in inverse proportion to its price. How many budding George Harrisons were permanently disenchanted when they couldn't play *She Loves You* on their plastic Beatle guitar?

The Lovin' Spoonful (*above*) were remodelled folkies inspired by the Beatles. Since their dissolution in 1968, only John Sebastian (front) has managed to retain even part of his reputation with the occasional flash of inspiration. The Turtles (*left*), one of the brightest Californian folk/rock outfits saw their potential curtailed in the wake of a series of acrimonious lawsuits.

striking girl of Red Indian extraction, was somewhat luckier. Together they survived the sixties as one of the most celebrated married couples in showbiz, but in the early seventies their professional and personal relationship disintegrated and, whilst Sonny appeared to go to ground, Cher continued to grab the headlines. *Half Breed* and *Dark Lady* both returned her to number one (which she'd reached with *Gypsies, Tramps And Thieves* in 1971) and though her chart appearances became less frequent, her romantic entanglements with the likes of Gregg Allman (whom she briefly married) and Gene Simmons of Kiss have kept her in the news.

Much to the horror of the pompous protesters of the early sixties, Bob Dylan also decided to 'go electric', thus greatly extending his popularity. By the end of the year, both *Like A Rolling Stone* and *Positively Fourth Street* had reached the top ten and *Rainy Day Woman* followed them a few months later.

Folk-rock wasn't the only American retaliation, however. After a string of six minor hits on the Moonglow label, the Righteous Brothers, residents on the T.V. series *Shindig*, were signed by Phil Spector. Bill Medley and Bobby Hatfield, who obviously weren't brothers at all, were the first white act to be signed to the Philles label – even though they sang with a pure black sound and inflection – and for their debut, Spector got together with Barry Mann and Cynthia Weil to create the perfect vehicle.

When *You've Lost That Loving Feeling* was issued, it was obvious that Spector had achieved new peaks in perfection and that nothing would stop the Righteous Brothers from topping charts all over the world – which they did in February 1965. It was an immaculate record which had no chance of being equalled, even though their three other singles for Philles all reached the top ten.

Worried that they were losing all their glory to Spector, they signed with Verve, for whom they made the magnificent *Soul And Inspiration* before fading into obscurity for several years.

The Beau Brummels, San Francisco's first nationally popular group, had five chart entries during 1965 including the top tenner *Just A Little*, and the Sir Douglas Quintet, a very Anglicised outfit from Texas, established themselves with *She's About A Mover. Wooly Bully*, their widely copied million selling debut, opened a two year chart run for Sam the Sham and the Pharoahs, who equalled their early success with *Lil' Red Riding Hood* the following year, and Gary Lewis (the son of comedian Jerry Lewis) and the Playboys started their career with seven top tenners, including their first, *This Diamond Ring*, which reached number one.

Of course, there was the usual flurry of activity on the soul scene, with the Temptations and Junior Walker coming in to replace some of the less durable artists on the Tamla Motown rostre.

In fact, the Temptations had been with Motown for several years, having formed from various earlier Detroit aggregations, but it wasn't until they recorded the Smokey Robinson song *The Way You Do The Things You Do* that they scored their first hit in early 1964.

However, it was in 1965 that they came to the fore

Above left: The Byrds (Jim, later Roger, McGuinn, Michael Clark, Chris Hillman, Gene Clark and David Crosby). In the course of an erratic nine year flight, many members came and went, though the distinctive 12-string trademark remained.

Below left: Sonny and Cher during their first British promotional visit in summer, 1965. The togetherness embraced in the lyrics of *I Got You Babe,* their first and biggest hit, was destined to be brief.

Right: Righteous Bros (Bill Medley (left) and Bobby Hatfield) enjoyed their greatest successes under the spectre of their producer Phil.

Far right: Autry DeWalt, or Junior Walker, enjoyed a steady stream of saxophone dominated dance hits.

Junior Walker and the All Stars were predominantly an instrumental unit, coming to the spotlight with *Shotgun* and maintaining their popularity with *Road Runner, How Sweet It Is* and *What Does It Take To Win Your Love?*

The year's two other major soul stars were Joe Tex, a Texan on Dial Records, and Wilson Pickett, who had started out in Detroit group the Falcons (who made the top twenty with *You're So Fine* in 1959).

Tex had recorded for several labels over the years, but it was only when he developed a fast talking gospel preacher's delivery that he began to make an impression. His first hit was *Hold What You've Got,* and *I Gotcha* and other fine follow-ups consolidated his success. Though now close to 50, he continues to record and tour.

Pickett found success with perhaps the most familiar song to emerge from the 1965 soul boom, *In The Midnight Hour,* which was the first of over 30 hits for Atlantic including his biggest, *Land Of A Thousand Dances* and *Funky Broadway.* Undoubtedly one of the sixties R&B/soul greats, Pickett is still recording though with rather less flair and exuberance.

Billy Joe Royal began his chart career with his biggest hit *Down In The Boondocks* and Roger Miller and Bobby Goldsboro both continued theirs with consistent appearances. Goldsboro, who'd started hesitantly in 1962, became firmly established as a result of *Little Things* and *Voodoo Woman,* whilst Roger Miller consolidated his previous hits with such offbeat smashes as *King Of The Road* and *England Swings.*

Indeed, this was the year of 'Swinging London', when the popular fashion centres of Carnaby Street and the Kings Road were added to the itinerary of every American tourist, and it was the Carnaby Street boutique of John Stephen which attracted and clothed the growing army of mods. They were soon to be lampooned in the Kinks' song *Dedicated Follower Of Fashion,* for they were a fairly mindless manifestation ... but out of the mod scene came a group destined to outlive all others save the Stones.

An early shot of the Temptations. Tuxedos and Brylcreem were later supplanted by psychedelic garb and accoutrements, but though styles and faces changed over the years, the group maintained their currency.

with their first number one, another Robinson classic, *My Girl,* which was followed by a stream of top tenners including *I'm Losing You, I Wish It Would Rain* and *I Can't Get Next To You.* During the seventies, though radically different in both personnel and musical approach, the Temptations continued to score with such number ones as *Just My Imagination* and *Papa Was A Rolling Stone,* before leaving the label for Atlantic.

The Who had started out as the Detours, a Tamla Motown/James Brown-influenced R&B band fronted by Roger Daltry on vocals and lead guitar. John Entwistle played bass, art student Pete Townshend played rhythm guitar, and a succession of temporary drummers preceded the arrival of Keith Moon, who was able to instal himself permanently.

After changing their name to the Who, then to the High Numbers – under which name they recorded their first single, *I'm The Face* – and then back to the Who, they began to emphasize their mod connections. They also started to write their own songs (or at least Townshend, who had now become sole guitarist – leaving Daltry to concentrate on vocals, did) and wear jackets cut from Union Jacks.

The long-term policies and deep pockets of their managers also allowed them to evolve a most exciting stage act, which usually culminated in the spectacular destruction of their equipment. Though not the cheapest way to launch a band, it proved to be one of the most successful: within weeks the Who were famous.

By the end of the year, they'd had three top ten hits: *I Can't Explain*, *Anyway Anyhow Anywhere* and *My Generation*, which became one of the most

Joe Tex testifies, alongside, Wilson Pickett (*above*) whose *In The Midnight Hour* has been part of the repertoire of every British soul band ever since its release in 1965.

Alligator Crawl or Crocodile Rock? As far as the Small Faces were concerned, it was just a good publicity stunt. Left to right Steve Marriott, Ian Maclagan, Kenny Jones and Ronnie Lane.

108

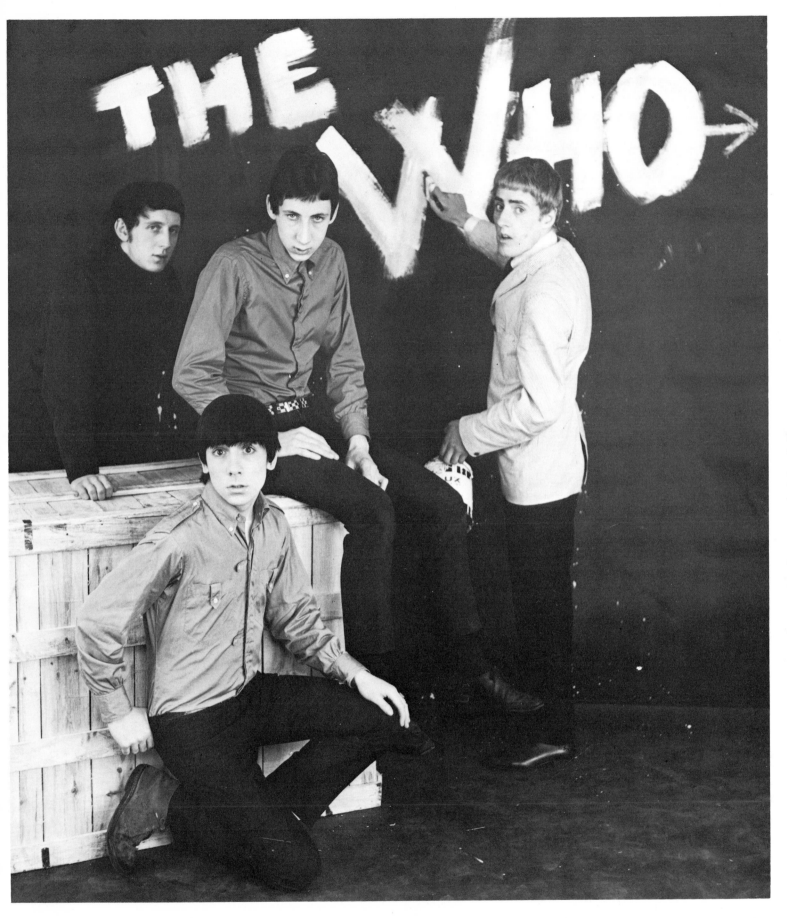

Youthful innocence. Left to right John Entwistle, Pete Townshend, Roger Daltrey and Keith Moon kneeling.

quoted songs of the sixties. As the hits continued – *Substitute*, *I'm A Boy*, *Happy Jack* – each of the group established his own instantly recognisable persona: Moon's drumming was the wildest in Britain, whilst no-one remained as motionless as Entwistle. Townshend developed an extraordinary guitar style, his right arm swinging windmill-like, and Daltrey swung his long-cabled microphone over the audience like a grappling hook.

Incredibly, their first significant American hit didn't come until 1967, by which time Pete Townshend had begun to move in less destructive and more creative directions as his subsequent masterwork *Tommy* was to prove.

The Who's early mod rivals were the Small Faces from the East End of London. In just over three years, they managed 10 top twenty entries including *All Or Nothing*, *Itchycoo Park* and *Lazy Sunday* –

all written by group members Steve Marriott and Ronnie Lane.

Unlike the Who, the Small Faces were unable to break out of their groove and found themselves restricted to the singles market – a factor which eventually influenced Marriott to leave and form Humble Pie. The other three cast about for a replacement, eventually coming up with two, as we shall see.

Three of the year's other big groups were blues practitioners: the Yardbirds, Them and the Spencer Davis Group, from whom superstars emerged in the shapes of Eric Clapton, Van Morrison and Stevie Winwood respectively.

The Yardbirds started in the Richmond area of London in the wake of the Rolling Stones, whose early route they followed, but their first two singles were too blues-oriented to have any wide appeal. For their third release, they were persuaded to record a more 'poppy' song, *For Your Love*, – written by Graham Gouldman, who was later to achieve stardom with 10cc – and they soon found themselves near the top of the charts.

Clapton, a staunch blues purist, found this overtly commercial approach most unseemly and left to play his guitar in John Mayall's Bluesbreakers, whilst the Yardbirds drafted in an astonishing replacement, the unknown Jeff Beck. His playing sizzled through their next four top tenners and Beck soon acquired a reputation as one of the most experimental and dazzling guitarists in the world, but the pressures of endless touring influenced him to leave in late 1966, after recording their last British hit, *Happenings Ten Years Time Ago* – by which time noted session player Jimmy Page had also come into the group.

The Yardbirds concentrated their activities in America, where their live following was particularly enthusiastic (even though subsequent record releases made little impact). Yet although they were certainly one of the most innovative of all sixties groups, few tears were shed in Britain when they disbanded in Summer 1968. From their ashes, Page surfaced with a new band, Led Zeppelin.

Already heroes in their native Belfast, Them were a raw and exciting R&B band led by blues-bawling Van Morrison, who moved to London for a crack at the national market. In early 1965 they made the top ten with *Baby Please Don't Go* and then number two with the follow-up *Here Comes The Night* – although it is the B-side of the first single, *Gloria*, by which the group is best remembered.

After a particularly rough ride, Morrison left the group for a solo career in mid-1966, and the quality of Them's music dwindled drastically as a result.

Stevie Winwood was the magic ingredient which enabled the Spencer Davis Group to move out of the Birmingham pub circuit and into the charts. Though only just 16, he possessed an outstandingly soulful voice and an intuitive feel for the American R&B material which comprised their repertoire.

Early singles chewed the edges of the chart until Chris Blackwell suggested they record a song written by Jackie Edwards (another artist attached to his fledgling company, Island Music). The resulting single, *Keep On Running*, reached number one as did its successor, *Somebody Help Me*. Late the following year, *Gimme Some Loving* made number

two in the U.K. and also gave the group its first American top tenner, and at the beginning of 1967 *I'm A Man* completed their worldwide run. At this point, Stevie Winwood left to form Traffic and the Spencer Davis Group went into sharp decline.

The other successful new British groups of 1965

The Spencer Davis Group. Left to right Stevie Winwood, Pete York, Spencer Davis and Muff Winwood.

were considerably softer in their musical approach. Herman's Hermits from Manchester were a very twee act who succeeded because of the all-round appeal of singer Peter Noone. Their impressive run of hits included 10 top tenners, the best of which were *I'm Into Something Good*, *A Must To Avoid* and *There's A Kind Of Hush* – but their British achievements paled beside their American track record, which included two number ones (*Mrs. Brown You've Got A Lovely Daughter* and *I'm Henry VIII, I Am*) and a total of eight top five entries. In 1971, Noone split for pastures new whilst the Hermits continued as a cabaret attraction.

The Walker Brothers were three unrelated Americans who used London as their operational base – as in the case of P. J. Proby, a move instigated by Jack Good. By embellishing Scott Walker's syrupy vocals with lavish orchestral arrangements, they became tremendously popular during 1965

and 1966, achieving two number ones with *Make It Easy On Yourself* and *The Sun Ain't Gonna Shine Anymore*, both diluted covers, like the majority of their output, of American soul classics.

The trio might have continued to score big hits in Britain, where their predominantly female following was close to fanatical, but turbulence within the group led to their separating for disappointing solo careers. In the mid-seventies, they reformed for a second assault but after their hit version of Tom Rush's *No Regrets*, all was silent once more.

The Fortunes from Birmingham scored two big hits in 1965 – *You've Got Your Troubles* and *Here It Comes Again* – before retreating into the night club circuit and Unit 4+2 also saw chart action with *Concrete And Clay* (a number one) and *You've Never Been In Love Like This Before.*

Chris Andrews, primarily a songwriter, broke into the top three with *Yesterday Man* and Hedgehoppers Anonymous, a bunch of R.A.F. recruits, enjoyed five-minute stardom with *It's Good News Week* – written by Jonathan King.

King was 1965's multi-talented boy wonder. Having established himself with *Everyone's Gone To The Moon*, he went on to get a finger in every pie and can justifiably claim to have 'discovered' the Bay City Rollers, whose first hit, *Keep On Dancing*, he produced in 1971.

After failing in the hands of Joe Meek, Tom Jones tried for a more sophisticated sound with Gordon Mills, who directed his career to astronomic heights. *It's Not Unusual* was released at the beginning of 1965, and reached the top of the British chart, as well as entering the American top ten and selling a million. Over the succeeding years, Jones accumulated dozens of hit singles, becoming a Las Vegas bill-topper and the tax-exile fantasy lover of millions of housewives.

After making numerous chart appearances since 1955, former child film star Petula Clark suddenly came into her own during 1965 when *Downtown*

'65 the year

Events

24 Jan. Sir Winston Churchill dies, aged 91.

7 Feb. The U.S. begins bombing North Vietnam.

8 Mar. President Johnson sends the first ground combat troops to Vietnam.

14 May Queen Elizabeth bequeaths 3 acres of Runnymede, the site of the signing of the Magna Carta, to the U.S. in memory of John Kennedy.

2 June The first Australian troops arrive in Vietnam.

3 June Astronaut Edward White leaves his Gemini capsule to become the first American to float in space.

11 June The Beatles are made Members of the Order of the British Empire in the Queen's Birthday Honours List.

6 Oct. The Post Office Tower opens in London.

9 Nov. New York, parts of New England and Canada are blacked out in the largest power failure in history.

11 Nov. Rhodesia under Ian Smith makes a Unilateral Declaration of Independence.

U.S. CHART TOPPERS – WEEKS AT TOP

I Feel Fine	Beatles
Come See About Me	Supremes
Downtown	Petula Clark
You've Lost That Lovin' Feeling	Righteous Brothers
This Diamond Ring	Gary Lewis and the Playboys
My Girl	Temptations
Eight Days A Week	Beatles
Stop In The Name Of Love	Supremes
I'm Telling You Now	Freddie and the Dreamers
Game Of Love	Wayne Fontana and the Mindbenders
Mrs. Brown You've Got A Lovely Daughter	Herman's Hermits
Ticket To Ride	Beatles
Help Me Rhonda	Beach Boys
Back In My Arms Again	Supremes
I Can't Help Myself	Four Tops
Mr. Tambourine Man	Byrds
Satisfaction	Rolling Stones
I'm Henry VIII, I Am	Herman's Hermits
I Got You Babe	Sonny and Cher
Help	Beatles
Eve Of Destruction	Barry McGuire
Hang On Sloopy	McCoys
Yesterday	Beatles
Get Off Of My Cloud	Rolling Stones
I Hear A Symphony	Supremes
Turn Turn Turn	Byrds
Over And Over	Dave Clark Five

U.K. CHART TOPPERS – WEEKS AT TOP

I Feel Fine	Beatles
Yeh Yeh	Georgie Fame
Go Now	Moody Blues
You've Lost That Lovin' Feeling	Righteous Brothers
Tired Of Waiting For You	Kinks
I'll Never Find Another You	Seekers
It's Not Unusual	Tom Jones
The Last Time	Rolling Stones
Concrete And Clay	Unit 4+2
The Minute You're Gone	Cliff Richard
Ticket To Ride	Beatles
King Of The Road	Roger Miller
Where Are You Now My Love?	Jackie Trent
Long Live Love	Sandie Shaw
Crying In The Chapel	Elvis Presley
I'm Alive	Hollies
Mr. Tambourine Man	Byrds
Help	Beatles
I Got You Babe	Sonny and Cher
Satisfaction	Rolling Stones
Make It Easy On Yourself	Walker Brothers
Tears	Ken Dodd
Get Off Of My Cloud	Rolling Stones
The Carnival Is Over	Seekers
Day Tripper/We Can Work It Out	Beatles

Films of 65

Cat Ballou · The Collector · Dr. Zhivago · Help!
The Sandpiper · The Sound Of Music · The Spy Who Came In From The Cold · Thunderball

Left: Ed White walks in space.
Opposite top right: natural enemies, a Mod and a Rocker.
Opposite centre right: the Beatles.

AUSTRALIA BANS TROGGS' LATEST

THE Troggs' single "I Can't Control Myself," currently number 8 in the MM Pop 50, has been totally banned in Australia.

A spokesman for the group told the MM on Monday: "The ban has been imposed by the Broadcasting Control Board in Australia and applies to both sales and to all the radio stations there. The official reason for the ban is Reg Presley's lyrics.

"Reg is upset that they should take the lyrics the wrong way. We are particularly disappointed because the record was in most of the charts before the ban."

The group signed for a three-week tour of Australia, New Zealand and the Far East last Friday. The tour, which will take the group to Australia for two weeks, will take place in February.

If no official reason for the ban can be obtained from Australia through Australia House in London, manager Larry Page, at present in America, will fly on to Sidney to try to get the ban lifted.

There will probably not be another Troggs' single this year but the group are hoping to release a new album at Christmas. Reg Presley is spending time on the present tour with the Walker Brothers writing material for the LP.

113

Jonathan King, captured sometime before his first million.

Donovan Leitch, originally touted as Britain's answer to Bob Dylan, later fell beneath the spell of the Maharishi.

heralded a string of big hits. Her career took off particularly strongly in America where both *Downtown* and *My Love* topped the charts during the year.

1965 was also the year the American 'folk boom' reached Britain. Bob Dylan and Joan Baez both made the singles charts with old album tracks (*The Times They Are A-Changing* and *There But For Fortune* respectively), while an ultra-commercial London-based Australian folk group called the Seekers cleaned up with such sentimental chart toppers as *I'll Never Find Another You* and *The Carnival Is Over*.

British folk talent, meanwhile, struggled to get beyond the club scene, but only Donovan succeeded. His debut single, *Catch The Wind*, was launched on the first of six consecutive appearances on *Ready Steady Go*. It flew into the top five as did its successor *Colours*. Donovan moved into folk-rock for his biggest success, *Sunshine Superman*, and though he maintained a consistent chart career until 1969, he seemed to lose his focus during the days of 'flower power' and his further output was not taken as seriously as the singer had intended.

Although the B.B.C. saw rock music as an abhorrent disease and accorded it the minimum of needletime, the record companies had no difficulty getting airplay for new product because pirate radio stations were now proliferating around Britain. Operating from converted ships outside territorial waters, or wartime defence forts, the pirates, by offering a livelier service than the B.B.C., made 24 hour broadcasting a practicable proposition and their audience was escalating furiously.

In 1967, Parliament introduced legislation to outlaw the pirates and broadcasting reverted to the monopoly of the B.B.C., who instituted a facelift which provided for the new *Radio One* to adopt a pirate format of pop music and personality disc jockeys. Of course, it was never the same.

While they lasted, the leading pirate stations (London and Caroline) were a joy: they featured adventurous programming, unprecedentedly breezy presentation, and they always played the best new records.

'66

'Good Vibrations'

The Association · Paul Butterfield Blues Band · Lou Christie · Dave Dee, Dozy, Beaky, Mick and Tich · Neil Diamond · Tommy James and the Shondells The Left Banke · The Mamas and the Papas · John Mayall · The Monkees Napoleon XIV · The Rascals · Otis Redding · Paul Revere and the Raiders Mitch Ryder · Simon and Garfunkel · Nancy Sinatra · Percy Sledge · Cat Stevens The Troggs · Frank Zappa

Whilst established stars, especially the Beatles three number ones: *We Can Work It Out*, *Paperback Writer* and *Eleanor Rigby*) and the Rolling Stones three top fivers: *Nineteenth Nervous Breakdown*, *Paint It Black* and *Have You Seen Your Mother, Baby?*), were releasing brilliant recordings, new British acts couldn't seem to come up with anything substantial in 1966. Most appeared to have an aura of novelty about them, as if they were just more products of the trite and ephemeral pop machine.

The Troggs were a prize example; ostensibly a bunch of country bumpkins from Wiltshire, they reached number two with their ludicrously inept debut, *Wild Thing*. The same naive enthusiasm pervaded the chart-topping *With A Girl Like You* and *I Can't Control Myself*, which reached number two though on their other big hits, *Anyway That You Want Me* and *Love Is All Around*, one could detect a definite sensitivity creeping in.

Unfortunately for the Troggs, they were all washed up, chartwise, by early 1968 – despite comeback attempts – but lead singer Reg Presley and his current cohorts still enjoy a considerable cult following in America, where their efforts seem to have been taken rather more seriously.

Also from the south-west of England, Dave Dee and the Bostons were a top local attraction with an interesting line in comedy to supplement their musical appeal. After signing with Ken Howard and Alan Blaikley, who had previously managed the Honeycombs, they changed their name to Dave Dee, Dozy, Beaky, Mick and Tich and embarked on a highly successful chart career which saw them in the top twenty no less than 10 times in the 31 months between March 66 and October 68. Best-remembered of their hits are *Bend It*, *Zabadak* and *Legend Of Xanadu*, their only number one.

In spite of their enormous popularity in Britain, they were unable to impress the Americans and parted in 1969, Dave Dee to go solo and the others to continue as a group. Neither recovered sufficient impetus to make it and Dee subsequently quit to become a record company executive.

If Dave Dee's television appearances had an air of contrivance about them, so, too, did those of the New Vaudeville Band. Their brassy oompah and megaphone vocals recalled the Temperance Seven, and though they weren't around for long they had a pair of sizeable hits in *Winchester Cathedral* and *Peek A Boo*.

Anyone who called himself Cat and sang a song called *I Love My Dog* had to be suspect, but Cat Stevens was the most durable of all British acts launched during the year. He really came into his own during 1967 with four chart entries including

the top tenners *Matthew And Son* and *I'm Gonna Get Me A Gun*, but was then laid up with a severe case of tuberculosis until 1970, when he made a dramatic return with *Lady d'Arbanville*.

During the seventies he established himself as one of the better singer/songwriters in an overstocked market and several of his albums, notably, *Catch Bull At Four* and *Buddha And The Chocolate Box*, were massive worldwide sellers.

Neil Christian, a rocker since the late fifties, had his first and last hit with *That's Nice*; New Yorker Roy C had a U.K.-only smash in *Shotgun Wedding*; Crispian St Peters had a quick fling with *You Were On My Mind* and *The Pied Piper*; and the Merseybeats reappeared as a trimmed-down duo known as the Merseys, but *Sorrow* was to be their only success.

Bringing a little more stability to the proceedings was Alan Price, a refugee from the Animals, who went on to carve a respectable solo career which took him into the top twenty six times following his 1966 debut, *I Put A Spell On You*. He subsequently snuggled into television and cabaret work and by the seventies had established himself as a film soundtrack writer.

Meanwhile, clubs around the country were still vibrating to the sound of blues from groups like John Mayall's Blues Breakers, the Graham Bond Organisation and Chris Farlowe and the Thunderbirds. All had released singles to little response, but in 1966 Farlowe broke through with the Jagger/Richard song *Out Of Time*, which was a surprise number one. He never repeated the feat and after a chequered career with Colosseum and Atomic Rooster, he retired to his London antique business. However, he continued to perform sporadically during the late seventies.

John Mayall's Blues Breakers were a permanent fixture. Oblivious to commercial considerations, Mayall pursued his chosen music through thick and thin, watching a succession of brilliant guitarists (including Eric Clapton, Peter Green and Mick Taylor) join and leave his band. After slogging around the clubs for many years, Mayall began to achieve album success and finally moved to Los Angeles where he continues to record.

Mayall's American counterpart was Paul Butterfield, a singer and harmonica player whose Chicago-based Blues Band included ace guitarist Mike Bloomfield by the time they first recorded for Elektra in 1965, and like Mayall's, his band spawned a spate of imitators. When Bloomfield left to work with Bob Dylan after which he formed Electric Flag in 1967, Butterfield's second guitarist Elvin Bishop stepped into the limelight before he

Left: Ringo went up in the world when he joined the Beatles.

Right: The Troggs led by the exuberant Reg Presley (far right and no relation), blundered their way to stardom with a series of raw sexual invitations.

Far right: Steven Georghiou (also known as Cat Stevens) established himself as a singles artist in the late sixties and graduated to worldwide album acclaim in the seventies.

Centre: Dave Dee, Dozy, Beaky, Mick and Tich, whose hit singles were often as contrived as their name, nevertheless had some catchy songs.

Below right: Frank Zappa masterminded several different versions of his group, the Mothers of Invention (*below*). Regarded at first as a hippy novelty act, Zappa has more recently gained recognition as a serious composer and musician.

too left to form his own group.

After his Blues Band had broken up, Butterfield formed the excellent Better Days but they, too, split and Butterfield's current appearances are rare.

If Butterfield's youth was steeped in Chicago blues, Frank Zappa's time was spent listening to R&B, and his first group excursion was with the Los Angeles-based Soul Giants in the early sixties. He soon gained control of the group, changed their name to the Mothers of Invention, and began to alter their musical direction quite radically.

By the time they recorded their first album in 1966, the Mother's music was a weird collage of styles incorporating parody, blues, social satire, classical music and avant-garde jazz. Critics assumed that drugs were behind the bizarre stage act which Zappa had evolved and the group's performances became known as 'freak outs' – a term which would soon be used to describe any drug-oriented musical event.

Of course, Zappa had the imagination and skill to survive adverse criticism and, despite literally dozens of musicians having been through his band, he continued to make powerful, idiosyncratic records which invariably reached the middle ranges of the American album charts. Over the years, he has become a respected and influential figure, but has never dropped his cynical tongue-in-cheek façade.

As Zappa crashed into the L.A. rock scene, Phil Spector made a discreet exit. His latest coup had been to sign Ike and Tina Turner, and he spared no effort to ensure that their debut, *River Deep Mountain High*, would be regarded as his finest creation. When it climbed no higher than number 88, he was destroyed . . . simply packed his bags and locked up shop.

During the seventies he re-emerged to lend this technical expertise on various occasions, but he has kept his creative profile distinctly low.

Ike and Tina weathered the trauma more stoically . . . *River Deep* had, after all, been a huge hit in Britain, and the follow-up, *A Love Like Yours*, had also made the top twenty. They went on to become one of the most successful album acts of the seventies, and their live performances were second to none in terms of excitement, but their eventual divorce did little to stimulate their individual careers.

Tina was the most explosive girl singer of 1966; the year's other female contenders were more reserved. Sandy Posey revealed herself to be the antithesis of Women's Lib with her string of under-some-man's-thumb singles, including *Born A Woman* and *Single Girl*, both of which reached number 12, while Frank Sinatra's daughter, Nancy, portrayed herself as a man-stomper in her chart-topping hit, *These Boots Are Made For Walkin'*.

Nancy returned to the top ten twice the same year, and in 1967 had two big duet winners – *Jackson* with Lee Hazlewood and *Something Stupid* (another number one) with her father – but after that her hits dried up all too quickly.

Bobby Hebb suffered the same fate. After an impressive start with *Sunny*, he disappeared almost immediately – as did a number of bright and not-so-bright prospects including Robert Parker with *Barefootin'*, the Capitols with *Cool Jerk*, Napoleon XIV with *They're Coming To Take Me Away, Ha Ha*, and the Count Five with *Psychotic Reaction*.

Bob Lind had a one-off folk hit with *Elusive Butterfly* and Simon and Garfunkel rang in the new year with the chart-topping *Sounds Of Silence*, a song they'd recorded back in 1964. During their absence (Simon was in England, Garfunkel at college), the original acoustic track had been embellished with suitable instrumentation to make it a chart winner – and Simon and Garfunkel found themselves folk rock stars!

They immediately set about capitalising on this new-found success, producing a series of best-selling albums including *Parsley, Sage, Rosemary And Thyme* and *Bookends*, and contributing to the soundtrack of the Academy Award-winning film *The Graduate*. The peak of their career came with the multi-million selling *Bridge Over Troubled Water*, but they parted soon after.

Garfunkel continued his movie and recording pursuits while the reclusive Simon worked at his songs and released the occasional (and inevitably platinum) album.

The Mamas and the Papas also tried their wings in folk music before breaking into the rock market. Leader and principal songwriter John Phillips had enjoyed limited success with the Journeymen before retiring to the Virgin Isles with his wife Michelle and two friends, Denny Doherty and Cass

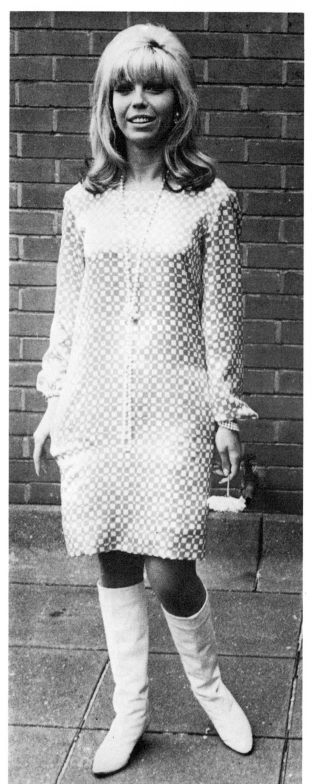

Left: Nancy Sinatra models her famous walking boots. Her photogenic appeal could not prevent her falling from chart favour.

Above: Paul Simon (right) and Art Garfunkel, who had scored their first, though minor, hit in 57 as Tom and Jerry. Folk music was a basis for a successful reunion, and Simon's socio-political songs carried them to the top.

Above right: In a career spanning a little over two years, the Mamas and the Papas (left to right: John Phillips, Michelle Phillips, Denny Doherty and Cass Elliott) captured the essence of sixties California.

Elliott, to write songs and formulate plans for a four-part harmony vocal group.

Through their friendship with Barry McGuire, they landed a contract with manager/producer Lou Adler and recorded some of the most inspired music to come out of the sixties. In a little over a year they released six top five singles – including *California Dreamin'*, the chart-topping *Monday Monday*, and *Creeque Alley*, which detailed their rise to fame – and four top five albums.

By 1968, however, they had burned out the combination and separated for solo careers. An early heart attack death terminated Mama Cass' progress; Denny slipped from sight after a poorly received album; John, after an excellent solo debut, relied on his skills as a producer and songwriter;

and as the sixties came to an end they moved into a fruitful cabaret career.

Paul Revere and the Raiders, from Portland Oregon, had been around since the turn of the decade but it wasn't until they recorded the Mann/Weil song *Kicks* in 1966 that they made the top ten. Similar winners were *Hungry*, *Good Thing* and *Him Or Me – What's It Gonna Be?*, and their reputation seemed assured. However, their onstage comedy routines and historical military uniforms had pegged them as a teeenybop group and they were unable to make the transition required by late sixties rock audiences. After dwindling sales and numerous personnel changes, they abbreviated their name to the Raiders and despite a surprise return with *Indian Reservation*, a number one in 1971, they faded away during the early seventies.

The story of Tommy James and the Shondells follows the same pattern: a string of creditable singles, unjust pigeonholing as an insubstantial bubblegum group, and an unsuccessful bid to meet changing tastes. The story behind their first hit, however, is unique. James and a bunch of schoolfriends recorded a version of the Barry/Greenwich song, *Hanky Panky* (which the composers had recorded as the Raindrops), for a small Michigan label in the early sixties. Several years later he was astonished to find that a Pittsburgh disc-jockey had recently been championing the record and that a pirated pressing was topping the local charts.

Roulette Records bought the legitimate rights and in Summer 1966, it became a national number one. Fronting a new Shondells, James became a huge star, acquiring another number one in *Crimson And Clover* and considerable hits with *I Think We're Alone Now*, *Mony Mony* (his only British success) and *Crystal Blue Persuasion*, among others.

In 1970 he split with the Shondells and, whilst they vanished after an ill-considered name change to Hog Heaven, he managed to score a final winner in *Draggin' The Line* before he too disappeared from the public eye.

Several other American bands made an impact during 1966. The Standells reached number 11 with *Dirty Water* and though follow-ups were less successful, they established themselves as prototypical punk rockers whose records influenced a new generation of musicians 10 years later. The Happenings, a harmony group in the Four Seasons mould, made their mark with *See You In September* and *I Got Rhythm*, and a young New York group, the Left Banke, made a stunning entry with *Walk Away Renne*. After a less powerful follow-up, *Pretty Ballerina*, the group's mainspring Michael Brown, left and their brilliance withered.

After building a strong local reputation, Mitch Ryder and the Detroit Wheels signed with producer Bob Crewe and recorded a million seller in the raucous medley *Jenny Take A Ride* – a combination of Little Richard's *Jenny Jenny* and the R&B standard *C. C. Rider*. The formula was even more successful for *Devil With The Blue Dress On/Good Golly Miss Molly*, but after *Sock It To Me Baby* he faltered and soon found himself on the slide, suffering from a throat infection which ended his career.

Working the same soul/R&B vein were another white group, the Young Rascals, three of whom had met as members of Joey Dee's band at the

The Association overcame accusations that their first U.S. hit, *Along Comes Mary*, had drug connotations, and went on to enjoy a string of classic harmony hits.

and Michelle went on to become one of Hollywood's better film stars.

Almost as successful as the Mamas and the Papas were the Association, Paul Revere and the Raiders, and Tommy James and the Shondells.

The Association, a West Coast six-piece, also relied on intricate vocal arrangements, as their top tenner, *Along Comes Mary*, testified. Their second release, *Cherish*, became the best-selling single of 1966 and was followed by another number one, *Windy*. *Never My Love* and *Everything That Touches You* marked the end of their chart run, however,

Above: Otis Redding, probably the most influential soul singer of the late sixties.

Above centre: Percy Sledge, who was unable to repeat the success of his classic *When A Man Loves A Woman.*

Above right: Ike and Tina Turner had been together for some years before their first chart success, and had put together a spellbinding stage show.

Centre below: Neil Diamond, initially a Brill Building song-smith, went on to capture the hearts of a million house-wives.

Peppermint Lounge. After their first tentative stabs they came up with a number one in *Good Lovin'* and another in *Groovin'*, which also became their only solid British hit. *A Girl Like You* and *How Can I Be Sure?* continued their run which peaked with a third number one, *People Got To Be Free*, in 1968 – by which time they preferred to be known as the Rascals. In 1972, the group broke up.

The Young Rascals had been one of the first white groups to appear on Atlantic Records, a label traditionally associated with black R&B and soul artists – two of whom came to the fore during 1966.

In fact, Otis Redding recorded for the Memphis-based Volt Records, but they were nationally promoted and distributed by Atlantic. The son of a minister, Redding grew up with gospel influences but, towards the end of his schooldays, became besotted with the works of Little Richard, whose style he copied in his early days. A white Atlanta school friend, Phil Walden (later owner of the Capricorn label), introduced him to another local performer, Johnny Jenkins, whose band he joined as chauffeur and part-time singer – and it was during some excess studio time that Redding got a chance to cut his own single *These Arms Of Mine*, which scratched the surface of the charts in 1963.

His solo career burgeoned with a succession of minor hits until *I've Been Loving You Too Long* and *Respect* brought him national recognition in 1965. His version of *Satisfaction* and *Try A Little Tenderness* consolidated his reputation and he was able to tour Europe to enthusiastic response in 1966 and 1967 – when he also broke through to the expanding 'underground' audience by appearing with the world's premier acts at the Monterey Pop Festival.

Redding seemed poised to conquer the world – but it was not to be: on 10th December 1967, he died when a plane carrying him and his band, the Bar Kays, crashed into a lake near Madison Wisconsin. Ironically, his biggest single came with the posthumous release *Dock Of The Bay*, which reached number one in early 1968.

Atlantic's other major success was Percy Sledge, who cut one of the finest soul records ever made: *When A Man Loves A Woman*. It was to be by far his greatest achievement but provided the base for a stage career which has remained buoyant.

James and Bobby Purify had a big soul hit with *I'm Your Puppet* and Sam and Dave began their chart career with *Hold On I'm Comin'* – though *Soul Man* and *I Thank You*, both released in 1967, represented the peak of their success. Stax stablemate Eddie Floyd also broke though for the first time, with *Knock On Wood*, which was to be his calling card for years to come.

Tamla's new star was Jimmy Ruffin, whose brother David was a member of the Temptations. His first hit, *What Becomes Of The Broken Hearted?* proved to be his biggest and label changes in the seventies did nothing to reverse his gradual decline.

Overall group dominance left little room for white solo singers, who were considered very passé in 1966, but two are deserving of mention: Lou Christie and Neil Diamond.

Christie, a balladeer who specialised in falsetto breaks, had achieved a spate of success in 1963 when three singles including the top tenner, *Two*

Paul Revere (second from right) and the Raiders ruled the U.S. air waves for a few years as America's answer to the British invasion.

The Monkees (left to right: Davy Jones, Peter Tork, Mickey Dolenz and Mike Nesmith) proved that a manufactured group could still inspire teen worship.

Faces Have I, reached the charts. He lay low during the British occupation, only to return with a number one, *Lightning Strikes*, in early 1966. A further top twenty entry, *Rhapsody In The Rain*, preceded another bleak spell which ended with his last major success *I'm Gonna Make You Mine* – a hit on both sides of the Atlantic late in 1969.

Neil Diamond, of course, was just beginning his career in 1966. *Cherry Cherry* was his first top ten entry, followed by *Girl You'll Be A Woman Soon*, *Sweet Caroline*, *Holly Holy*, *Cracklin' Rosie*, *I Am . . . I Said* and *Song Sung Blue*. By this time, 1972, Diamond's potential as a singer/songwriter was such that C.B.S. had signed him to a million dollar contract a full year before his contract with Uni was due to expire.

He subsequently became an international megastar with gold and platinum albums covering his walls – but in 1966, he was holed up in Don Kirshner's New York song factory trying his best to turn out some hit songs. Two of these, *I'm A Believer* and *A LIttle Bit Me, A Little Bit You*, provided smashes for the year's biggest group . . . the Monkees.

The Monkees were a totally contrived group, comprising four talented but disparate individuals who were chosen from thousands of applicants. They were brought together primarily to make a television comedy series about being in a rock group; the songs would be ultra-commercial, the group would have all the requisite teen-appeal, and many of the visual ideas would derive from the Beatles' films.

It was a recipe to set the cash registers ringing. The series began transmission during the last quarter of 1966 and by the end of the year the Monkees had become the most popular group in America, racking up two number one singles in *Last Train To Clarksville* and *I'm A Believer* (which had advance orders exceeding a million), and a best-selling album, *The Monkees*, which found its way into over three million American homes.

During 1967, they scored five more hits and within 18 months of forming had won 10 gold discs – though it subsequently transpired that the group had little to do with the records, which were largely manufactured by seasoned session musicians. Eventually, they were allowed to sing and play on their records, but by this time their novelty was wearing thin and their days at the top were numbered.

Peter Tork, the first to leave the group, was seldom heard of again, whilst Davy Jones and Mickey Dolenz returned to their acting careers. Michael Nesmith persevered as a singer/songwriter and after a series of critically acclaimed albums enters the eighties a respected musician.

All in all, 1966, was not the most auspicious year for new musical talent – but revolution was just around the corner.

'66 the year

Events

14 Feb. Two Soviet writers, Sinyavsky and Daniel, are sentenced to hard labour for publishing 'anti-Soviet' works abroad.

1 Mar. The Soviet spacecraft Venus 3 lands on Venus – the first man-made object to reach another planet.

29 June American planes bomb Hanoi, North Vietnam.

30 July England wins the World Cup, beating West Germany 4–2 in the final.

29 Aug. In San Francisco, the Beatles play their final 'live' performance.

6 Sept. South African Prime Minister Verwoerd is assassinated, and is succeeded by John Vorster.

21 Oct. 144 people (mostly children) are killed in a slag tip disaster in Aberfan, South Wales.

12 Dec. Lone yachtsman Francis Chichester arrives in Sydney, Australia on his round-the-world solo journey in Gypsy Moth IV.

Films of 66

Alfie · Blow Up · Born Free · The Fortune Cookie · The Fantastic Voyage · Grand Prix · A Man For All Seasons · Who's Afraid Of Virginia Woolf

Below right: Neil Diamond's first royalty cheque.

Below: Michael Caine in *Alfie.*

Opposite bottom: North Vietnamese troops.

U.S. CHART TOPPERS – WEEKS AT TOP

The Sounds Of Silence	Simon and Garfunkel
We Can Work It Out	Beatles
My Love	Petula Clark
Lightnin' Strikes	Lou Christie
These Boots Are Made For Walkin'	Nancy Sinatra
The Ballad Of The Green Berets	Barry Sadler
Soul And Inspiration	Righteous Brothers
Good Lovin'	Young Rascals
Monday Monday	Mamas and the Papas
When A Man Loves A Woman	Percy Sledge
Paint It Black	Rolling Stones
Paperback Writer	Beatles
Strangers In The Night	Frank Sinatra
Hanky Panky	Tommy James and the Shondells
Wild Thing	Troggs
Summer In The City	Lovin' Spoonful
Sunshine Superman	Donovan
You Can't Hurry Love	Supremes
Cherish	Association
Reach Out, I'll Be There	Four Tops
96 Tears	Question Mark and the Mysterians
Last Train To Clarksville	Monkees
Poor Side Of Town	Johnny Rivers
You Keep Me Hangin' On	Supremes
Winchester Cathedral	New Vaudeville Band
Good Vibrations	Beach Boys

U.K. CHART TOPPERS – WEEKS AT TOP

Day Tripper/We Can Work It Out	Beatles
Keep On Runnin'	Spencer Davis Group
Michelle	Overlanders
These Boots Are Made For Walking	Nancy Sinatra
The Sun Ain't Gonna Shine Anymore	Walker Brothers
Somebody Help Me	Spencer Davis Group
You Don't Have To Say You Love Me	Dusty Springfield
Pretty Flamingo	Manfred Mann
Paint It Black	Rolling Stones
Strangers In The Night	Frank Sinatra
Paperback Writer	Beatles
Sunny Afternoon	Kinks
Get Away	Georgie Fame
Out Of Time	Chris Farlowe
With A Girl Like You	Troggs
Eleanor Rigby/Yellow Submarine	Beatles
All Or Nothing	Small Faces
Distant Drums	Jim Reeves
Reach Out, I'll Be There	Four Tops
Good Vibrations	Beach Boys
Green Green Grass Of Home	Tom Jones

BROADCAST MUSIC, INC.
589 FIFTH AVENUE   ●   NEW YORK, N.Y.

CHECK NO. RD 058267

1-12
210

A

PAY TO THE ORDER OF

NEW YORK MAR 31, 1966

NEIL LESLIE DIAMOND
140-21 BURDEN CRESCENT
JAMAICA 35 L. I.
NEW YORK

$••.73

EXACTLY $50 AND 73 CTS DOLLARS

ROYALTY ACCOUNT

TO CHEMICAL BANK NEW YORK TRUST COMPANY
30 ROCKEFELLER PLAZA
NEW YORK

⑆0210-0012⑆   601-103025⑈

Small Faces in a tight green circle

WHO boss attacks Beach Boys

"EVERYBODY do the paranoia!" hissed Steve Marriott as he sloped across the room of the Small Faces' Pimlico pad. Resembling an unlikely gang of underwater karate experts, mimicking the great Wilson, Keppel, and Betty, the remaining Faces followed about the room in slow motion.

The squeamish may find the Small Faces latest warcry a little cruel—Napoleon XIV didn't stay unbanned—but then the Faces live in a compact, happy, air-tight little world of life, thought, ideas, and music.

Steve, Mac, Plonk, and mate Mick—a kind of hidden Small Face you never hear about—lounged about in front of the TV. Drummer boy Kenny was out underneath his mini. Someone stealthily moved to the record player and put on a sound. After about one third of a bar the Faces were all grooving along with the record, listening hard and digging.

Downstairs, faint shuffling, step-treading and the occasional "eeeeek", came floating under the front door. "They must be soaking wet by now, they've been out there for hours," thought Stevie of the handful of fans clustered under the front porch.

STEVIE, 'must be soaking wet'.

NICK JONES at a Small Faces recording session

PETE TOWNSHEND this week attacked **Brian Wilson**, musical brain behind the **Beach Boys**, for "making pop music too complex."

"Brian Wilson lives in a world of flowers, butterflies and strawberry flavoured chewing gum," the Who star declared.

"His world has nothing to do with pop. Pop is going out on the road, getting drunk, meeting the kids.

" 'Good Vibrations' was probably a good record but who's to know? You had to play it about ninety bloody times to even hear what they were singing about."

As the musical brain behind the Who, the group that last year **Paul McCartney** predicted would probably be the biggest influence on pop music in 1966, Pete Townshend finds himself concerned about the state of pop music in general, and especially about the British pop scene.

His attitude to pop is that it is getting so complicated nobody knows what's happening—least of all the fans. And it is the fans that Pete is most concerned about.

In his manager's office last week he yanked off the scarf that had been half covering his face against the cold like a Bedouin let loose in London, and slumped in a handy chair.

"Look, the kids just don't know what's going on, everything's so involved. Next year is going to be worse. We're going to have a batch of over-produced Beach Boys records and over-produced records in general.

"**Andy Warhol** (leader of America's plastic pop brigade) will come over and start on his psychedelic bit and everyone will walk around saying 'oh yeah that's what I thought all the time'. And the first person to explain it like that will cop the money.

Decline

"The thing that hung me up this year about British pop was the decline of British groups in America. **Herman** coming out with clever records. It's sad. And the English public now want what the Americans want. Groups to wear gaudy clothes and sing fa la la. The biggest bring down for me was **Dave Dee** and that lot.

"Even **Herb Alpert** was a better influence this year. He knew where he was going. He was producing light music. And the Mamas and Papas too.

"It needs the Beatles to come out of their hole and make a really simple pop record to sort things out. I'd prefer to see a reversion to pop for a pop audience. It's all wrong to elevate a pop audience to what you're doing.

"We made that mistake earlier on. We had no plans to escalate as quickly as we did musically. We used ideas we didn't even understand ourselves never mind anyone else not understanding them."

And indeed what of the Who? Do they think Beatle Paul was right when 12 months ago he prophesied such a glowing future for them?

"We're doing what we want. At least with the last single and the LP. But I don't think the group regard themselves as having any status. It used to give us a surprise when we saw our name top of the bill."

'We need Beatles to sort things out'

'67

'Let's Go To San Francisco'

Amen Corner · Jeff Beck · Captain Beefheart · The Bee Gees · Big Brother and the Holding Company · The Box Tops · Buffalo Springfield · Canned Heat Arthur Conley · Country Joe and the Fish · Cream · The Doors · Fleetwood Mac Aretha Franklin · Bobbie Gentry · The Grateful Dead · Jimi Hendrix The Herd · Jefferson Airplane · Love · Scott McKenzie · The Move Pink Floyd · Procol Harum · Sly and the Family Stone · Traffic · Vanilla Fudge

By 1967, rock music and the complementary hi-fi leisure industry had developed to the point where, for the first time, albums began to outsell singles, leading to the swift decline of many singles-oriented groups, though the more adventurous and musical were already established album artists too ... none more so than the Beatles, whose June release *Sergeant Pepper's Lonely Hearts Club Band* was a cornerstone in the album takeover.

1967 was also the year when the use of drugs, previously widespread but covert, suddenly became de rigeur for rock musicians – and much of the music reflected this, particulary that originating from the latest centre of excitement, San Francisco.

Until the drug was outlawed in 1966, writer Ken Kesey and 'his merry pranksters' had been touring California in a converted bus inviting interested parties to sample the hallucinogenic drug L.S.D. (whose effects he'd first felt as a guineapig volunteer, under psychiatric conditions); since he was based near San Francisco, a local band, the Grateful Dead, often played at his gatherings.

A drug-related culture started to develop in the city, which, due to abundant sensationalist publicity, began to attract a steady influx of long-hairs, drop-outs and musicians (collectively known as 'hippies'), who more or less took over a rundown quarter called Haight Ashbury ... and numerous rock groups began to emerge, together with appropriate venues.

At the Fillmore Auditorium and the Avalon Ballroom, instead of experiencing a formal concert hall atmosphere, the audience was sucked up and integrated into the whole fabric of sight and sound. Strobe lights flashed, light-shows bubbled over every surface, and bands played at a volume designed to achieve sensory overload ... and the style of music, largely inspired by L.S.D., became known as 'psychedelic' or 'acid' rock.

As soon as news of 'The San Francisco Sound' leaked out, every label sent scouts to sign a piece of the action ... and the first group to achieve national success were the Sopwith Camel, who reached the top thirty early in 1967, with *Hello Hello.* Illness and arguments fragmented the group before they could capitalise on their breakthrough, however, and they were destined to remain one-hit wonders.

If the Sopwith Camel weren't altogether typical of the San Francisco Sound, the next group were. After a mildly successful first album the year before, the Jefferson Airplane had two top ten hits during the summer of 67: *Somebody To Love* and the classic *White Rabbit.* The catalyst was a girl singer called Grace Slick, whose clear soaring voice integrated perfectly with the fluid runs of Jorma Kaukonen,

one of the city's most inventive guitarists.

After eight top twenty albums including a number three in *Surrealistic Pillow*, the Airplane was grounded by a plethora of personal problems but, after a brief hiatus, the principal members re-emerged with Jefferson Starship and went on to become one of the most successful bands of the mid-seventies.

For Moby Grape, whose leader Skip Spence had drummed with the early Airplane, the flight was considerably rougher. The group was launched with an unprecedented barrage of publicity which saw the simultaneous release, in May 1967, of an album and five singles, but the Grape were unable to sustain their initial success. By the end of the sixties they were just a memory.

By mid-1967, *Newsweek* magazine, in a lavish investigation of the San Francisco scene, estimated that the city's electricity was being used by several hundred bands, most now only names on a list – including two of the pioneering groups, the Charlatans and the Mystery Trend, both, sadly, squeezed out in the commercial stampede ... but the Grateful Dead and Country Joe and the Fish managed to establish themselves as international stars.

Beatle John Lennon expanded his horizons when he co-starred in the controversial Dick Lester film *How I Won The War.*

124

The Grateful Dead enjoyed a huge live following but, due to difficulties in transferring their psychedelic ramblings to tape, took longer to achieve significant album sales, which didn't come until the release of *Workingman's Dead* and *American Beauty* in the early seventies – after which they appeared to lose the drive which had powered them through so many crises. Diverse interests led them into spin-off projects and though the band periodically reformed to record and tour, they were widely regarded as relics of a bygone era by the eighties.

Country Joe and the Fish, a Berkeley-based quintet, produced one of the most imaginative albums of the period in *Electric Music For The Mind And Body*, designed, they said, as the perfect musical accompaniment to an acid trip Although patchy in quality, four subsequent albums made the charts and the group was able to make a resounding impression at the Woodstock Festival, which was filmed for posterity. Country Joe subsequently went solo, though his artistic and commercial achievements were never to equal his 1967 peak.

The other major San Franciscan group was Big Brother and the Holding Company, whose main

Above: Jefferson Airplane (left to right: Marty Balin, Spencer Dryden, Jorma Kaukonen, Grace Slick, Paul Kantner and Jack Casady).

Right: The Grateful Dead (left to right: Bill Kreutzmann, Phil Lesh, Jerry Garcia, Bob Weir and Ron 'Pigpen' McKernan).

Below: Big Brother and the Holding Company (left to right: David Getz, Janis Joplin, Sam Andrew, James Gurley and Peter Albin). These three groups spearheaded the San Francisco sound.

attraction was their raunchy singer Janis Joplin. Initially she was not given star-billing, but by the time of their second album, *Cheap Thrills*, in 1968, it was obvious that the rest of the band were functioning as her backing group. The album sold a million and topped the charts, prompting Janis to leave for a solo career – a move which ultimately finished off the group.

Despite spectacular success, Janis Joplin's subsequent life was punctuated with misery and heroin finally killed her in October 1970. She didn't live to see her final album, *Pearl*, outstrip all competition to reach number one.

The euphoric atmosphere induced many visitors – including Steve Miller, Boz Scaggs, the Sir Douglas

Quintet and Mother Earth – to make San Francisco their permanent residence, whilst other groups, like Kaleidoscope from Los Angeles and the Thirteenth Floor Elevators from Texas, made it their second home ... but musical activity in the Bay Area reached a peak in June 1967 when a wealth of international talent converged on Monterey to mount America's first rock festival. Among the performers was Scott McKenzie, whose single *San Francisco (Wear Some Flowers In Your Hair)* was riding high in the charts. The lyric, by John Phillips of the Mamas and the Papas, coaxed the youth of America to visit the 'gentle people' of the city – which they did in droves.

Meanwhile, the drug culture was affecting the music of Los Angeles and London. L.A.'s second leaguers included Clear Light, the Seeds, the Misunderstood, the Peanut Butter Conspiracy, and Spanky and Our Gang, while those destined for greater heights included Love, Buffalo Springfield, Canned Heat, Captain Beefheart, and the Doors.

The Doors (who took their name from Aldous Huxley's psychedelic exploration *The Doors Of Perception*), led by the intense and theatrical Jim Morrison, had been rejected by various record companies before being signed by Elektra, a folk label trying out its rock wings. Within five years the Doors had accumulated seven top ten albums, including a number one in *Waiting For The Sun.*

Their first single, the swirling *Light My Fire*, had also reached number one though subsequent offerings fared less well because Morrison's anarchic lyrics and heavily sexual image did not endear him to radio programmers. Nevertheless, the group became one of the biggest draws in the world – until Morrison allegedly exposed himself on stage in Miami in March 1969. The resultant furore marked the beginning of their decline.

After completing a final album, *L.A. Woman*, Morrison moved to Paris – ostensibly to pursue his creative writing in a suitably sympathetic environment – where he died in July 1971, reportedly suffering a heart attack whilst taking a bath. His erstwhile colleagues tried but failed to recapture the magic of one of the best and most adventurous bands to come out of the sixties, disbanding in 73.

Equally interesting, though considerably less successful, were Love, fronted by the enigmatic Arthur Lee. After a derivative first album they developed a distinctive style of their own, which flowered in their masterpiece *Forever Changes* – regarded by many as the finest in the West Coast genre – but drug problems and internal bickering resulted in their speedy disintegration. Lee subsequently formed several new versions of Love, and still enjoys a strong cult following in Europe, but later albums afforded only occasional glimpses of his former radiance.

Canned Heat and Captain Beefheart and his Magic Band were blues bands with psychedelic overtones. Though their main vocalist was Bob 'The Bear' Hite, Canned Heat's biggest hits, *On The Road Again* and *Goin' Up The Country*, were both sung by transplanted Bostonian Al Wilson, who later added to the growing number of deaths due to drug overdose.

His debut album, *Safe As Milk*, established a small but fanatical following for Captain Beefheart, whose British devotees have remained particularly

Jim Morrison, charismatic vocalist and leader of the Doors.

Arthur Lee, leader of Love, one of the most under-rated West Coast groups of the late sixties.

Don Van Vliet, better known as Captain Beefheart, remains one of the most enigmatic but influential rock figures of all time.

The original line up of Procol Harum (left to right: Bobby Harrison, Matthew Fisher, Gary Brooker, Dave Knights and Ray Royer). While their debut single, *Whiter Shade Of Pale*, was still climbing the charts, B. J. Wilson and Robin Trower replaced Harrison and Royer in the first of many personnel changes.

loyal. A childhood friendship with Frank Zappa was reaffirmed when he recorded his most celebrated work, *Trout Mask Replica*, for Zappa's Straight label in 1969 since when he has continued to make bizarre and idiosyncratic albums with a succession of puzzled musicians.

The latest in a long line, the Buffalo Springfield were folk-rockers of the highest calibre, though only after they split up in May 1968 were they fully appreciated. Stephen Stills and Richie Furay, both veterans of the Greenwich Village folk scene, coerced Canadian Neil Young to join them in Los Angeles, where they soon won acclaim for the quality of their songs, singing and instrumental work – eventually achieving a hit single in *For What It's Worth*, their account of an anti-curfew demonstration on Sunset Strip. Despite the hit, Springfield attracted only limited recognition and,

after stumbling through three albums and innumerable internal hassles, decided that theirs was an ill-fated combination. Furay left to form Poco and Young, after laying the foundation for his subsequent solo success, joined Stills in Crosby, Stills, Nash and Young.

Until 1966, what was known as 'the underground' in Britain had been a very shaky and diverse movement comprising poets, film makers, painters, beatniks jazz musicians, folk singers, students, writers and so on – but in October of that year, Britain's first nationally distributed underground newspaper, the *International Times*, was launched with a party held at the Roundhouse in Chalk Farm, and for the first time all the different factions were together, literally under one roof.

Rock music, soon to emerge as the strongest element, had not been considered important but, nevertheless, two of the handful of rock groups who were accepted by the movement were brought in to provide music for the assembled throng. One was called Pink Floyd, the other the Soft Machine.

The Floyd had already developed their strange, spaced-out music, but it wasn't until they became regular headliners at the newly opened UFO Club that their fame began to spread – and such was the pandemonium they caused that they were able to sign a wildly lucrative recording deal before they'd even played outside London.

Their first single, *Arnold Layne*, made number 24 whilst the follow-up, *See Emily Play*, reached the top ten – but two subsequent releases (the last singles they ever put out) missed the chart altogether. When their leader and principal songwriter, Syd Barrett, left the group in Spring 1968, most people were ready to write them off ... but the Floyd climbed back with ever escalating album sales to the point where they are now one of the most popular groups in the world. Their mid-seventies releases, *The Dark Side Of The Moon* and *Wish You Were Here*, were particularly well received and allowed them to withdraw from the unsavoury business of constant touring.

Syd Barrett, meanwhile, disappeared completely after releasing two mildly successful solo albums.

After trying to harness their experimental wanderings into a commercially acceptable single, and slogging around America to find stardom, the Soft Machine decided to go their own way. The resulting developments were too inaccessible to impress a mass audience but the group enjoyed reasonable success until the late seventies when they finally threw in the towel. Founder members Kevin Ayers and Daevid Allen, who both left during the group's early days, went solo.

The UFO Club became a breeding ground for new talent, launching the careers of the Purple Gang (who recorded the excellent *Granny Takes A Trip*), the Social Deviants (led by writer Mick Farren), the Crazy World of Arthur Brown (soon to break out with *Fire*), Tomorrow (featuring Steve Howe on guitar), John's Children (who made some of the year's best non-selling singles) and Nirvana (who also watched good singles go unheeded).

All had something different to offer, but none scored as dramatically as Procol Harum, who crawled from the bowels of UFO to the top of the world's charts in a few days; *Whiter Shade Of Pale*, extolling the dreamy ecstasy of the drugged mind, ended up selling over six million copies.

Formed from the remnants of Southend R&B group the Paramounts, Procol Harum based their style on the melodies and distinctive vocals of pianist Gary Brooker and the cryptic lyrics of Keith Reid, but after the reasonably successful follow-up, *Homburg*, they fell on hard times and only single-minded determination saw their eventual recovery in the early seventies. Several solid-selling albums, notably *Live In Concert With The Edmonton Symphony Orchestra*, ensured healthy live audiences until they came off the road in 1977.

Other successful groups whose lyrics alluded to drugs included the Jimi Hendrix Experience and Traffic.

Jimi Hendrix, an extraordinarily skilful black guitarist, was spotted by Animals bassist Chas Chandler playing in a New York club. Chandler, who had just left his group to move into management, convinced Hendrix to move to England, where his full potential could be realised ... and with English sidemen, Mitch Mitchell on drums and Noel Redding on bass, he made an immediate impact with a dramatic version of *Hey Joe*.

By the end of the year, three more top twenty hits cemented his British success and incessant U.S. tours, including a devastating performance at Monterey, made him a superstar in America, where his double album *Electric Ladyland* reached number one. Overcoming drug, management and personnel problems, he returned to England to play a particularly ragged set at the Isle of Wight festival in Summer 1970. It was his final public performance; in September he died in his London hotel, choking on his own vomit whilst in a drug-induced coma. It was an ignoble end for such a gifted and influential musician, and his memory was further sullied by a flood of exploitation albums which showed him in less than inspired form. *Voodoo Chile*, released posthumously in November 1970, became his only number one.

Traffic was formed by ex-Spencer Davis Group star Stevie Winwood, who gathered three Midlands mates together to come up with a wonderfully creative combination. They wasted little time in racing up the charts with their first single, *Paper Sun*, which was followed into the top ten by *Hole In My Shoe* and *Here We Go Round The Mulberry Bush* ... but disagreements resulted in the departure of guitarist Dave Mason, who subsequently made it on his own.

In 1969, the group dissolved altogether when Winwood joined Blind Faith, But that group's truncated career enabled him to resurrect Traffic for another assault. In common with most revitalisations, their output lacked the spark which characterised their earlier works and they eventually ground to a halt. Since then Winwood and drummer Jim Capaldi have pursued solo careers which have so far delivered rather less than they promised.

By the summer of 67, the underground had blossomed into a thriving industry, and all the trappings of flower power – kaftans, bells, beads, incense and assorted drug paraphernalia – were on display at the annual British jazz and blues festivals. So, too, were two groups who were helping to

Opposite above: The most successful variation of Canned Heat (left to right standing: Fito de la Parra, Al Wilson, Henry Vestine; seated: Larry Taylor and Bob Hite).

Opposite below: Pink Floyd as psychedelic pioneers (clockwise from top left: Rick Wright, Nick Mason, Roger Waters, Syd Barrett).

Above: Fleetwood Mac in their *Albatross* period. Top: Jeremy Spencer; left to right: Peter Green, Danny Kirwan, John McVie and Mick Fleetwood.

instigate a blues boom in the British clubs: Cream and Fleetwood Mac.

Both were offspring of John Mayall's pioneering Blues Breakers, which at various times had included Eric Clapton and Jack Bruce of Cream, and John McVie, Mick Fleetwood and Peter Green of Fleetwood Mac.

Cream, a trio of highly respected musicians completed by Ginger Baker, were the first to attract the label 'supergroup' – and deservedly so: they became one of the most successful groups of the decade, with Clapton becoming the most influential guitarist of his generation.

After an unexpectedly slow start, they gathered impetus with the hit single *I Feel Free* before finally finding their stride with the chart-topping album *Wheels Of Fire*, which as well as showcasing their studio skills, captured the drawn-out improvisation of their live performances. However, over the months a growing incompatibility created tensions which eventually splintered the group in late 1968.

Clapton and Baker remained together to form Blind Faith whilst Jack Bruce embarked on a chequered solo career, but Cream re-issues and compilations continue to sell and their achievements are still remembered with affection.

Fleetwood Mac's lifespan was destined to be somewhat longer, though of the current line-up only Mick Fleetwood was present at the beginning. By the time their first album was released, guitar hero Peter Green was flanked by Jeremy Spencer, John McVie and Fleetwood, and when they began to move out of their original strict blues framework they took on another guitarist, Danny Kirwan.

Their chart-topping single, *Albatross*, enabled them to leave the club circuit and three further smashes, *Man Of The World*, *Oh Well* and *The Green Manalishi*, saw them headlining bills around the world – but they took a severe knock when Peter Green suddenly quit the band in May 1970.

McVie's wife Christine, who had also participated in the 1967 blues boom as pianist/singer with Chicken Shack, stepped into the breach and the group began a holding action which was not assisted by numerous personnel changes. Their fortunes

steadily declined until 1975 when they began an extraordinary recovery.

Another band with blues roots was the Jeff Beck Group, led by the former Yardbird who shared the spotlight with a refugee from several semi-successful groups, including Steampacket and Shotgun Express ... Rod Stewart. In their shadow was another musician who would later find fame and fortune – bassist Ron Wood.

Early pop-inclined singles like *Hi Ho Silver Lining* and *Love Is Blue* gave little indication of Beck's real penchant for the 'heavy heavy heavy' rock which permeated his stage act and his first album *Truth* – but although tne group's potential was boundless, Beck allowed it to crumble in Summer 1969, by which time Led Zeppelin were heading for super-stardom on the formula he'd devised.

Stewart and Wood helped the remaining Small Faces to pick up the pieces, while Beck was involved in a car crash which set his career back two years. In 1971, he returned with a new group which he soon dismissed in favour of an association with two ex-Vanilla Fudge members – but Beck, Bogert and Appice also proved unsatisfactory and Beck began to use session musicians for both recording and live work. Despite several successful albums, his refusal to compromise has prevented Beck from sharing the stardom of his peers.

The year's new mainstream British acts included Amen Corner, whose three-year hit run was climaxed by the chart-topping *Half As Nice*; the Herd, who did fairly well until Peter Frampton ('The face of 67') left to start Humble Pie; the Tremeloes, who (without Brian Poole) came back to start a 14-hit run with *Here Comes My Baby* and *Silence Is Golden*; and Engelbert Humperdinck, who secured his future with *Release Me* and *The Last Waltz*. The Bee Gees and the Move also made a considerable impression.

The Bee Gees – three brothers, Barry, Maurice and Robin Gibb – were born in Britain but emigrated with their parents to Australia, where they formed a singing group. Several hit singles in Australia resulted in their own television show and their eventual return to England to attack the British and American markets. It was an impressive campaign: by the end of 1969, they'd achieved six top ten entries including number ones in *Massachusetts* and *I Gotta Get A Message To You*, but then squabbles temporarily ended their partnership.

By the end of 1970 they'd resolved their differences and were back on the hit-making trail, though it was assumed that their greatest successes were behind them. That wasn't the case as will be seen.

The Move, from Birmingham like the Moody Blues before them, made a startling impact on London audiences by smashing television sets, destroying effigies and letting off smoke bombs during their stage acts. Fortunately, they also possessed abundant musical skill, which was evident from their series of classic hits including *Night Of Fear*, *Flowers In The Rain*, *Fire Brigade* and the chart-topping *Blackberry Way* – all written by the group's mainspring Roy Wood.

The 1970 arrival of Jeff Lynne from the Idle Race heralded more hits including their only American

success, *Do Ya* (which he wrote) but it also saw the development of a parallel group, The Electric Light Orchestra – which eventually took precedence over the activities of the Move, whose swansong was the top tenner *California Man* in Summer 1972.

The year's one-off hits included *The First Cut Is The Deepest* by P. P. Arnold, *Let's Go To San Francisco* by the Flowerpot Men, *I Was Kaiser Bill's Batman* by Whistling Jack Smith, *Death Of A Clown* by Kink Dave Davies, *Let The Heartaches Begin* by Long John Baldry, *Kites* by Simon Dupree and *Al Capone* by Prince Buster.

America also produced the usual array of one-off hits: *Judy In Disguise* by John Fred and his Playboy Band, *Snoopy Versus The Red Baron* by the Royal Guardsmen, *98·6* by Keith, *Little Bit Of Soul* by the Music Explosion, *Brown-eyed Girl* by Van Morrison, *Get On Up* by the Esquires, *Feelin' Groovy* by Harper's Bizarre, *That Acapulco Gold* by the Rainy Daze, *I Had Too Much To Dream Last Night* by the Electric Prunes and *Incense And Peppermint* by the Strawberry Alarm Clock.

The Box Tops, a white soul act from Memphis, began a short but sweet chart romance with *The Letter* (the year's biggest single) and *Cry Like A Baby* and *Soul Deep*; the Buckinghams, from Chicago, had three massive hit singles in *Kind Of A Drag*, *Don't You Care* and *Mercy Mercy Mercy* but couldn't find the album audience necessary for survival; the Classics IV from Florida also had three big hits – *Spooky*, *Stormy* and *Traces* – before fading away and evolving into a successful late seventies group, the Atlanta Rhythm Section; the Fifth Dimension, a black vocal quintet who formerly comprised part of the Ray Charles Soul Revue, broke out on their own with the first in a long line of best sellers, *Up Up And Away*; the Cowsills jumped onto the Bubblegum Bandwagon (drawn by the Monkees and Herman's Hermits) with the first of their three top tenners, *The Rain, The Park, And Other Things*; and Bobbie Gentry, previously a Las Vegas nightclub dancer, launched a singing career with her murder-mystery smash, *Ode To Billie Joe*.

Top left: The Jeff Beck Group suffered much upheaval over the years, seen here in an early seventies incarnation. Beck is on the far right.

Centre left: The Bee Gees were a quintet when they relocated in England. Left to right: Robin Gibb, Maurice Gibb, Vince Melouney, Colin Peterson and Barry Gibb.

Below left: Moody Blues mark two. Left to right: Justin Hayward, Graeme Edge, Ray Thomas, Mike Pinder and John Lodge.

Bottom left: Traffic (left to right: Dave Mason, Stevie Winwood, Chris Wood and Jim Capaldi).

Above: Cream (left to right: Eric Clapton, Ginger Baker and Jack Bruce), the first supergroup.

Opposite top left: 'Lady Soul', Aretha Franklin.

Opposite top right and below: Jimi Hendrix, American guitar genius, who moved to London to launch his all too brief solo career.

'67

the year

Events

27 Jan. Three astronauts (Chaffee, Grisson and White) die in a fire in their spacecraft at Cape Kennedy.

12 Feb. Keith Richard and Mick Jagger are arrested for drug possession.

18 Mar. The Torry Canyon runs aground and spills a massive oil slick into the English Channel.

27 Apr. Expo 67 opens in Montreal.

28 Apr. Muhammad Ali is stripped of his title for refusing to enter the Army.

5 June The Six-Day War between the Arabs and Israel begins.

16 June The Monterey pop festival begins.

24 July De Gaulle calls for 'Free Quebec' in a speech in Montreal.

3 Dec. Christiaan Barnard performs the first heart transplant.

25 Dec. The Beatles' *Magical Mystery Tour* is shown on television.

Films of 67

Accident · Bonnie And Clyde · Doctor Dolittle · The Graduate · Guess Who's Coming To Dinner · In The Heat Of The Night · A Man And A Woman · Thoroughly Modern Millie

U.S. CHART TOPPERS – WEEKS AT TOP

I'm A Believer	Monkees
Kind Of A Drag	Buckinghams
Ruby Tuesday	Rolling Stones
Love Is Here And Now You're Gone	Supremes
Penny Lane	Beatles
Happy Together	Turtles
Something Stupid	Nancy Sinatra and Frank Sinatra
The Happening	Supremes
Groovin'	Young Rascals
Respect	Aretha Franklin
Windy	Association
Light My Fire	Doors
All You Need Is Love	Beatles
Ode To Billie Joe	Bobbie Gentry
The Letter	Box Tops
To Sir With Love	Lulu
Incense And Peppermints	Strawberry Alarm Clock
Daydream Believer	Monkees
Hello Goodbye	Beatles

U.K. CHART TOPPERS – WEEKS AT TOP

Green Green Grass Of Home	Tom Jones
I'm A Believer	Monkees
This Is My Song	Petula Clark
Release Me	Engelbert Humperdinck
Something Stupid	Nancy Sinatra and Frank Sinatra
Puppet On A String	Sandie Shaw
Silence Is Golden	Tremeloes
A Whiter Shade Of Pale	Procol Harum
All You Need Is Love	Beatles
San Francisco	Scott McKenzie
The Last Waltz	Engelbert Humperdinck
Massachusetts	Bee Gees
Baby, Now That I've Found You	Foundations
Let The Heartaches Begin	Long John Baldry
Hello Goodbye	Beatles

New Musical Express

EVERY FRIDAY 6ᴰ

TOM JONES ✦ LENNON MYSTERY

— by a Squire

TOP POP NEWS

- ALAN PRICE • BACHELORS

WINDSOR FESTIVAL

- HENDRIX, HUMP, BURDON

new discs reviewed

WHY CAT IS SAD

Popword

PINK FLOYD LIFE-LINES

GET THIS HIT DISC
FIVE LITTLE FINGERS
BY
FRANKIE McBRIDE
ON
EMERALD MD 1081

K.P.M. MUSIC, 21 DENMARK STREET, W.C.2 TEM 38...

975   Week ending August 19, 1967

...D'S LARGEST CIRCULATION OF ANY MUSIC PAPER

Below: Julie Andrews in *Thoroughly Modern Millie.*

Bottom: Christiaan Barnard immediately after the first heart transplant.

burning of the midnight lamp

The Jimi Hendrix Experience

MOJO   35 cents

NAVIGATOR ROCK • ROLL NEWS

A New York quartet, Vanilla Fudge, impressed and influenced almost every musician who heard them. Their speciality was to take a pop classic, slow it down, and convert it into a heavily dramatic piece. *You Keep Me Hangin' On* was their only big single but their albums and live performances won great acclaim.

Soulwise, little new was happening. Arthur Conley had his first and biggest hit with *Sweet Soul Music*, but the only major act to emerge from the traditional soul belt was Aretha Franklin, a minister's daughter from Memphis.

Aretha recorded for several labels without spectacular results – but in November 1966 she signed with Atlantic and immediately found a winner in the Jerry Wexler production *I Never Loved A Man*. Three more 1967 million sellers included her chart-topping version of Otis Redding's *Respect*, and by the end of 1968 her supremacy seemed settled.

Over on the West Coast, soul music was undergoing some strange changes in the hands of Sly and the Family Stone. Sly Stone (born Sylvester Stewart) and his overdressed gypsy musicians played a distinctive brand of 'psychedelicised soul' which stole the show everywhere they played.

In 1967 they entered Epic's studios to cut *Dance To The Music*, the first in a stream of hits which included three chart-toppers, *Everyday People*, *Thank You (Falettin Me Be Mice Elf Agin)* and *Family Affair*, but also managed to cross over into the album market, and become one of the most successful groups of the early seventies.

Their influence on such groups as the Temptations, Funkadelic, and Earth, Wind and Fire was considerable, and though they went into self-imposed limbo at the height of their popularity they may still possess the base for a comeback.

Top: The Move (left to right: Trevor Burton, Bev Bevan, Ace Kefford, Roy Wood and Carl Wayne).

Above: Bobbie Gentry wrote and recorded one of the year's most distinctive singles, *Ode To Billie Joe*, before teaming up with country star Glen Campbell (*right*) for a series of albums and concerts.

Far right: Former disc-jockey and record producer Sly Stone led his group through uncharted areas of psychedelic soul.

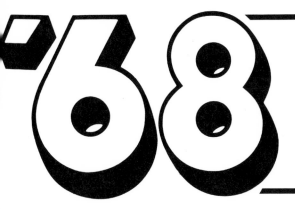

'68

'Jumping Jack Flash'

The Band · Tim Buckley · Joe Cocker · Leonard Cohen · Julie Driscoll
Mary Hopkin · Jethro Tull · Led Zeppelin · The Steve Miller Band
Joni Mitchell · Johnny Nash · Randy Newman · The Nice · Laura Nyro
Poco · Quicksilver Messenger Service · Spirit · Status Quo
Ten Years After · The Velvet Underground · Jimmy Webb

Drugs and flowers were still profuse in 1968, but the drugs were getting harder, the flowers were wilting . . . and the music was getting heavier. The sparkling sixties had peaked, and less effervescent times were ahead. The Beatles had long since stopped performing and were now spending much of their time with their guru Maharishi Mahesh Yogi, and the overall innocence of 1967 had been replaced by cold-blooded commerce.

At the time, however, it all seemed exciting enough. The Rolling Stones had returned to top form, Hendrix and Cream were at their peak, Dylan released his first record in two years, and the Beatles found time to record an excellent double album despite all their meditative noodling.

In Britain, the billowing underground/hippie movement kept any mainstream pop groups out of the clubs, but three significant new acts managed to emerge nevertheless.

Decked in the obligatory flower power gear, Status Quo looked like another here-today gone-tomorrow affair; in fact they'd already been together since 1962 when guitarist Francis Rossi, bassist Alan Lancaster and drummer John Coghlan formed a group at school. By 1966 they'd added another guitarist, Rick Parfitt, and gone professional – and two years later they made their debut with *Pictures Of Matchstick Men*, a top twenty entry on both sides of the Atlantic.

After the inevitable follow-up hit, they lost popularity at an alarming rate – though another isolated winner, *Down The Dustpipe* in 1970, temporarily stemmed their decline. By 1972, most people had written the group off . . . but 1973 would see a remarkable recovery.

The Love Affair, on the other hand, never recovered from the press revelation that session musicians had recorded their chart-topping *Everlasting Love*. Despite having an excellent singer in Steve Ellis, they were doomed to go under, which they did in 1969 after three further top ten hits.

Marmalade, already established in Scotland, broke nationally with *Lovin' Things*, though it was their number one version of the Beatles' *Ob-la-di Ob-la-da* which really established them. Distinctly at odds with current trends, they still made the singles charts regularly until 1972 when they turned to cabaret, although they had an isolated top tenner in 1976 with *Falling Apart At The Seams*.

Other pop-oriented acts had considerably less success. The Equals scored a number one with *Baby Come Back*, but had only two more hits in the next two years; the Honeybus reached the top ten with *I Can't Let Maggie Go* – their first and last hit; Cupid's Inspiration came and went with *Yesterday Has Gone*

Above and left: The psychedelic five-piece Status Quo, some years before their conversion to denim and heads down all out boogie.

Alvin Lee, leader of Ten Years After, in characteristic guitar hero pose.

as did the Plastic Penny with *Everything I Am*, the Casuals with *Jesamine* and the Marbles with *Only One Woman*.

Leapy Lee leapt in and leapt out with *Little Arrows*; Esther and Abi Ofarim waltzed *Cinderella Rockafella* to number one; ex-Walker Brother Scott made a brief return to the top ten with *Joanna*; street busker Don Partridge had two big hits with *Rosie* and *Blue Eyes*; and musical-comedy madmen the Bonzo Dog Doo Dah Band had a freak hit with *I'm The Urban Spaceman*.

Julie Driscoll, formerly in Steampacket with Rod Stewart, was unable to find an adequate successor to *This Wheel's On Fire*, but Mary Hopkin, discovered on the television talent show *Opportunity Knocks*, returned with three more top tenners after her smash debut *Those Were The Days*. The only other new girl singer to make an impression was Christine McVie, later a Fleetwood Mac star but then vocalist with the blues band Chicken Shack, who the following year made the singles chart with *I'd Rather Go Blind*.

Chicken Shack stayed second leaguers, but two other groups surfaced from the current clubroom blues boom to become international stars: Ten Years After and Jethro Tull.

Ten Years After, from Nottingham, first emerged in 1966, their main attraction being the good looks and fluent guitarpicking of Alvin Lee. Playing the right music in the right place at the right time, it was their lengthy performance of *Goin' Home* in the film *Woodstock* which sealed their superstar status.

The group toured America solidly during the early seventies, continuing to release commercial albums, but by 1975 had grown tired of continually retreading the same ground and disbanded to embark on rather less successful solo projects.

Their management, the Chrysalis Agency, noting the vogue for the blues guitar hero, cast around for a second string to their bow and found Jethro Tull, formerly a floundering soul outfit from Blackpool called the John Evan Band. The disintegration of the Evan Band induced singer Ian Anderson and bassist Glenn Cornick to move to Luton, where two local musicians, guitarist Mick Abrahams and drummer Clive Bunker, joined them to form Jethro Tull.

Abraham's Claptonesque guitar, complemented by Anderson's distinctive vocals, jazzy flute playing and intuitive theatricality, made them the unexpected hit of the 1968 National Jazz and Blues Festival and their fortunes soared. After their first album, *This Was*, had reached the top ten, however,

Abrahams was ousted in the first of several personnel shuffles which ultimately saw several of the Evan Band playing behind Anderson, who was now the sole survivor and undisputed leader. By the end of the seventies they had accumulated 15 hit albums, including three compilations, all of which had achieved gold or platinum status.

The two other major underground breakouts were the Nice and Joe Cocker.

The Nice originally assembled to back pop/soul singer P. P. Arnold but decided to strike out on their own. Initially, the limelight was shared by guitarist Davy O'List and keyboard wizard Keith Emerson, but when the former left in 1968 he was not replaced, and Emerson dominated the trio for the rest of their extraordinarily successful career, directing them into classical music and other areas previously considered beyond the scope of rock musicians.

Their adventurous music, flashy showmanship and controversial stance resulted in three top five albums in the U.K. – though they had difficulty bridging the Atlantic. Their onstage burning of an American flag did not endear them to the authorities and composer Leonard Bernstein was so affronted by their treatment of his song *America* that he vetoed its release.

A comparatively brief life ended in 1969, when they split up to launch three new groups, though only Emerson, Lake and Palmer was to eclipse the achievements of the Nice.

After several abortive attempts to escape the Sheffield pub circuit, ex-gas fitter Joe Cocker suddenly found himself at the top of the charts with his Vanilla Fudge – style adaptation of *With A Little Help From My Friends* – almost unrecognisable from Ringo Starr's original on the previous year's *Sergeant Pepper* album. It enabled him to convince a huge audience, including witnesses of Woodstock (the festival and the film), that his was one of the best soul voices to come out of England and he rode into the seventies on the crest of a wave.

An alliance with Leon Russell enabled him to scale new heights but the genial Cocker had no defences for the pressures of the business, which effectively halted his progress.

Though Ian Anderson and Keith Emerson were both able to negotiate a smooth and successful passage into the eighties, by far the biggest and most durable new British stars of 1968 were Led Zeppelin.

Following the dissolution of the Yardbirds, remaining member Jimmy Page wasted no time in pulling together a new group (originally known as the New Yardbirds) to fulfill their outstanding tour obligations. His choice of musicians, particularly

Led Zeppelin (left to right: John Paul Jones, John Bonham (obscured by drums), Jimmy Page and Robert Plant) rose from the ashes of the Yardbirds to become the most spectacularly successful rock band in history.

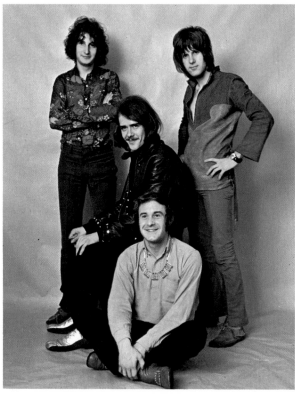

Far left above: With A Little Help From My Friends took Joe Cocker from the backstreets clubs of Sheffield to international stardom.

Far left below: The Nice (standing: Davy O'List, Keith Emerson; centre: Lee Jackson; front: Brian Davison).

Above left: The Steve Miller Band (left to right: Boz Scaggs, Jim Peterman, Steve Miller, Lonnie Turner and Tim Davis). After two classic albums, Scaggs left for a solo career.

Below left: Quicksilver Messenger Service (left to right: Greg Elmore, Gary Duncan, John Cipollina, Jim Murray and David Freiburg). Murray had left by the time they recorded the classic Happy Trails.

vocalist Robert Plant, who was practically unknown outside the Birmingham area, was inspired – as an exceptional first album, completed in only 30 hours, demonstrated.

Though initial progress in England was slow, they took off immediately in America, where they were headlining within three months and their second album *Led Zeppelin II*, became the fastest selling record in Atlantic's history. Subsequent albums sold even more speedily and their seventies supremacy is evidenced by their one hundred percent platinum record.

Though the first Jeff Beck Group evolved the blueprints on which they based their early pyrotechnics, Led Zepplin are widely credited as being the originators of a rock style to become known as 'heavy metal' – later characterised by a bare-chested screaming singer, long songs built around repetitive guitar riffs, and pain-threshold volume. Other pioneers of this genre include three American

groups who also came to prominence in 1968: the Velvet Underground, Iron Butterfly and Blue Cheer.

While others were more belligerent, the Velvet Underground had artistic aspirations, which won them the patronage of Andy Warhol, who was subsequently credited as producing their classic debut album on which Lou Reed intoned his drug songs *Heroin* and *I'm Waiting For The Man* over a backing of sinister intensity. Despite considerable media interest, relatively few people bought their albums and it was only after their frustrated, disillusioned break-up that the extent of their influence (on David Bowie, Mott the Hoople, Patti Smith and the punks, among others) became clear

Of the original members, three established themselves as solo artists: Nico gained a devoted cult following with several obscure albums, John Cale made his mark as a composer, musician, singer and producer, and Lou Reed experienced triumphs and failures in a particularly erratic career.

Iron Butterfly, from San Diego, reached a commercial peak into their second album *In-a-gadda-da-vida*, whose 17-minute title track propelled it into the top five, whilst Blue Cheer, from San Francisco, are best remembered for their first release, *Vincebus Eruptum*, containing their only top twenty single, a savage distortion of Eddie Cochran's *Summertime Blues*.

The loudest and least subtle of San Franciscan groups, Blue Cheer spearheaded the city's second wave, though the Steve Miller Band and Quicksilver Messenger Service were more successful in the long run. Both bands had resisted the temptations of early contracts, holding out for optimum deals which afforded them financial security and adequate studio time. In each case it was their second album, *Sailor* and *Happy Trails* respectively, which

took them into the top thirty.

Miller, a Texan schooled in Wisconsin, had moved to San Francisco after a brief group sortie in Chicago. His early blues style quickly gave way to a softer psychedelic approach and his early albums, produced by Glyn Johns and featuring Boz Scaggs, are some of the finest to come out of the West Coast scene.

After a bleak spell, he came back stronger than ever with *The Joker*, a single which topped the charts in 1973, taking the eponymous album to number two ... and though his output slowed drastically during the rest of the seventies, he never missed the bullseye. He remains one of the few flower-power survivors whose credibility is intact.

Conversely, Quicksilver Messenger Service came to a creative standstill after their acid-rock masterpiece, *Happy Trails*, in 1969, though they continued, in various configurations, into the mid-seventies. Founder-member David Freiberg currently powers the Jefferson Starship.

A record industry attempt to create a 'Boston sound' to follow the San Francisco explosion was an expensive failure which almost finished M.G.M. Records and the groups involved – notably the Ultimate Spinach, Orpheus, and the Beacon Street Union – but meanwhile, a Philadelphia sound was evolving without artificial boosting.

The Philly sound was characterised by the soft soul of the Delfonics, who opened their long chart run with the top five hit *La La Means I Love You*, and the Intruders, who also reached the top ten for the first time in 1968 with *Cowboys To Girls*. The latter group were protegés of the Gamble and Huff producing team, in whose hands the Philadelphia sound would soon blossom – but at this time they were still struggling for recognition, though they did assist Archie Bell and the Drells to number one with *Tighten Up*.

Other soul hits were *Girl Watcher* by the O'Kaysions, *The Son Of Hickory Holler's Tramp* and *Little Green Apples* by O. C. Smith, *Hold Me Tight* by Johnny Nash and *You're All I Need To Get By*, the

last of four top tenners by Marvin Gaye and Tammi Terrell.

Main stream pop hits included *Green Tambourine* by the Lemon Pipers, *Turn Around, Look At Me* by the Vogues (relatively dormant since their 1965 hit *Five O'Clock World*), *Harper Valley P.T.A.* by Jeannie C. Riley, *This Guy's In Love With You* by Herb Alpert and *Captain Of Your Ship* by Reparata and the Delrons (which, though a considerable U.K. success, sank completely in America).

Songwriter Jim Webb won acclaim for a number of hit songs, principally *MacArthur Park*, a worldwide smash for Richard Harris, and *By The Time I Get To Phoenix* and *Wichita Lineman* for Glen Campbell, who was now concentrating on singing after some years as a session guitarist. In addition, Webb gathered five Grammy awards for *Up Up And Away*, a hit for the Fifth Dimension the previous year.

A Los Angeles group, Gary Puckett and the Union Gap, were the most successful new pop act: *Young Girl* and *Lady Willpower* were the biggest of seven hits which took their chart career into 1970 – though a reissue of *Young Girl* returned them to the British top ten during Summer 1974, by which time

Above: Marvin Gaye united with Tammi Terrell to make a string of soulful Motown duets.

Below: Country rock pioneers Poco. Tom Schmit (left) subsequently joined the Eagles, Richie Furay (centre) flew briefly with the Souther-Hillman-Furay supergroup, but Rusty Young (right) piloted the group to eventual well-deserved success.

Below right: The Band's farewell concert attracted a star-studded cast of friends, including Joni Mitchell, Neil Young, Van Morrison and Bob Dylan. All were captured for posterity by Martin Scorsese in his film *The Last Waltz.*

Top right: Ian Anderson, charismatic mastermind behind the long-term success of Jethro Tull.

'68 the year

Events

23 Jan. The US spy-ship Pueblo is boarded by North Koreans; the crew are imprisoned but freed on 23 December.

17 Feb. Jean-Claude Killy, the French ski champion, wins his third gold medal at the Winter Olympics.

3 Apr. Martin Luther King is assassinated.

7 Apr. Pierre Trudeau becomes Prime Minister of Canada.

4 May The teachers and students of Sorbonne University, Paris go on strike sparking off widespread strikes throughout France.

29 July A Papal encyclical forbids use of artificial birth control by Roman Catholics.

20 Aug. Soviet troops invade Czechoslovakia.

26 Aug. Police and demonstrators fight the 'Battle of Chicago' outside the Democrat party convention, which nominates Humphrey and Muskie.

30 Sept. The Boeing 747 Jumbo jet makes a test flight.

12 Oct. The Olympic Games begin in Mexico City.

Films of 68

Bullitt · Belle De Jour · The Good, The Bad And The Ugly · Jungle Book · Oliver · Rosemary's Baby · The Thomas Crown Affair · Yellow Submarine

U.S. CHART TOPPERS – WEEKS AT TOP

Hello Goodbye	Beatles
Judy In Disguise	John Fred and His Playboy Band
Green Tambourine	Lemon Pipers
Love Is Blue	Paul Mauriat
The Dock Of The Bay	Otis Redding
Honey	Bobby Goldsboro
Tighten Up	Archie Bell and the Drells
Mrs. Robinson	Simon and Garfunkel
This Guy's In Love With You	Herb Alpert
Grazing In The Grass	Hugh Masakela
Hello I Love You	Doors
People Got To Be Free	Rascals
Harper Valley P. T. A.	Jeannie C. Riley
Hey Jude	Beatles
Love Child	Supremes
I Heard It Through The Grapevine	Marvin Gaye

U.K. CHART TOPPERS – WEEKS AT TOP

Hello Goodbye	Beatles
The Ballad Of Bonnie And Clyde	Georgie Fame
Everlasting Love	Love Affair
The Mighty Quinn	Manfred Mann
Cinderella Rockafella	Esther and Abi Ofarim
Legend Of Xanadu	Dave Dee, Dozy, Beaky, Mick and Tich
Lady Madonna	Beatles
Congratulations	Cliff Richard
Wonderful World	Louis Armstrong
Young Girl	Garry Puckett and the Union Gap
Jumping Jack Flash	Rolling Stones
Baby Come Back	Equals
I Pretend	Des O'Connor
Mony Mony	Tommy James and the Shondells
Fire	The Crazy World of Arthur Brown
Do It Again	Beach Boys
I Gotta Get A Message To You	Bee Gees
Hey Jude	Beatles
Those Were The Days	Mary Hopkin
With A Little Help From My Friends	Joe Cocker
The Good The Bad And The Ugly	Hugo Montenegro
Lily The Pink	Scaffold

Left: 2001: A Space Odyssey.

Opposite top: a shop in Carnaby Street.

Opposite bottom: Czechoslovakians stone Soviet tanks.

Representing lady singer/ songwriters were Canadian Joni Mitchell (*top*) and Bronx-born Laura Nyro (*above*). Joni was popular in her own right, while Laura won greater acclaim as a songwriter, providing hits for Barbra Streisand, the Fifth Dimension and Blood, Sweat and Tears.

jazzer; pianist John Locke lent both classical and jazz influences; while bassist Mark Andes had played blues with the embryonic Canned Heat.

Consistent innovation culminated in their classic fourth album, *The 12 Dreams Of Dr. Sardonicus*, but audience response remained abysmally low and vocalist Jay Ferguson left to set up a new group, Jo Jo Gunne, with Andes. After unhappy attempts to pick up the pieces, Spirit fell into disarray until 1975, when California and Cassidy masterminded a determined but only partially successful revival.

Across the country, in upstate New York, Bob Dylan's backing group, the Band, released their widely praised debut album *Music From Big Pink*. The maturity and traditional feel of the work stemmed from their having played together since the early sixties when they were hired, one by one, to play in Ronnie Hawkins' Toronto-based band the Hawks. After striking out on their own, they were invited to join Dylan, who had just 'gone electric' — but the 1966 motorcycle accident laid Dylan up for almost two years and afforded them plenty of time to work on their own material.

By the time they disbanded in 1977, they had won the respect not only of audiences but rock musicians the world over — as their final concert testified. Mounted in San Francisco, *The Last Waltz* as it was called, featured guest appearances by Neil Young, Eric Clapton, Van Morrison and Ringo Starr among others — and a movie of the event proved to be one of the most successful rock films ever made.

Another of the guest stars bidding the Band a fond farewell was Joni Mitchell. After local success she moved to New York and several of her songs had already been popularised by Judy Collins and Tom Ruch by the time her first album, *Song For A Seagull* — produced by ex-Byrd David Crosby, was released in 1968.

Well-publicised romances with several leading rock stars added to her charisma, and in 1974 two of her albums, *Court And Spark* and *Miles Of Aisles* reached number two. Since then releases have been infrequent and increasingly esoteric — factors which do not appear to have reduced her following.

Singer/songwriter activity was soon to reach epidemic proportions, with every kid on the block turning his diary into media cornflakes, but in 1968 the trend was only beginning and quality was still the name of the game. Tim Buckley, Laura Nyro, Randy Newman and Leonard Cohen all turned out fine albums which attracted praise rather than sales — though all saw their songs reach the charts in the hands of more commercial interpreters.

Meanwhile the bubblegum market was lapping up the flimsy creations of two New York producers, Jerry Kasenetz and Jeff Katz, who were almost single-handedly responsible for bubblegum music, light pop jingles played by characterless groups and aimed at the teen and pre-teen market. Monkeemania had already subsided dramatically — mainly because the group was bent on establishing some sort of musical credibility — but teenyboppers were soon singing along to hits by such anonymous groups as the 1910 Fruitgum Company and the Ohio Express, who between them racked up four top tenners. *Yummy Yummy Yummy, I've Got Love In My Tummy*... no wonder they weren't around for long.

Puckett had given up singing in favour of acting.

Also from L.A. were Poco, Steppenwolf and Spirit. Poco, a Buffalo Springfield spring-off, specialised in country rock, which, despite simultaneous pioneering by the Byrds, and subsequent development by excellent groups like the Flying Burrite Brothers, only took flight with the Eagles four years later. Though their 13 albums all enjoyed a modicum of success, Poco remained in the second division until a decade of unflagging optimism was rewarded by a 1979 top twenty hit in *Legend* which also produced their hottest single, *Crazy Love*.

Members who pulled out during the barren years included Jim Messina (later of Loggins and Messina), Richie Furay (of Souther, Hillman and Furay), Randy Meisner and Tim Schmit (both to become Eagles).

Steppenwolf and Spirit were both psychedelically-oriented, though the former's drug/outlaw references were more overt, as their most celebrated songs, *Born To Be Wild*, *Magic Carpet Ride* and *The Pusher*, indicate. After eight gold albums, they split for ill-fated solo ventures in 1972.

Spirit's music displayed more sophistication — a result, no doubt, of the disparity in their backgrounds: Randy California's guitar style, later brazenly Hendrixian, was melodic and subtle; his stepfather Ed Cassidy's drumming showed the technical expertise of many years as a modern

'69

'Space Oddity'

The Archies · Black Sabbath · Blind Faith · Blood, Sweat and Tears
David Bowie · Chicago · Creedence Clearwater Revival · Crosby, Stills and Nash
The Faces · Fairport Convention · Family · The Flying Burrito Brothers
Grand Funk Railroad · Hawkwind · Humble Pie · King Crimson
Love Sculpture · The MC5 · Mott the Hoople · The Plastic Ono Band
Santana · Sha Na Na · The Stooges · Thunderclap Newman · War
Johnny Winter · Neil Young

As the sixties shuddered to a close, the many aspects of rock music, whose sub-styles were diffusing more furiously by the hour, were drawn together under the open skies: 1969, more than any other, was the year of the rock festival. Spectacular, star-studded bills attracted huge audiences who were prepared to brave the elements, contend with primitive toilet facilities and accept overpriced hot dogs in order to escape into their own world for a few days.

A rare performance by Bob Dylan and the Band brought about a dramatic overpopulation of the Isle of Wight, the site for Britain's most illustrious festival, and the even rarer appearance of John Lennon's Plastic Ono Band iced the cake at Toronto, but both were overshadowed by events in the United States.

Almost half a million people converged on a small town in upstate New York for 'three days of peace and love' at the Woodstock Music and Art Fair – certainly the biggest and best festival ever mounted – but the summery vibes had turned sour by December when the overall unpleasantness at an outdoor gathering on the Altamont Speedway near San Francisco climaxed in the brutal murder of an innocent spectator.

The bill-topping attraction at Altamont, the Rolling Stones, had earlier in the year drawn the largest crowd ever seen in London to a free concert in Hyde Park – which also provided the setting for the public unveiling of the year's most anxiously awaited supergroup, Blind Faith.

Following Cream's dissolution, Eric Clapton and Ginger Baker recruited Stevie Winwood from Traffic and Rick Grech from Family for what was planned as the ultimate rock group. The combination was ill-fated: after one album and a coolly received American tour, they simply fizzled out. Winwood returned to Traffic, Grech became the archetypal rock'n'roll gypsy, Baker involved himself in a series of unhappy group ventures, and Clapton retreated into a shadowy solo career.

Blind Faith's failure did not deter the two other British hybrid groups who formed during the year. Steve Marriott had left the Small Faces to launch Humble Pie with Peter Frampton, previously of the Herd, but though they started convincingly, disagreements over musical policy resulted in Frampton's replacement by Colosseum guitarist Dave Clempson. Their subsequent loud, direct and frill-free style took them high into the American album charts during the early seventies but after a total of 22 U.S. tours they ground to a halt in 1975.

The remaining Small Faces, meanwhile, found themselves facing abject penury – despite a dozen hit singles – but the timely arrival of the ebullient duo Rod Stewart and Ron Wood saved their bacon. For a couple of years, Stewart and Wood had toiled

Below: Humble Pie, latest in a line of fashionable super-groups. Left to right: Greg Ridley, Peter Frampton, Steve Marriott and Jerry Shirley.
Bottom left: Rick Grech jumped from the comparative obscurity of Family to achieve instant recognition as bass player with the notorious Blind Faith. This shot was taken at the band's only British concert, their world debut in Hyde Park.
Bottom: Other members of Blind Faith, snapped on the same occasion, were left to right: Ginger Baker, Eric Clapton and Stevie Winwood.

in the shadow of Jeff Beck but they now became the centres of attraction in the Faces, as the quintet renamed themselves. After a surprisingly slow start, they took off and though their albums lacked the flair and excitement of their stage shows they still sold in quantity. However, their album success was totally eclipsed by that of Stewart's concurrent solo output and his standing escalated; the Faces were increasingly relegated to a subordinate role.

The inevitable split came at the end of 1975, when Stewart put together a new backing group to negotiate the final steps to superstardom. Ron Wood also reached the top when he accepted an invitation to join the Rolling Stones. The remaining Faces reunited with Steve Marriott in an attempt to resurrect the Small Faces and when that ended in ignominy, drummer Kenny Jones joined the Who whilst Ian McLagen became keyboard player in the Stones touring party.

Down the scale at club level, several new groups were struggling for recognition. Among the best were Family, Fairport Convention, Mott the Hoople and King Crimson.

Family, an adventurous five piece from Leicester, made a significant impression with their second album *Family Entertainment* but constant personnel changes robbed them of any real consistency and they lurched to a frustrated conclusion in 1973. Since then, only grainy vocalist Roger Chapman has been able to maintain a visible profile.

Strangely, line-up changes did little to impair the popularity of Fairport Convention, who, in the two years after their formation, refined their early eclecticism into a folk-rock style deeply rooted in traditional English music. Their 1969 masterpiece *Liege And Lief* marked the permanent arrival of fiddler Dave Swarbrick and the temporary departure of their gifted singer Sandy Denny. Among the other notable musicians who passed through the group were Ian Matthews, who left to form Matthews Southern Comfort, a briefly successful band with a chart topping single, *Woodstock*, to their credit; Ashley Hutchings, subsequent founder of Steeleye Span and the Albion Band, and a respected figure in the folk music field; and Richard Thompson, a remarkable guitarist who, in partnership with his wife Linda, went on to restrained

album and concert success during the seventies. After a marvellous career spanning 12 years, 15 line-ups, 17 albums and 20 musicians, Fairport finally disbanded in August 1979.

King Crimson went on the rocks in 1974 after surviving founder Robert Fripp had almost driven himself to distraction in his attempts to keep the group afloat. Redolent of the Moody Blues but hippier and heavier, their mellotron-dominated arrangements were the highlight of an imaginative stage act which won them an appreciable following months before their first album, *In The Court Of The Crimson King*, was released – but within a year of their London debut, Greg Lake had left to conspire with Keith Emerson, and Ian McDonald had embarked on the winding road which would eventually lead him to Foreigner.

In direct contrast to the denim/t-shirt streetwear of the underground groups, Mott the Hoople were as flashy and exciting as their music, which on a good night was exceptional. Their early career was

Opposite above: In early 1969 Fairport Convention were (left to right) Ian Matthews, Simon Nicol, Ashley Hutchings, Martin Lamble, Sandy Denny and Richard Thompson. Over the next 10 years, 20 musicians passed through their ranks.

Opposite below left: Ian Hunter, flamboyant frontman for Mott the Hoople, led the group through several bleak years to eventual worldwide success. After fluctuating fortune as a solo artist, Hunter enters the eighties with his reputation restored.

Opposite below right: 'Ground control to Major Tom' – David Bowie, after fleeting chart success with *Space Oddity*, retreated to evolve his plan for world domination in the seventies.

Left: Humble Pieman Steve Marriott. Humble Pie's massive American popularity was never reflected in their native Britain.

Below: The Faces (left to right: Kenny Jones, Ronnie Lane, Rod Stewart and Ron Wood. Not in this picture: Ian McLagan). Their good-time party music was far more acceptable on stage than on vinyl, and Stewart subsequently renounced their loose style in favour of a more disciplined and less democratic approach.

particularly traumatic, however, and in early 1972 they dejectedly decided to split up after four albums had failed to gather any commercial momentum. Getting wind of their intention, David Bowie suddenly declared himself a hard-core Mott fan and his enthusiasm encouraged them to try again.

A Bowie-penned single, *All The Young Dudes*, took them to number three and Mott were suddenly overnight stars. *All The Way From Memphis* and *Roll Away The Stone* returned them to the top ten and their albums, especially *The Hoople* and *Live*, broke through on the American charts. Bt this time, guitarist Mick Ralphs had left to set up Bad Company, but his absence didn't detract from their popularity which peaked in a full week of sold-out shows on Broadway.

At the end of 1974, front man Ian Hunter left for a solo career, taking the recently arrived Mick Ronson as his righthand man. Mott never recovered from the loss, but Hunter went on to cement his reputation as a singer, composer and producer ... and the extent of his influence was only revealed when the 1976 new wavers credited him as a major inspiration.

Mott's saviour and benefactor, David Bowie, had himself come to prominence in 1969 when his eerie *Space Oddity* nosed its way into the top five. Though he'd been leading bands since the early sixties, any success had been localised and his novel hit was presumed to be a flash-in-the-pan. In fact, his subsequent disappearance was self-imposed; he chose to channel his energies into running a small arts laboratory in his hometown of Beckenham, where he remained until his dramatic re-emergence three years later.

Bowie's was one of several isolated hits which included *Where Do You Go To My Lovely?* by Peter Sarstedt, *Something In The Air* by Thunderclap Newman, *Je T'Aime* by Jane Birkin with Serge Gainsbourg and *Hare Krishna Mantra* by the Radha Krishna Temple.

Caribbean music saw more chart activity than in previous years: Desmond Dekker and the Aces reached number one with *The Israelites* and number seven with *It Mek*, Jimmy Cliff made the top ten with *Wonderful World, Beautiful People*, the Upsetters put *The Return Of Django* into the top five, and Harry J. and the All Stars scored with *The Liquidator*.

Blue Mink began their chart career with *Melting Pot* and John Lennon and the Plastic Ono Band began theirs with *Give Peace A Chance*, but for Love Sculpture *Sabre Dance* was their first and last hit. Their driving force, guitar ace Dave Edmunds, gave up performing when the group fell apart after an ill-organised American tour. Instead, he spent most of his time holed up in Rockfield Studios, either producing other groups or working on his own elaborate recordings: *I Hear You Knocking, Baby I Love You* and *Born To Be With You* all reached the top ten.

His eventual return to live work, with Rockpile in the late seventies, was prefaced by a short British tour in Summer 1974. On this he was backed by another of 1969's hopefuls, Brinsley Schwarz.

The Brinsleys had outgrown the limitations of

their previous identity, Kippington Lodge, and were struggling to survive when a small ad connected them with a management company who changed their name and their lives. Unable to attract

Top left: The Faces in characteristic party pose.

Far left below: Bob Fripp, sole constant factor in the ever-changing face of King Crimson.

Above: Roger Chapman, manic vocalist with Family, one of the most distinctive British underground groups.

Left: Love Sculpture featured the guitar pyrotechnics of Dave Edmunds (centre), while Brinsley Schwarz (*below left*) (left to right: Billy Rankin, Bob Andrews, Brinsley Schwarz and Nick Lowe) relied heavily on Nick Lowe's songwriting skills. In the late seventies, Lowe and Edmunds combined to front Rockpile.

Opposite top: Creedence Clearwater Revival (left to right: Tom Fogerty, Stu Cook, Doug Clifford and John Fogerty).

Opposite centre: The Chicago Transit Authority abbreviated their name to Chicago, and were among the pioneers of the jazz–rock movement.

Opposite below: Sha Na Na specialised in recreating the music and excitement of fifties rock'n'roll.

146

a record deal, gigs or publicity, they devised a plan which involved 150 media being flown to New York to witness the group's appearance at the Fillmore East, where they were third on the bill below Quicksilver Messenger Service and Van Morrison.

The resulting press deluge succeeded in bringing Brinsley Schwarz to the notice of the public but the accompanying cries of 'contrived hype' effectively dashed any chances of their ever achieving credibility in the rock world. In fact, they were a capable and inventive outfit but their albums were ignored and their 5½-year career was more like a prison sentence.

They broke up in 1975, since when they've found the respect they deserve.

The other significant British newcomers were Hawkwind, a drug-oriented bunch of hippies who dumfounded detractors by achieving a massive hit single, *Silver Machine*; Caravan, who sprang from the same Canterbury scene which spawned the Soft Machine; Blodwyn Pig, a blues band fronted by former Jethro Tull guitarist Mick Abrahams; Wishbone Ash, whose twin lead-guitar attack peaked on their biggest album, *Argus*; and Black Sabbath, heavy metallurgists of the basest stripe, who nevertheless attracted colossal audiences and phenomenal album sales.

Heavy metal merchants were also on the rampage in America, nowhere more so than in Detroit, where the Amboy Dukes, Bob Seger, Frost, the Stooges, the MC5 and Grand Funk Railroad had all established themselves.

Though the Amboy Dukes had enjoyed brief national success with their 1968 hit, *Journey To The Centre Of The Mind*, leader Ted Nugent would have to plug away for a few more years before his talents were fully appreciated and the same fate lay in store for Bob Seger. Frost, despite some creditable albums, achieved only marginal success beyond their home city – though guitarist Dick Wagner became a noted session guitarist – and the Stooges were widely regarded as a bad joke until singer Iggy Pop's subsequent re-emergence led to their being re-examined as a serious musical/socio-political venture. The MC5 rode to fame on a wave of revolutionary hysteria, much of it dreamed up by their manager John Sinclair. The group's first album, *Kick Out The Jams*, was an extremely powerful and totally uncompromising live recording which took them into the top thirty but their follow-up, *Back In The U.S.A.*, was a commercial failure which set them on a collision course for obscurity.

Grand Funk Railroad had a patently undiscerning but nonetheless enormous audience as their astonishing track record attests. Two number one singles (*We're An American Band* and *Locomotion*) and six top ten albums confirmed their heavy metal supremacy throughout the first half of the seventies, when constant critical abuse had absolutely no effect on their chart and concert blitzkreig.

Johnny Winter, a guitar hero who fell from grace, managed to pick himself up and restore his reputation after being written off as a has-been.

An albino from Texas, Winter led a blues band which became legendary in his home state during the mid-sixties, but it was only after *Rolling Stone* magazine, in an article on the Texan scene, drew

Heavy metal trio Grand Funk Railroad (left to right: Mel Schacher, Mark Farner and Don Brewer).

Above right: Albino blues guitar star Johnny Winter.

attention to his prowess that his fame began to spread. Impressed by what he'd read, a New York entrepreneur and club owner signed Winter and secured him a contract with C.B.S., who launched him on a massive publicity campaign. Albums and concerts were immediately successful and Winter rode into the seventies as the hottest blues act ever ... but the transition from bar entertainer to superstar created pressures which culminated in drug addiction and Winter, whose band was now the remains of *Sloopy* hitmakers the McCoys, entered hospital to recuperate.

After two years away from music, he emerged with a new band and a new positivity, but as well as effecting his own comeback, Winter was instrumental in returning Muddy Waters to the front rank, as will be seen.

The other American blues guitarist to break through in 1969 was Carlos Santana, a San Franciscan who'd first come to notice when he replaced Mike Bloomfield in a 'supersession' with Al Kooper. Soon after forming his own band, the first of many different line-ups to appear as Santana, an impressive display at Woodstock assisted his debut album into the top five and the follow-up, *Abraxus*, to number one.

Santana's distinctive blend of blues, rock and Afro-Cuban rhythms was flexible enough to facilitate short-term unions with guest musicians (notably John McLaughlin), a sustained religious diversion, a particularly transient personnel, and a long and happy chart career which was still active in the late seventies.

The aforementioned Al Kooper, famed for his organ work on several seminal Dylan tracks and his leadership of New York group the Blues Project, pioneered a new musical direction when he formed Blood, Sweat and Tears, a unique jazz-rock fusion where a traditional rock quartet was augmented by a four-piece brass section. When Kooper left after their fairly well-received debut, the group was presumed doomed but they confounded critics by returning stronger than ever in 1969, breaking into the big time with two chart-topping albums and a series of sold-out national tours.

During 1971, mounting internal dissention led to a major line-up shuffle and a considerably weaker band reaped the benefit of earlier triumphs. By this time, however, Blood Sweat and Tears were being overshadowed by Chicago, a group of similar construction and style. Specialising in double albums, triple albums and quadruple boxed sets, Chicago became a multi-million dollar industry with five consecutive number ones, but in the late seventies there were signs that their audience was beginning to tire of their predictable flatulence. Their increasing homogeneity was interrupted only by the occasional hit single, like the chart topping *If You Leave Me Now* in 1976, and guitarist Terry Kath's Johnny Ace-styled death in 1978.

Gram Parsons' life was like one long game of Russian roulette, but in moments of relative lucidity he produced some of the best country rock ever heard. After joining the Byrds and taking them on a country excursion, Parsons and founder/bassist Chris Hillman left to form the Flying Burrito Brothers, an excellent group whose potential was never to be realised. Their 1969 debut, *The Gilded Palace Of Sin*, attracted rave reviews but sold as poorly as its successors and, hampered by financial problems and a rapid turnover of musicians, they threw in the towel in 1972. Bernie Leadon went on to form the Eagles and Rick Roberts to form Firefall, whilst Parsons, after completing two fine solo albums, died from a drug overdose in 1973.

Perhaps if the Burritos had taken a leaf out of Creedence Clearwater Revival's book their trail-

lazing efforts would not have gone unheeded.
Creedence's music had country edges but was
crunchier, rockier, more disciplined and more
direct ... and they hit the bullseye every time.
Theirs was not an overnight success, however; as
the Blue Velvets and the Golliwogs they'd lurched
round the San Francisco area at bare survival level
since the early sixties. It wasn't until 1969 that John
Fogerty, a remarkable singer/lead guitarist/
composer/producer, perfected the watertight formula which took them to the top and although their
candle only burned for three years, theirs was the
brightest flame on both the singles and album
charts.

Their first eponymous L.P. opened the door for
five platinum albums, including two number ones
in *Green River* and *Cosmo's Factory*, and seven top
five singles (all of which were also hits in Britain),
including such classics as *Proud Mary*, *Bad Moon
Rising* and *Up Around The Bend*.

Like all great groups should (but seldom ever do),
Creedence quit at the top. Fogerty, presumed to be
planning a spectacular solo career, released two
modest albums before spending the last half of the
decade in seclusion.

Vying with Creedence in the singles charts were
Canadian group the Guess Who, whose three top ten
entries paved the way for their chart-topping
American Woman the following year; Three Dog
Night, whose similar achievements were to lead to
three number ones in *Mama Told Me Not To Come*,
Joy To The World and *Black And White*; the

Above: Despite numerous
personnel changes, Carlos
Santana (with face visible)
led Santana to consistent
acclaim.

Left: Ex-Byrd and Flying
Burrito Brothers founder
Gram Parsons, the original
cosmic cowboy.

'69 the year

Events

20 Jan. Richard Nixon is inaugurated as the 37th President of the U.S.A.

2 Mar. Concorde makes its maiden flight from Toulouse.

11 Mar. Golda Meir becomes Prime Minister of Israel.

1 July The Investiture of Charles as Prince of Wales takes place.

12 July There is rioting in Londonderry, Northern Ireland, following a civil rights march.

20 July Neil Armstrong and Edwin Aldrin become the first men on the moon.

5 Sept. Liet. Calley is charged with the My Lai massacre of 109 civilians.

9 Dec. Charles Manson is arrested for the murder of Sharon Tate.

22 Dec. Bernadette Devlin is jailed for six months.

Films of 69

Butch Cassidy And The Sundance Kid · The Damned · Easy Rider · If · Midnight Cowboy · The Prime Of Miss Jean Brodie · They Shoot Horses Don't They? · True Grit

U.S. CHART TOPPERS – WEEKS AT TOP

I Heard It Through The Grapevine	Marvin Gaye
Crimson And Clover	Tommy James and the Shondells
Everyday People	Sly and the Family Stone
Dizzy	Tommy Roe
Aquarius/Let The Sun Shine In	Fifth Dimension
Get Back	Beatles
Love Theme From Romeo And Juliet	Henry Mancini
In The Year 2525	Zager and Evans
Honky Tonk Women	Rolling Stones
Sugar Sugar	Archies
I Can't Get Next To You	Temptations
Suspicious Minds	Elvis Presley
Wedding Bell Blues	Fifth Dimension
Come Together/Something	Beatles
Na Na Hey Hey Kiss Him Goodbye	Steam
Leaving On A Jet Plane	Peter, Paul and Mary
Someday We'll Be Together	Supremes

U.K. CHART TOPPERS – WEEKS AT TOP

Ob-La-Di Ob-La-Da	Marmalade
Lily The Pink	Scaffold
Albatross	Fleetwood Mac
Blackberry Way	Move
Half As Nice	Amen Corner
Where Do You Go To My Lovely	Peter Sarstedt
I Heard It Through The Grapevine	Marvin Gaye
The Israelites	Desmond Dekker
Get Back	Beatles
Dizzy	Tommy Roe
Ballad Of John And Yoko	Beatles
Something In The Air	Thunderclap Newman
Honkey Tonk Women	Rolling Stones
In The Year 2525	Zager and Evans
Bad Moon Rising	Creedence Clearwater Revival
Je T'Aime Moi Non Plus	Jane Birkin and Serge Gainsbourg
I'll Never Fall In Love Again	Bobbie Gentry
Sugar Sugar	Archies
Two Little Boys	Rolf Harris

Right: Dennis Hopper and Peter Fonda in *Easy Rider*.

Opposite top left: man lands on the moon.

Opposite top right: the Apple boutique.

fontana

CENSORED
CENSORED

We wanted to illustrate 'JE T'AIME·· ·· MOI NON PLUS' the sexational single by JANE BIRKIN & SERGE GAINSBOURG (on Fontana TF 1042). But they wouldn't let us. Listen to it – and you'll see why.

ERIC CLAPTON STEVE WINWOOD GINGER BAKER RICK GRECH

FREE CONCERT HYDE PARK JUNE 7 3 P.M.

BLIND FAITH

Crosby, Stills, Nash and Young were the last super-group of the sixties . . . but here it's (left to right) Stephen Stills, David Crosby, Graham Nash and Neil Young.

Youngbloods, whose *Get Together* briefly improved their third division status; and Johnny Cash, who had the biggest hit of his career in *A Boy Named Sue*. Successes also came to Mountain, Kenny Rogers and Jackie de Shannon..

The Edwin Hawkins Singers had their heydey with *Oh Happy Day*, the Cuff Links with *Tracy*, Zager and Evans with *In The Year 2525*, Steam with *Na Na Hey Hey Kiss Him Goodbye* and R. B. Greaves with *Take A Letter Maria*. Bobby Sherman became the biggest of the pre-Osmonds teenybop stars when *Little Woman* became the first of his four top tenners, and bubblegum fans also went for *Sugar Sugar* by the non-existent cartoon group, the Archies.

At the other end of the scale, Delaney and Bonnie came out into the open after years working the back streets; War, originally fronted by Eric Burdon, began their sweep to the top; and Sha Na Na, boosted by their appearance at Woodstock, launched a thousand imitators when they broke through with their rock'n'roll revival act.

Biggest of all the groups to emerge in 1969, however, was another Woodstock winner . . . Crosby, Stills, Nash and Young.

Whilst Neil Young was making a brief exploratory solo excursion, his Buffalo Springfield colleague Stephen Stills was conspiring with David Crosby, formerly of the Byrds, and Graham Nash, soon to leave the Hollies – and the three of them came together to make one of the summer's better albums. However, knowing that his pals were only average rhythm guitarists, Stills blanched at the instrumental burden he would have to carry on the road, and Neil Young was invited, along with a bassist and drummer, to share the load.

After two long tours, they spent some 800 studio hours crafting *Déjà Vu* and then returned to the road as 'the highest paid group in the world'. Tapes from the tour were subsequently edited into a double album, *Four Way Street*, which, like its predecessor, flew straight to number one. Having conquered the planet, they successfully chased their solo ambitions . . . though periodically reuniting. With commercial considerations ranking low in Neil Young's list of priorities, it was natural that his albums should sell fewer than those of his cohorts: though *After The Gold Rush* reached number eight in 1970 and *Harvest* (together with its single choice *Heart Of Gold*) reached number one in 1972, it was not until the beginning of 1979 that he would reach the top twenty again. Nevertheless, the consistent artistic superiority of Young's work did much to brighten the gloom of the early seventies.

'70

'Bridge Over Troubled Water'

The Allman Brothers · Badfinger · Bread · The Carpenters · Dawn
Deep Purple · E.L.P. · Free · The J. Geils Band · Norman Greenbaum
Hot Chocolate · The Jackson Five · Kris Kristofferson · Little Feat
Curtis Mayfield · The Partridge Family with David Cassidy · Leon Russell
Shocking Blue · James Taylor · R. Dean Taylor · T. Rex · Uriah Heep

n 1970, the British rock scene was suffering a hangover from the excesses of the swinging sixties, as the overall flippancy of the singles chart suggests.

Rolf Harris opened the year with his heartbursting *Two Little Boys* and Clive Dunn was waiting to push his woeful *Granddad* into the top slot 12 months later. In between, we saw the arrival of the England World Cup Squad, Dana, the Pipkins, Pickettywitch, Hotlegs, Christie, Lee Marvin, Chairman of the Board, Mungo Jerry, McGuiness Flint, the Brotherhood of Man, and those two anonymous groups with interchangeable components, White Plains and Edison Lighthouse. Some were O.K.; some were terrible.

We also saw the arrival of Arrival, who weren't at all bad, and Badfinger, who were quite good, but the two major entrants to the pop stakes were Hot Chocolate and T. Rex.

Hot Chocolate was formed in 1970 as a vehicle for the considerable songwriting talent of Errol Brown, although their debut single, released on the Beatles' Apple label, was a cover of John Lennon's *Give Peace A Chance*. When they signed with Mickie Most's Rak label later in the year, the group began a chart career which would bring them 12 top twenty hits over the next eight years. Their sporadic American success was finally cemented by their 1979 album, *Every One's A Winner*, and its title track was also a hit single.

T. Rex, composed of Marc Bolan and his ever changing sidemen, became one of the most flamboyant hit makers of the early seventies. *Ride A White Swan*, which reached number two towards the end of the year, was only their beginning: over the next 18 months they scored another number two and four number ones: *Hot Love*, *Get It On* (which, reaching the American top ten, gave them their biggest Stateside success), *Telegram Sam* and *Metal Guru*. As a teenage idol of considerable imagination, Bolan soon established himself as a leading light in the 'glitter-rock' craze and his unbroken run of top tenners, 11 in all, continued until Summer 1973, when he began to relax his relentless work schedule. In 1977 he returned with a new T. Rex and his own television series. The final episode had yet to be transmitted when he died in a car accident.

Prior to his decisive conversion to blatant electric rocker, Bolan, a wordy lyricist and acoustic strummer in a duo called Tyrannosaurus Rex (unpronounceable to the audience he later attracted), had been minstrel by appointment to the London hippy scene, wherein he had languished for some years.

Also struggling to escape 'underground' re-

strictions were a group of groups, including the Pink Fairies, the Edgar Broughton Band, Van der Graaf Generator, the Groundhogs, Quintessence, Barclay James Harvest, Atomic Rooster and Medicine Head. None succeeded like Free, who rode to stardom on their magnificent smash, *All Right Now*. They followed it with four top ten albums and an annual hit single for the next three years, during which time they broke up and reformed incessantly. Their turbulent history came to a permanent conclusion in Summer 1973, when vocalist Paul Rodgers and drummer Simon Kirke convened Bad Company. Paul Kossoff, their brilliant but erratic guitarist, embarked on numerous projects, all of which foundered because of his

T. Rex, Personified by Marc Bolan (front) progressed from an underground cult band in the late sixties to become the teenybop sensation of the early seventies.

The late '60s

NEW FILLMORE
PROCOL HARUM
PINK FLOYD
H.P. LOVECRAFT

NOV 10-11 WINTERLAND
WAIT & SEE

TICKETS
Valid Friday Only $3.00

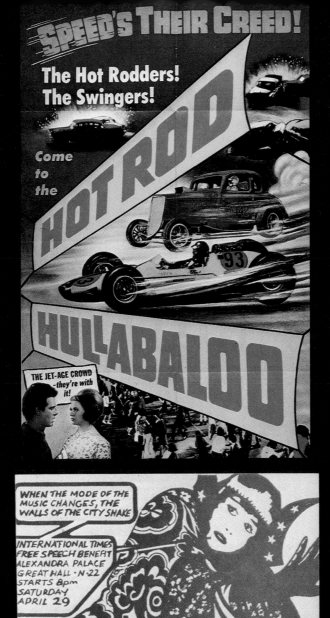

SPEED'S THEIR CREED!

The Hot Rodders!
The Swingers!

Come to the

HOT ROD
HULLABALOO

THE JET-AGE CROWD
—they're with it!

INTERNATIONAL TIMES

£1
advance
tickets
only
FROM HIP SOURCES & BOOK SHOPS

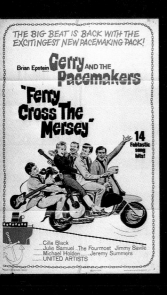

THE BIG BEAT IS BACK WITH THE
EXCITINGEST NEW PACEMAKING PACK!

Brian Epstein
Gerry AND THE Pacemakers

"Ferry
Cross The
Mersey"

14
Fabtastic
song
hits!

Cilla Black
Julie Samuel .. The Fourmost .. Jimmy Savile
Michael Holden .. Jeremy Summers
UNITED ARTISTS

WHEN THE MODE OF THE
MUSIC CHANGES, THE
WALLS OF THE CITY SHAKE

INTERNATIONAL TIMES
FREE SPEECH BENEFIT
ALEXANDRA PALACE
GREAT HALL · N·22
STARTS 8pm
SATURDAY
APRIL 29

POSTE RESTANTE

RTL

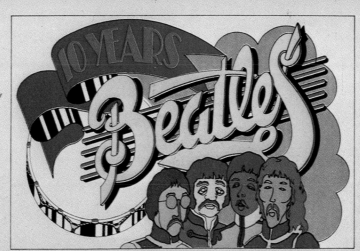

10 YEARS
Beatles

THE BIKINI-
BUNNIES
are BUSTIN' OUT
ALL OVER!

TRANS AMERICAN presents

IT'S A
Bikini
World
by CINEMASCOPE

DEBORAH TOMMY
WALLEY and KIRK
BOBBY PICKETT and SUZIE KAYE

THE ANIMALS
THE CASTAWAYS
THE TOYS

insoluble drug problem which had complicated Free's progress, and in March 1976, when for once his future looked optimistic, he died in his sleep on a plane.

Also entering the big league in 1970 were new groups, Emerson, Lake and Palmer; Uriah Heep; and Deep Purple, who, like Free, had been trying to establish themselves for a couple of years.

Purple, ultimately one of the most influential and successful heavy metal groups ever, took off quickly in America where they achieved a top five single in *Hush*, but British recognition came only after a major personnel shuffle which saw Ian Gillan installed as vocalist. Of the six albums recorded by this line-up, two, *Deep Purple In Rock* and *Fireball*, reached number one in Britain and two, *Machine Head* and *Made In Japan* reached the American top ten. They eventually ground to a halt in early 1976; the inevitable spin-offs all suffered from comparisons with their forebears but, after shaky beginnings, three looked towards the eighties with optimism. Gillan now led his own band, while Whitesnake, fronted by his successor, David Coverdale, contained two other Purple people.

Curtis Mayfield emerged from the relative anonymity of the Impressions to become one of the decade's first black superstars.

Rainbow, driven by their uncompromising guitaris[t] Ritchie Blackmore, had seen four albums creepin[g] up the charts since their inception, but a late 197[9] hit single, *Since You've Been Gone*, boosted thei[r] value and enthusiasm considerably.

Like Deep Purple, Uriah Heep were launched o[n] large injections of money from commercial in[-] vestors, and while this alienated certain critics, i[t] did propel them to 'instant' stardom – though th[e] musicians involved had all paid appropriate dues i[n] undernourished sixties groups. In a hard-workin[g] career spanning 14 albums Uriah Heep went int[o] gradual decline after their 1972 album *Demons An[d] Wizards*, but despite the departure of singer Davi[d] Byron they still retain a reasonable following eve[n] though the music is now irretrievably obsolescent.

Emerson, Lake and Palmer, similarly redundant after ringing the changes on the same restricted formula for ten years, unveiled themselves in spectacular style at the 1970 Isle of Wight festival. Keyboard wizard Keith Emerson (from the Nice), bassplayer/singer Greg Lake (from King Crimson) and drummer Carl Palmer (from Atomic Rooster) had no difficulty convincing the world of their worth and their first four albums all went top five, but their early vitality gave way to over-indulgence which eventually peaked on the pompously titled double album *Works – Volume One*, where each had a whole side to demonstrate his technical expertise. On the remaining side, they united for a noteworthy intepretation of Aaron Copeland's neo-classical *Fanfare For The Common Man*, an edited version of which reached number two in the U.K. singles chart during Summer 1977.

Since then, however, instrumental dexterity has been washed out of vogue by the New Wave and rumours of E.L.P.'s semi-retirement have been strengthened by the infrequency and declining popularity of subsequent 'works'.

1970 was a good year for European groups, three of whom found chart success on both sides of the Atlantic. The Rattles scored with *The Witch*, Frijid Pink with their revamped *House Of The Rising Sun*, and, most convincingly of all, Shocking Blue with *Venus*.

Jimmy Ruffin, relatively inert since his 1966 hit, *What Becomes Of The Broken Hearted*, suddenly found his feet with *Farewell Is A Lonely Sound*, the first of four British top tenners, none of which made any impression in his homeland.

In fact, the American soul scene had been static for some time but now there were distinct signs of rejuvenation: Eddie Holman reached number two with *Hey There Lonely Girl*, the Five Stairsteps reached number eight with *O-o-h Child*, Freda Payne had her first and biggest hit with *Band Of Gold*, Edwin Starr made the top with *War* and Clarence Carter had a smash in *Patches*.

Curtis Mayfield left the Impressions to concentrate on his record label, Curtom, and a solo career, which started hesitantly but moved into high gear when he wrote the score for the black streetlife movie, *Superfly*. The soundtrack album not only went gold on its day of release but also provided two top ten singles in *Freddie's Dead* and the title track, and though their success tended to overshadow his later output, he is still a highly respected singer, songwriter and producer.

However, the year's major soul discovery were he Jackson Five, who, not surprisingly, appeared on the Tamla Motown label. The sons of a former musician, the five were brothers who had already made several obscure singles before being spotted by Diana Ross at a charity show. Ms. Ross, now a solo singer and the star of the newly founded Motown Picture Corporation, lent her advice, encouragement and patronage and within one year, they had hit the top of the charts with four singles: *I Want You Back*, *ABC*, *The Love You Save* and *I'll Be There*.

All featured the incredible voice of the youngest of the brothers, Michael, who was only 11 when they cut *I Want You Back*, and he remained their focal point as well as branching out on a concurrent solo career which, after a couple of near misses, brought him a number one, *Ben*, in 1972. The mid-seventies saw the five, now known as the Jacksons, on a downhill slide but in 1977 they fought back with *Show You The Way To Go* followed by *Blame It On The Boogie* the year after, and were as ebullient as ever.

The same could not be said of the Partridge Family, who ceased to exist when their television series folded up. Whilst together, the Partridges scored only three top ten hits (including a number one, *I Think I Love You*) but their popularity acted as a springboard for David Cassidy, who continued his career as a teen idol in the seventies.

Rare Earth had their first hit with *Get Ready*, and B. J. Thomas had his biggest with *Raindrops Keep Falling On My Head*, as did Ray Stevens with *Everything Is Beautiful* – though by far the best selling single of the year was *Bridge Over Troubled Water* by Simon and Garfunkel.

R. Dean Taylor, the first white act in the Tamla Motown stable, appeared with *Indiana Wants Me* and Dawn began their long chart association with *Candida* and *Knock Three Times*, but the biggest of the new pop acts were the Carpenters and Bread.

Often dismissed as bland pap churners, Richard Carpenter and his sister Karen took more pains than most, and their efforts were rewarded with a string of hits familiar to anyone who switched on a radio during the early seventies. *Close To You*, a number one in 1970, was followed by *We've Only Just Begun*, *For All We Know*, *Goodbye To Love* and several other top tenners and by 1977, they'd accumulated some 20 gold discs.

Bread, initially a trio of songwriters, singers and session musicians, were helping on an album by a group called Pleasure Faire when they decided to start helping themselves, and it was a track from their second album, *Make It With You*, which secured their future – though at this point the group lost one member and added two. *Baby I'm-A-Want You* and *Guitar Man* took them high into the album charts and also furnished such top twenty singles as *Everything I Own*, and *Sweet Surrender*, but when founder members David Gates and James Griffin fell out, the group broke up. Despite its demise, the group's enduring popularity was shown when a 1977 compilation album, *The Sound Of Bread*, sold over two million copies in Britain alone.

Meanwhile on the American long-haired front, underground groups were surfacing in profusion, though most, like the Flock, It's A Beautiful Day,

Stars of a popular T.V. series, the Partridge Family later achieved significant success as recording artists. David Cassidy (top right) subsequently emerged as a teen idol.

David Gates (top left) was the leading light behind Bread's consistent hit output.

Hot Tuna, and Dan Hicks and His Hot Licks, would soon submerge again. Amongst those who stayed afloat were two blues groups, the Allman Brothers and the J. Geils Band.

The star of the Allman Brothers was undoubtedly Duane Allman, who'd earned his reputation as a studio guitarist, decorating late sixties recordings by Wilson Pickett and Aretha Franklin among others. By 1970, he'd teamed up with brother Gregg to form a six-piece powerhouse who, after attracting a huge following in the south, broke nationally with their live double album *At Fillmore East*.

Above: From bopping elf to electric warrior, Marc Bolan's transformation from non-entity to megastar was cemented by 11 consecutive top ten singles.

Left: The remarkably consistent Hot Chocolate, fronted by Errol Brown (third from left).

Below far left: The most successful Deep Purple line-up right to left: Ian Gillan, Jon Lord, Roger Glover and Ritchie Blackmore, with Ian Price in front.

Left: Free (left to right: Simon Kirke, Paul Kossoff, Paul Rodgers and Andy Fraser) may have failed to realise their full potential because of their incessant internal strife.

Opposite: Keith Emerson wonders how to switch on his instrumental array.

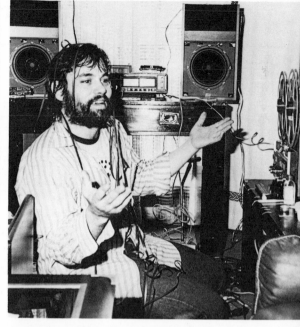

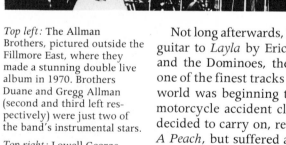

Top left: The Allman Brothers, pictured outside the Fillmore East, where they made a stunning double live album in 1970. Brothers Duane and Gregg Allman (second and third left respectively) were just two of the band's instrumental stars.

Top right: Lowell George, ringleader of Little Feat, demonstrates his studio expertise.

Right: Kris Kristofferson on-stage at the Isle of Wight Festival in 1970, when he opened the proceedings as an unknown.

Above: When Joe Cocker parted company with his Grease Band in Spring 1970, Leon Russell stepped into the breach to organise an all-star touring band known as *Mad Dogs And Englishmen*.

Not long afterwards, Duane added his unique slide guitar to *Layla* by Eric Clapton's new group Derek and the Dominoes, the result being recognised as one of the finest tracks ever cut, but just as the rock world was beginning to acknowledge his genius a motorcycle accident claimed his life. The Allmans decided to carry on, reaching the top five with *Eat A Peach*, but suffered a second setback a year later when bassist Berry Oakley was killed in an accident almost identical to Duane's.

Strangely, the depleted band then released their most successful album, *Brothers and Sisters*, which reached number one in 1973. Dominating the proceedings was guitarist Richard Betts, who had previously worked in Duane's shadow, and his exciting, tour de force, *Ramblin' Man*, provided the band with a top three single.

The last half of the seventies saw the band dissolve into relatively unsuccessful solo enterprises which inevitably led to a regrouping, though subsequent output lacked the cachet of earlier recordings. Gregg Allman's credibility slumped when he testified against one of the band's employees (being tried for drug offences), and his misfortunes continued in 1975 when he married Cher (of 'Sonny and' fame), who filed for divorce after only nine days of connubial bliss.

Whereas the Allmans specialised in drawn-out surging improvisation, the J. Geils Band from Boston favoured shorter, tighter R&B numbers. Led by guitarist Geils and dynamic singer Peter Wolf they came be regarded as the best group of their type though *Bloodshot*, in 1973, was their only top ten album.

Little Feat, similarly admired by the cognoscente, had even greater difficulty fattening their cult

During his reign as number one teen heart-throb, David Cassidy incited the most fervent fan worship since the Beatles.

ollowing. Despite their excellence, their first three lbums made no impression whatsoever on the harts and it was only a last ditch attempt, *Feats Don't Fail Me Now*, which took them into the top orty and rescued them from oblivion in 1974 – four ears after guitarist Lowel George had put the band ogether. Despite continued critical acclaim, their ubsequent albums were only moderately successul, a factor which finally induced George to try his olo wings in 1979. A few days into his first tour he was found dead in his hotel room.

James Taylor, the latest singer/songwriter, not only cured his drug addiction but also wrote about t to achieve his first hit single, *Fire And Rain*, which eached number three towards the end of the year. Ie had been among the first acts to be signed to the Beatles' Apple label in 1967 and though it was a varticularly uneventful phase, his guardian angel here, Peter Asher (formerly of Peter and Gordon), ubsequently organised a contract with Warners, which resulted in the hit single and the platinum lbum *Sweet Baby James*. A second smash album, *Mud Slide Slim And The Blue Horizon*, provided nother hit single in *You've Got A friend*, which

reached number one, and the ultra-relaxed Taylor established himself as one of the most consistent and enduring of the singer/songwriter genre.

Working a similar vein was Kris Kristofferson, a Texan who graduated from Oxford University with an English literature degree – a qualification which helped him secure a job as janitor in a Nashville studio during the mid sixties. His musical prowess

Following their record success, the Jackson Five became the subject of a television cartoon series. Lead singer Michael Jackson (second from right), only 11 when the group first hit the charts, rode into the eighties as one of the biggest solo acts in the world.

'70 the year

Events

2 Feb. Bertrand Russell dies.

18 Feb. The 'Chicago Seven' are acquitted of conspiring to incite riots, but are found guilty of other charges.

29 Apr. U.S. and South Vietnamese troops invade Cambodia.

4 May Four students die when national Guardsmen open fire on demonstrators at Kent State University, Ohio.

19 June Edward Heath becomes the British Prime Minister.

21 June In soccer, Brazil beat Italy 4–1 to win the World Cup for the third time.

8-12 Sept. Arab commandoes hijack three airliners and blow them up in the Jordanian desert.

8 Oct. The Nobel Prize for literature is awarded to Alexander Solzhenitsyn.

15 Oct. The Baltimore Orioles defeat the Cincinatti Reds to win the baseball World Series.

23 Oct. Gary Gabelich sets a new land speed record of over 622 m.p.h. at Bonneville Salt Flats.

Films of 70

Catch 22 · Five Easy Pieces · Let It Be · M.A.S.H. · Performance · Women In Love · Woodstock · Zabriskie Point

Right: Bertrand Russell, who died in 1970.

Opposite top left: Glitter became the craze.

Opposite top right: the Beatles in *Let It Be.*

Opposite below: M·A·S·H.

U.S. CHART TOPPERS – WEEKS AT TOP

Raindrops Keep Fallin' On My Head	B. J. Thomas
I Want You Back	Jackson Five
Venus	Shocking Blue
Thank You	Sly and the Family Stone
Bridge Over Troubled Water	Simon and Garfunkel
Let It Be	Beatles
ABC	Jackson Five
American Woman	Guess Who
Everything Is Beautiful	Ray Stevens
The Long And Winding Road	Beatles
The Love You Save	Jackson Five
Mama Told Me Not To Come	Three Dog Night
Close To You	Carpenters
Make It With You	Bread
War	Edwin Starr
Ain't No Mountain High Enough	Diana Ross
Cracklin' Rosie	Neil Diamond
I'll Be There	Jackson Five
I Think I Love You	Partridge Family
The Tears Of A Clown	Smokey Robinson and the Miracles
My Sweet Lord	George Harrison

U.K. CHART TOPPERS – WEEKS AT TOP

Two Little Boys	Rolf Harris
Love Grows	Edison Lighthouse
Wanderin' Star	Lee Marvin
Bridge Over Troubled Water	Simon and Garfunkel
All Kinds Of Everything	Dana
Spirit In The Sky	Norman Greenbaum
Back Home	England World Cup Squad
Yellow River	Christie
In The Summertime	Mungo Jerry
The Wonder Of You	Elvis Presley
The Tears Of A Clown	Smokey Robinson and the Miracles
Band Of Gold	Freda Payne
Woodstock	Matthews Southern Comfort
Voodoo Chile	Jimi Hendrix
I Hear You Knocking	Dave Edmunds

eventually landed him a recording contract and 1970 saw the release of *Kristofferson*, an album which contained a number of classic songs, including *Help Me Make It Through The Night* and *Me And Bobby McGee*, the enormous popularity of which established him in the front line.

During the seventies, Kristofferson focussed his attention on the silver screen and escalating acclaim culminated in his most celebrated success, *A Star Is Born*, in which he shared starring roles with Barbra Streisand. The demands of Hollywood now leave little time for musical pursuits, a trend strengthened in 1979 by his divorce from his wife Rita Coolidge. Rita, however, is still performing.

Rita's old flame Leon Russell (who immortalised her as the *Delta Lady*) had been a respected L.A. studio musician for many years and came to Joe Cocker's aid when his group deserted him on the eve of an American tour in 1970. Russell organised a massive backing band known as Mad Dogs And Englishmen, and the tour was completed in spectacular style – spawning a successful double album and a full length film, from which it was obvious that the charismatic Russell was stealing much of Cocker's thunder.

As Joe slunk back to England, Russell launched his own solo career, releasing a series of hit albums on his own label, Shelter, and consorting with such superstars as Bob Dylan and George Harrison, whom he supported at the concert for Bangla Desh. The southern drawl and keyboard virtuosity which

had made his early albums so attractive soon began to wear a little thin, however, and an extraordinarily self-indulgent triple album, issued in 1973, marked a turning point in his popularity.

All in all, the decade opened hesitantly: the pandemonium surrounding the two major festivals (Bath and the Isle of Wight) ensured that only comparatively modest events would ever take place in Britain in the future, Jimi Hendrix and Janis Joplin died, and Paul McCartney confirmed what had long been suspected ... the Beatles were no more. It was not the most illustrious of rock years.

James Taylor assumes a typically sensitive singer/songwriter pose.

Like many of her contemporaries, Janis Joplin was a victim of sixties excess.

164

'My Sweet Lord'

Curved Air · John Denver · Al Green · George Harrison · Isaac Hayes
The Honey Cone · Elton John · Carole King · John Kongos · John Lennon
Paul McCartney and Wings · The New Seekers · Olivia Newton-John
Harry Nilsson · The Osmonds · Carly Simon · Slade · Ringo Starr
Rod Stewart · Sweet · Yes

The break-up of the Beatles, made official in April 1970, put pressures on the individuals to prove themselves. John Lennon, of course, had already recorded singles under the banner of the Plastic Ono Band, but his *Imagine* album, which topped both British and American charts late in 1971, confirmed that his mop-top genius had not evaporated.

Imagine was the best and most accessible of Lennon's albums, which ranged from mysterious *Two Virgins* whose cover showed him and his second wife, Yoko Ono, in full frontal nudity) to revelatory (*John Lennon/Plastic Ono Band*), but he pursued a straighter line with *Mind Games* and *Walls And Bridges* – another American number one. After completing *Rock'n'roll* in 1975, the ever enigmatic Lennon began to retreat from the public eye, quickly effecting a total disappearance and almost unbroken silence. Fantastic financial inducements for the Beatles to reform for a quick killing have failed to lure him from his lair.

Ringo, too, adopted a shadowy lifestyle after his solo success had begun to deteriorate. A numbingly self-indulgent album of songs that his mother enjoyed preceded *Beaucoups Of Blues* and *Ringo* – his most successful collection, which also furnished him with two American number ones, *Photograph* and *Your Sixteen*. Subsequent albums were a good deal less profitable though Ringo was now being acclaimed as a natural screen actor following starring roles in *The Magic Christian* and *That'll Be The Day*.

George Harrison reached an artistic zenith with his triple album *All Things Must Pass* from which came his most celebrated single, *My Sweet Lord*, a worldwide chart topper at the beginning of the year, and a few months later his spiritual beliefs prompted him to organise an extravagant benefit concert for Bangla Desh, whose population was suffering as a result of political uprisings. The concert was a huge success aesthetically and financially and an album of the event, featuring Bob Dylan, Eric Clapton, Leon Russell, Ravi Shankar and various others besides Harrison, enjoyed brisk sales.

Although a single, *Give Me Love*, returned him to the top ten in 1973, Harrison's religious interests appeared to eclipse his enthusiasm for rock and his work became progressively less interesting. In 1979, the imaginatively titled *George Harrison* indicated some desire to return to the mainstream though its curious dedication to the motor racing drivers of the world was illustrative of his latest consuming passion.

Paul McCartney was to achieve more in chart terms than the other three put together. After two

Ron Wood (left) and Rod Stewart, stars of the Faces, who made the big time in 1971.

transitional albums, *McCartney* and *Ram*, he formed Wings, a group whose fluctuating personnel has always revolved around the permanent core of McCartney, his wife Linda, and ex-Moody Blueboy Denny Laine, and their early career peaked with *Band On The Run*.

Released at the end of 1973, this album made number one across the record buying world and was to remain in the American chart for several years.

Jimmy Page (left) and Robert Plant of Led Zeppelin.

Right: 'Success didn't change me a bit' says Olivia Newton-John, ironing her favourite pinafore.

Below: The Moody Blues in early seventies guise (left to right: John Lodge, Graeme Edge, Ray Thomas, Justin Hayward and Mike Pinder).

As lead singer of the Faces, Stewart was basking in escalating praise, but it was very noticeable that his concurrent solo albums were vastly superior to those of the group, both in terms of performance and choice of material. His major breakthroughs, both achieved in 1971, were *Every Picture Tells A Story*, the first of six consecutive chart topping albums, and *Maggie May*, which preceded four other number one singles: *You Wear It Well, Sailing, I Don't Want To Talk About It* and *Do Ya Think I'm Sexy.*

As previously mentioned, Stewart left the Faces in 1975 to concentrate on a solo career which has taken him to the dizziest heights of superstardom – a stratum in which very few singers are fortunate enough to operate. One of his peers is Elton John who, coincidentally, also spent part of his ill-paid apprenticeship in the shadow cast by Long John Baldry.

Unable to negotiate the obstacle course to fame, Elton's first group, Bluesology, had to back visiting American soul stars as well as blues singer/cabaret artist Baldry in order to survive. Dissatisfied with this, he applied for a job as tunesmith at Dick James Music, where a partnership with lyricist Bernie Taupin was sufficiently productive to warrant an album, *Empty Sky*, released to little effect in 1969.

A second album, *Elton John*, not only revealed his growth as singer and pianist but also provided his first hit single, *Your Song*, a top tenner on both sides of the Atlantic, and limited British recognition was boosted by the rapturous response which greeted his first American tour. *Tumbleweed Connection* and *Madman Across The Water* replaced *Elton John* in the U.S. top ten during 1971 and the following year he sealed his superstar status with *Honky Chateau*, a number one instant platinum album in America, and three smash singles, *Rocket Man, Honky Cat* and *Crocodile Rock.*

Until 1974, McCartney, unable to obtain an American visa due to a small blot on his copybook, was forced to restrict Wings' touring schedule to Britain and Europe – but once he had resolved his differences with the U.S. Embassy, he was able to plan the most spectacular and comprehensive tour ever undertaken by a rock group. Lasting 13 months, from September 1975 to October 1976, Wings played in 11 countries to over two million people, recording a triple album and filming a T.V. documentary along the way.

By 1978, McCartney had seen six of his eight post-Beatle albums reach number one in America and all of them make the British top ten. Additionally he'd enjoyed an abundance of worldwide hit singles, including *Mull Of Kintyre*, his late 1977 release, which became the biggest-selling record in the history of British music.

Paul McCartney, John Lennon, the Who, the Rolling Stones, E.L.P., the Moody Blues, Deep Purple, T. Rex and Led Zeppelin all had number one albums in Britain during 1971, and so too did Rod Stewart.

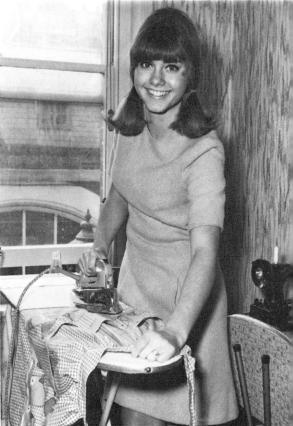

Between 1973 and 1976, there was little doubt that Elton was the biggest rock star on the planet, though reverence was far greater in America, where *Bennie And The Jets*, *Lucy In The Sky With Diamonds*, *Philadelphia Freedom*, *Island Girl* and *Don't Go Breaking My Heart* (a duet with Kiki Dee) all reached number one on the single charts.

As a chart-topping album artist he was unapproachable: *Don't Shoot Me I'm Only The Piano Player*, *Goodbye Yellow Brick Road*, *Caribou*, *Greatest Hits*, *Captain Fantastic And The Brown Dirt Cowboy*, and *Rock Of The Westies* all rang the bell within days of release – the first four reaching number one in Britain too.

During the last years of the decade, Elton concentrated on his soccer and record company interests, but a historic Moscow concert heralded his return to the boards in 1979.

Olivia Newton-John, no relation, also made waves in 1971. After emigrating to Australia with her family, she won a T.V. talent contest, the prize for which was a trip back to England, where she sang to little avail before being selected by Don Kirshner to become part of Toomorrow, a manufactured film star quartet whom Kirshner hoped would repeat the success of the Monkees. The group was a dismal failure but a romance with Shadow Bruce Welch led to his producing the first of several hit singles by her, a cover of Bob Dylan's *If Not For You*, which crept into the top ten to be followed by *Banks Of The Ohio* later in the year.

Her subsequent progress was erratic but in late 1973 Olivia broke into the American market with *Let Me Be There*, the title of a gold single and a platinum album. *I Honestly Love You* and *Have You Never Been Mellow* were equally successful and snowballing popularity induced her to move permanently to America.

Olivia's earliest *Top Of The Pops* appearances were shared by the year's less durable chart newcomers including Hurricane Smith, Jonathan King's Piglets, Middle Of The Road, the Mixtures, Greyhound, the Pioneers, Dave and Ansell Collins, Ashton Gardener and Dyke and John Kongos.

Gilbert O'Sullivan and the New Seekers began

Above left: Gilbert O'Sullivan early in his career.

Above: Elton John achieved worldwide recognition following his stunning American debut in 1970.

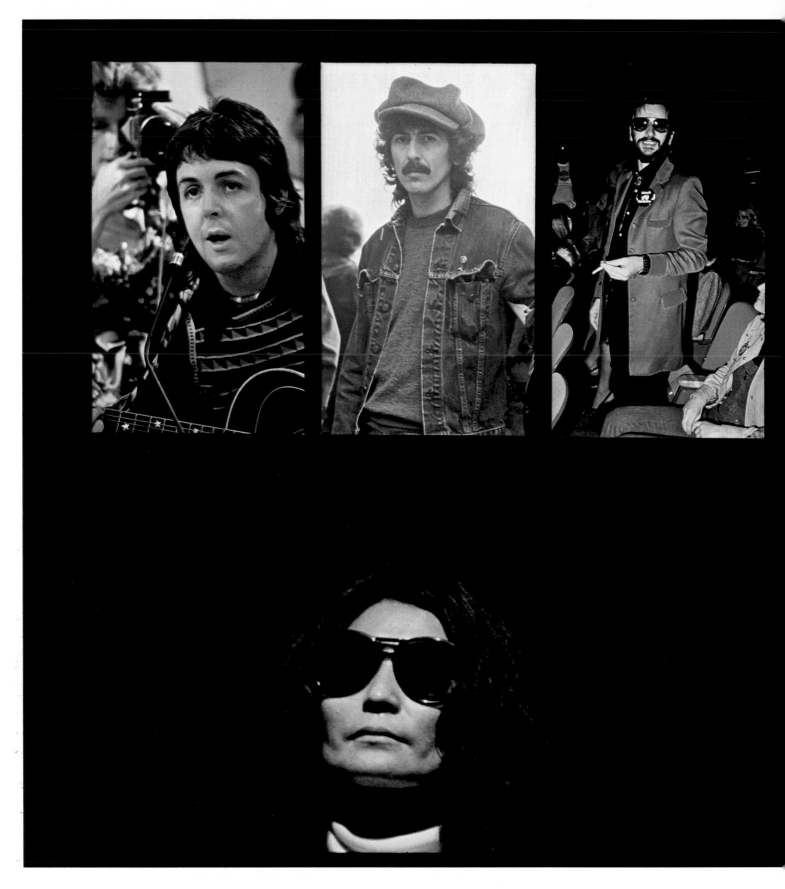

their spells of glory, a group called the Bay City Rollers had an isolated hit with *Keep On Dancing*, Scott English made an impression with *Brandy* (which Barry Manilow was soon to turn into gold as *Mandy*), and Benny Hill unfolded the saga of *Ernie*, the fastest chart-topping milkman in the west.

Soul fans, rooting for buried treasure, unearthed old American hits by the Elgins and the Tams, which took them to number three and number one respectively, and mainstream pop fans fell for Slade and Sweet.

After their first hit, *Get Down And Get With It*, Slade became the most consistent and successful pop group of the early seventies with an unbroken run of a dozen top five singles, including six number ones, the titles of which demonstrate their penchant for bad spelling: *Coz I Luv You*, *Take Me Bak Ome*, *Mama Weer All Crazee Now*, *Cum On Feel The Noize*, *Skweeze Me Pleeze Me* and *Merry Xmas Everybody*.

During this period, Slade also released three chart-topping albums, *Slayed*, *Sladest* and *Old, New,*

Yoko Ono (bottom left) was widely blamed for the break up of the Beatles following John Lennon's increasing involvement with her. Meanwhile, former Beatles (top left to right: Paul McCartney, George Harrison and Ringo Starr) embarked on separate solo projects. John Lennon (bottom right) had already seen chart action on his own account when *Give Peace A Chance*, credited to the Plastic Ono Band, made the top three in 1969.

Sweet (*top left*) were leading glitter and glam rock exponents, whilst Slade (*top right*) employed a more direct rabble-rousing technique.

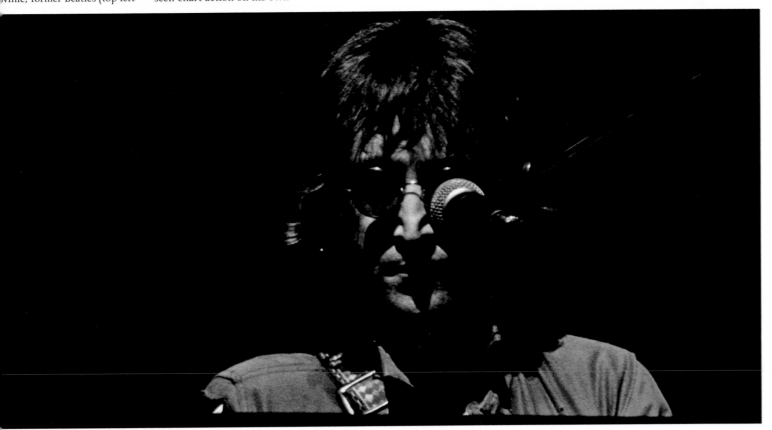

Borrowed, Blue, but their carefully cultivated illiterate/plebeian/cartoon image meant nothing in America and their consequent saturation of the British market began to have an adverse effect by 1975, though they still manage to cling to their headlining status.

Sweet, formed in 1968, released several unsuccessful singles before accepting the guiding hands of master songwriters and producers Nicky Chinn and Mike Chapman who gave them a 'glitter rock' image. The liaison bore fruit immediately as eight catchy and powerful top tenners, including *Co Co, Hell Raiser, Ballroom Blitz* and the number one *Blockbuster*, proved but relationships began to sour in 1974 and the group decided to assert their independence. The international success of *Fox On The Run*, one of their early self-written and produced efforts, augured well but the promise was short lived: by 1976 their overt sexuality and make-up had begun to pall and a sharp decline in fortune reached its nadir when lead singer Brian Conolloy left for a solo career.

'71 the year

Events

25 Jan. A coup d'état by Major-General Idi Amin deposes Ugandan President Milton Obote.

15 Feb. Britain adopts a decimal currency system.

9 Aug. Internment without trial begins in Ulster.

13 Sept. 28 prisoners are killed in a riot at Attica Prison, New York.

24 Sept. 105 Soviet representatives are accused of espionage and expelled from the U.K.

12 Oct. The celebration of 2500 years of Persian Empire began in Persepolis, Iran.

5 Nov. The three editors of *Oz*, an underground magazine, have sentences for obscenity quashed on appeal.

3 Dec. War breaks out between India and Pakistan; Bangla Desh (formerly East Pakistan) becomes independent.

15 Dec. Princess Anne, who had won the European Individual Championship at the Burghley Horse Trials, becomes B.B.C. Sports Personality of the year.

Films of 71

A Clockwork Orange · Fiddler On The Roof · The French Connection · The Go-Between · Klute · The Last Picture Show · Soldier Blue · Sunday Bloody Sunday

Left: a teenybopper.

Right: Malcolm McDowell in *A Clockwork Orange.*

Opposite top: a disco 1971-style.

Opposite below left: General Idi Amin.

Opposite below right: George Harrison and Bob Dylan at the concert for Bangla Desh.

U.S. CHART TOPPERS – WEEKS AT TOP

My Sweet Lord	George Harrison	3
Knock Three Times	Dawn	
One Bad Apple	Osmonds	5
Me And Bobby McGee	Janis Joplin	2
Just My Imagination	Temptations	2
Joy To The World	Three Dog Night	6
Brown Sugar	Rolling Stones	2
Want Ads	Honey Cone	1
It's Too Late	Carole King	5
Indian Reservation	Raiders	1
You've Got A Friend	James Taylor	1
How Can You Mend A Broken Heart	Bee Gees	4
Uncle Albert/Admiral Halsey	Paul and Linda McCartney	1
Go Away Little Girl	Donny Osmond	3
Maggie May	Rod Stewart	5
Gypsies, Tramps And Thieves	Cher	2
Theme From Shaft	Isaac Hayes	2
Family Affair	Sly And The Family Stone	3
Brand New Key	Melanie	1

U.K. CHART TOPPERS – WEEKS AT TOP

I Hear You Knocking	Dave Edmunds	2
Grandad	Clive Dunn	3
My Sweet Lord	George Harrison	5
Baby Jump	Mungo Jerry	2
Hot Love	T. Rex	6
Double Barrell	Dave and Ansell Collins	2
Knock Three Times	Dawn	5
Chirpy Chirpy Cheep Cheep	Middle of the Road	5
Get It On	T. Rex	4
I'm Still Waiting	Diana Ross	3
Hey Girl Don't Bother Me	Tams	3
Maggie May	Rod Stewart	5
Cos I Love You	Slade	4
Ernie	Benny Hill	3

171

While the mainstream pop groups relied on hit singles for continuity, the underground bands pinned their faith on increasing album sales – though Curved Air and East of Eden both saw their horizons widened by freak chart entries. However, newer contenders like Stone the Crows and Home were submerged by the ever-swelling deluge of record releases and the intense competition for dates.

One group who did manage to weather deprivation and despondency were Yes, who struggled for two and a half years before achieving recognition with *The Yes Album* in 1971. Once in motion, however, they rapidly gained momentum, and *Fragile*, featuring their new keyboard player Rick Wakeman and the recently arrived guitarist Steve Howe, winged its way into the top ten on both sides of the Atlantic. *Close To The Edge* followed suit and *Yessongs* (a triple live album), *Tales From Topographic Oceans* and *Going For The One* all flew to number one in Britain, helping Yes to consistent board-sweeping poll awards throughout the mid-seventies.

As overwhelming success became routine, their sense of proportion seemed to become somewhat scrambled and individual members felt obliged to work on solo albums. Predictably they were fairly insubstantial except for Rick Wakeman's, who had temporarily left the group when he recorded his widescreen epics *Journey To The Centre Of The Earth* and *The Myths And Legends Of King Arthur*.

Their convoluted, pseudo-majestic, quasi-mystical music appeared rather anachronistic by

Above: Yes evolved a colourful and complex sound, centred around founder members Jon Anderson (vocals) and Chris Squire (bass).

Below: Fronted by sex-symbol Sonja Kristina, Curved Air

enjoyed brief fame, and had the dubious distinction of being featured on the first modern picture disc.

Opposite top left: Isaac Hayes helped transform soul music into disco in the early 70s.

Top right: Carole King found a new lease of life with the *Tapestry* album.

Opposite: The Osmond Family who hit the chart in several permutations: (inset) Donny and Marie.

Rocky Mountain troubadour John Denver was the year's most successful newcomer.

widely ignored, suddenly bubbled up with the number one single, *Without You*, but Nilsson soon slumped back into a comfortable and fairly successful album career.

The American singles chart was also visited by Lobo, who had his first hit with *Me And You And A Dog Named Boo*, the Nitty Gritty Dirt Band with *Mr. Bojangles*, and Redbone whose only hit was *The Witch Queen Of New Orleans*. On the soul scene, two distinguished artists, Isaac Hayes and Al Green, had the biggest hits of their careers, *Theme From Shaft* and *Let's Stay Together* – both chart toppers – but no significant new acts came to light.

Girls were represented by Lynn Anderson, who reached the top five with *Rose Garden*, Joan Baez, who got as high as number three with *The Night They Drove Old Dixie Down*, the Honey Cone, who made the top with *Want Ads*, and Janis Joplin, who went out with her number one version of *Me And Bobby McGee*.

There was also the discovery of Carly Simon and the return of Carole King. After abortive recordings with Dylan's manager Al Grossman, Carly lay low for four years before re-entering the fray with her eponymous debut album in January 1971. Supported by the hit single *That's The Way I've Always Heard It Should Be*, the album moved slowly towards the top ten, paving the way for a number one single, the classic *You're So Vain*, and the smash album *No Secrets*, which remained in the chart for over a year. After her 1973 marriage to James Taylor her output slowed dramatically but her occasional album releases continue to charm American audiences.

As previously noted, Carole King was primarily a songwriter, working in conjunction with her then husband Gerry Goffin, though she made a brief but stimulating appearance as a singer in 1962, scoring with *It Might As Well Rain Until September*. Nine years later, following a spell of session work and a fruitless attempt to launch a group (the City, which also contained her current husband Charles Larkey), she returned to solo work, striking gold with a number one single, *It's Too Late*. Although her first album, *Writer*, was a comparatively moderate success, the follow-up, *Tapestry*, sold over 13 million. It remained on the chart for over six years, becoming one of the most successful albums ever. Later albums, *Music* and *Wrap Around Joy*, also reached number one, though her subsequent efforts were doomed to languish in the shadow of her major triumph.

The year's most successful new American group was, by several miles, the Osmonds, who climbed out of *The Andy Williams Show* and up the chart with a very convincing Jackson Five rip-off, *One Bad Apple*. It heralded the most comprehensive teenybop market exploitation programme ever seen, as the Osmonds swamped the media with every combination they could devise, including the introduction of Sister Marie and the pre-teen Jimmy (fortunately the final offspring borne by Mrs. Osmond).

Within five years, over 25 Osmond-shaped singles had peppered the British charts, but at least their essentially antiseptic and soulless output provided the perfect excuse for the introduction of punk rock . . .

the late seventies and a growing body of critics were calling Yes dinosaurs, but a group who have remained in the first division for almost ten years can only smile at such denigration.

Constant critical abuse had done little to impair the sustained success of John Deutschendorf, who beat 250 applicants to replace the retiring leader of the Chad Mitchell Trio, a hokum folk group who remained popular across American campuses until 1969. After providing Peter, Paul and Mary with their biggest hit, *Leaving On A Jet Plane*, Duetschendorf, who had long since changed his name to the more American sounding John Denver, embarked on a solo career which blossomed in 1971 with the smash single *Take Me Home Country Roads* and the gold album *Poems And Promises* and peaked three years later when *Sunshine On My Shoulder* and the contagious *Annie's Song* both reached number one.

Denver was by far the biggest star to emerge in America during the year, though for a time it looked as though Harry Nilsson was going to run him close. A simmering fascination, critically regarded but

'72

'American Pie'

Alice Cooper · America · Argent · Jackson Browne · The Chi-Lites · Derek and the Dominoes · Dr. Hook · The Doobie Brothers · The Eagles The Electric Light Orchestra · Roberta Flack · Genesis · Gary Glitter Lindisfarne · Don McLean · The New York Dolls · The O'Jays · Billy Paul Roxy Music · Steely Dan · The Stylistics · 10cc

The terrifying power of television advertising became apparent when K-Tel and Arcade began plugging hit compilation albums during the summer. In Britain, for the rest of the year their albums were missing from the top slot for only two weeks – when Rod Stewart's *Never A Dull Moment* temporarily deposed them in September. Before they arrived, Neil Young and Paul Simon each spent a week heading the list, but Britain's biggest selling (non-T.V.) album was quite a surprise. *Fog On The Tyne* by Lindisfarne hit the chart like a bolt from the blue, remaining at number one for four weeks.

A Newcastle group rooted in folk music, Lindisfarne established themselves on the club circuit soon after signing with Charisma Records in 1970, and their first album *Nicely Out Of Tune*, made a respectable chart showing. However, it was their follow-up, supervised by noted American producer Bob Johnston and propelled by two conterminous smash singles, *Meet Me On The Corner* and *Lady Elanor*, which really put them on the map.

Their third album, *Dingly Dell*, followed its predecessors into the top ten but, containing no hit singles, soon dropped from sight and subsequent internal disputes, aggravated by the release of a solo album by leader Alan Hull, bisected the group. One faction became Jack the Lad, who promised much but delivered little, whilst the other recruited new members to carry on as an uninspired Lindisfarne. The fall of both parties was inevitable.

In 1978, following riotously successful reunion gigs in Newcastle, the original members buried the hatchet and reformed on a permanent basis, reinstating themselves with a hit single, *Run For Home*.

The rumpled, unassuming Lindisfarne were in direct contrast to the year's major trend which was towards 'costume rock' as purveyed by three serious up-market acts – David Bowie, Roxy Music and Genesis – and one tongue-in-cheek down-market act, Gary Glitter.

As his pseudonym suggests, Glitter came on silvered and spangled to the hilt, determined to advertise himself rather better than he had as Paul Raven in the early sixties. Embarrassment prevailed as he waited in the wings, perspiring under cooking foil and wobbling on platform boots, watching his first single hover outside the chart . . . but after four months it began to rise, finally peaking at number two. In fact, *Rock And Roll (Part Two)* was little more than a rather monotonous rhythm riff repeated incessantly below Glitter's grunts, but it rocketed him to instant stardom and giant colour posters were soon gracing the bedrooms of girls a third of his age.

Though his trashy singles were often quite interesting, Glitter was symptomatic of the state of the British singles market, which was plagued by novelty – as chart-dominating items by the Royal Scots Dragoon Guards and Lieutenant Pigeon confirm. More ephemeral frivolity was scattered by Judge Dread and Terry Dactyl and the Dinosaurs, whilst mainstream pop prospered in the hands of Peter Skellern, Lynsey de Paul, Blackfoot Sue and Chicory Tip, whose *Son Of My Father* was one of the year's best sellers.

The Strawbs (*Lay Down*) and Argent (*Hold Your Head Up*) escaped the confines of the withering underground, and *Horse With No Name* laid the foundation for America's long and successful career. Rod Stewart, disguised as Python Lee Jackson, made the top three with *In A Broken Dream* and Eric Clapton, masquerading as Derek and the Dominoes, had his finest moment of glory with the scorching *Layla*. However, the overall paucity of talent led record companies to raid their vaults, as a result of which oldies by the Chiffons, Neil Sedaka, Little Eva, Jeff Beck, Procol Harum, Chris Montez and the Shangri-Las all reached the top twenty.

Jonathan King, in the habit of throwing as much as possible in the general direction of the charts, was delighted to see two of his groups managing to hold on. Nothing was ever heard of the dubious Shag after their first lucky hit, but 10cc turned out to be rather more than the one-hit-wonder suggested by *Donna*, which reached number two towards the end of the year.

In fact, 10cc were music-biz veterans: hit songwriter Graham Gouldman, ex-Mindbender Eric Stewart and songwriters/instrumentalists/ studio whizkids Lol Creme and Kevin Godley. The last three had achieved a modicum of success as Hotlegs, but before meeting King had been unable to secure a recording contract for their new group.

After a string of hits for King's U.K. label and then

Lindisfarne (left to right: Ray Jackson, Alan Hull, Rod Clements, Ray Laidlaw and Simon Cowe) took their name from an island off the north-east coast of England. They were the first group to break out of Newcastle since the Animals.

Mercury, 10cc split up when Creme and Godley left to develop an instrument they'd invented, the Gizmo which is best described as a guitar attachment producing an orchestral effect. Gouldman and Stewart kept the 10cc name, recruited new musicians, and continued making hits like *Things We Do For Love*, *Good Morning Judge* and a third chart topper, *Dreadlock Holiday*, while their erstwhile partners emerged from a long studio silence with the absurdly overstated triple album, *Consequences*, which despite its enormous production cost was a commercial disaster.

By the end of the decade, the Godley/Creme axis had, to a great extent, been forgotten by the fickle record-buying public, and a serious car accident involving Eric Stewart was temporarily preventing any further progress by 10cc . . . but in view of their finest moments having appeared on albums like *The Original Soundtrack* and *How Dare You*, critics were hoping for the eventual reunion of the founder members.

10cc's arrival was concurrent with that of an even more impressive group, the Electric Light Orchestra (E.L.O.), who rose from the ashes of the Move as soon as the latter's final hit, *California Man*, had dropped from the chart. E.L.O.'s initial premise (to which they've since adhered) was to develop the sound originated by the Beatles on *I Am The Walrus*, a track from the *Magical Mystery Tour* project, which featured intriguing string arrangements over a traditional rock rhythm section, but soon after the release of their first album and single, Roy Wood and two others left to start another group, Wizzard.

After masked employees had bolstered the depleted E.L.O. on television shows promoting their hit *10538 Overture*, Jeff Lynne, now the unequivocal leader, and Bev Bevan returned the seven man complement to full strength and began a serious assault on the American market, where, after long, grinding tours, their fourth album, *Eldorado*, went gold in 1975. *Face The Music* took them into the American top ten for the first time and *A New World Record*, which stayed on the chart for over a year, was declared gold on its day of release. By the end of 1977, when *Out Of The Blue* was released, they had become one of the most successful groups in the world – as advance orders in excess of 47 million dollars verified.

Whilst they were primarily known as an album band in the States, E.L.O. were better known for their singles in Britain, where a total of nine, including *Livin' Thing*, *Mr. Blue Sky* and *Sweet Talkin' Woman*, reached the top ten before the start of 1979.

Genesis, on the other hand, experienced the utmost difficulty securing a hit single, though their albums eventually swept them into the first division.

They had originally formed at the exclusive public school, Charterhouse, during the late sixties and had launched their recording career under the aegis of another ex-pupil, the ubiquitous Jonathan King, who produced their debut album, *From Genesis To Revelation*, in 1969. Miserable sales showed the album to be ahead of its time, but despite feeling daunted by the overwhelming success of the similarly motivated King Crimson, they persevered with ill-paid live work until their

Opposite top: The Rolling
Stones, now recording for
their own label, returned to
the top five in 1972 with
Tumbling Dice.

Opposite below: Gary Glitter,
almost unrecognisable in an
off-duty pose.

Above: Public schoolboys
who eschewed careers in
banking, Genesis (left to
right: Steve Hackett, Mike
Rutherford, Tony Banks,
Peter Gabriel and Phil
Collins).

Above right: Manchester
studio magicians 10 cc (left to
right: Eric Stewart, Lol
Creme, Graham Gouldman
and Kevin Godley).

Right: Roxy Music (left to
right: Paul Thompson, Bryan
Ferry, Brian Eno, Phil
Manzanera, Rik Kenton and
Andy Mackay) produced
some of the most com-
pelling and intelligent music
of the early seventies.

efforts won the patronage of Charisma Records.

An increase in morale and better working conditions were not reflected in sales until the release of their third album, *Foxtrot*, in 1972, by which time their theatrical stage act and idiosyncratic material had attracted a huge and devoted following. However, the subsequent departure of star vocalist Peter Gabriel left Genesis in a predicament from which few believed they could extricate themselves.

The crisis was conveniently alleviated when drummer Phil Collins revealed himself to be a fine singer after more than 400 hopefuls had failed the audition, and their next album, *A Trick Of The Tail*, cruised effortlessly into the top three, as did their 1978 offering *And Then There Were Three*. As the title indicates, the group has now been reduced to a core of three, and were augmenting the line-up with session musicians as necessary.

Departed members Gabriel and guitarist Steve Hackett worked hard to establish themselves as solo artistes, while Collins amused himself playing with Brand X during holes in Genesis' schedule. The two remaining members, Mike Rutherford and Tony Banks, both spent 1979 putting together solo albums, and combining with Collins to prepare a new group album for early 1980 release.

In Summer 1971, a penniless Bryan Ferry sat in his council flat and explained that his embryonic group, Roxy Music, was going to make it 'in as civilised a way as possible'. All he wanted was the best management, the best agency, the best record company, and adequate finance. A year later he had secured them all, and a first album *Roxy Music* was in the top ten, while *Virginia Plain* stood at number four in the singles chart.

It was an impressive start, one on which the group capitalised with four top five albums (including a number one in *Stranded*), three top ten singles, and various tours of Europe, America and the Far East, before breaking for an extended sabbatical in mid 1976.

During this four-year success period, several of the group had begun sideline careers, on which they now began to concentrate. Guitarist Phil Manzanera led his own group, 801, Andy Mackay wrote and produced music for television, including for the rabidly received *Rock Follies* series, and Bryan Ferry toured with a new band, as well as releasing a fourth and fifth solo album. Synthesizer player Brian Eno, who had left the group after a personality conflict some years earlier, diversfied widely, gaining respect as a composer, musician, eccentric, patron of the arts, record company proprietor and producer.

Ferry's solo career did nothing to enhance the reputation he'd earned during the first half of the decade and in Summer 1978 he reconvened Roxy Music in a bid to restore his credibility. The move produced the desired effect: an album, *Manifesto*, returned him to the top ten and two smash singles, *Dance Away* and *Angel Eyes*, saw him riding out of the seventies on the crest of a wave.

Like Ferry, David Bowie spent 1971 planning a spectacular entrance. He'd laid low since his *Space Oddity* hit but a union with ambitious manager Tony De Fries secured him a new recording contract and an extremely colourful and somewhat androgynous public image, which soon began to attract attention around the world.

Meanwhile Bowie had formed a band, who, alon with Rick Wakeman, played on his 'comeback album. Popular though it was, the success of *Hunk Dory* was slight compared to that of a second album *The Rise And Fall of Ziggy Stardust And The Spider From Mars*, which really broke down the barrier and showered him with international acclaim *Starman*, from the album, was the first in a lon series of top ten singles including *Jean Genie*, *Life O Mars* and *Sorrow*, a track from his *Pin Ups* album o which Bowie interpreted some of his favourit sixties hits.

Not content with his status as rock superstar, h began to diversify, working as mentor and produce to regenerate the flagging careers of Mott th Hoople, Lou Reed and Iggy Pop, as well as taking hi own music towards uncharted areas. However despite the apparently inaccessible and uncom mercial nature of some of his ideas, albums lik *Young Americans*, *Station To Station* and *Lodge* found his followers in close pursuit and hi charisma undiminished, though the suave an confident late seventies Bowie was in direct contras to the technicolour dreamer of 1972.

Bizarre though it was, Bowie's persona seeme restrained beside American's prime glitter manifes tations, Alice Cooper and the New York Dolls.

Their early R&B-inclined music displayed littl proficiency, but a rave article in *Melody Make* rocketed the Dolls from the back streets of Nev York to the Empire Pool, Wembley where they supported the Faces, who had been impressed by their description as 'subterranean sleazoid flash' Despite their drummer dying from a heroin over dose during their flying visit, the Dolls were able t sign a lucrative recording contract on their retur and this resulted in their first album – which i where the Dolls' troubles really began.

It showed them wearing women's clothes backbrushed bouffants and make-up, and th music, violent, uncontrolled and badly produced alienated many of those who had dared to explor further than the sleeve. A second album, accuratel titled *Too Much Too Soon*, displayed similar weak nesses though the group was reportedly nov excellent on stage, but disenchantment led to rapid deterioration and by the middle of 1975 combination of drink and drug problems ha rendered most of the band incapable of standing up let alone making music.

Lead singer David Johansen subsequently sur faced as a solo act and seems an interesting prospec for the eighties, but the Heartbreakers, forme around guitarist Johnny Thunders and drumme Jerry Nolan, foundered after a career which almos parodied that of the Dolls.

Despite their comparative insignificance in th American rock dream, the Dolls were a majo influence on the British punk pioneers, who dote on their excesses. Conversely, Alice Cooper wa dismissed as an inferior Gary Glitter, though hi status in America was awesome.

Vincent Furnier formed his band in Phoeni Arizona, going through various name change before arriving at Alice Cooper (a name whicl applied to him and the group) and migrating t Hollywood in a vain attempt to secure a recordin

contract. The group were living on the breadline until 1969 when, after seeing them empty a nightclub with their repugnant act, Frank Zappa signed them to his record company, Straight.

Contrary to Zappa's perverse reasoning, their first two albums were resounding failures and Alice Cooper dropped from sight, only to resurface in Detroit a year later. A new record label and a new producer turned the tide and, almost immediately, the hits began to come – starting with *Eighteen* and climaxing, in Summer 1972, with *School's Out*, a top tenner in the States but a number one in Britain, where his singles continued to do better: *Elected*, *Hello Hurray* and *No More Mr. Nice Guy* all reached the top ten.

In America, the group achieved gold albums with *Killer, School's Out, Billion Dollar Babies* and *Muscle Of Love* among others, while their lurid stage act, which at various times involved chickens, snakes, straight jackets, an electric chair and a hanging, continued to provoke the desired revulsion.

After dispensing with his band, who launched an unsuccessful career as the Billion Dollar Babies, Cooper hired top flight session musicians to increase the musicality of his albums and shows, but during the late seventies he mellowed considerably, spending much of his time on the golf course or in residential clinics curing his alcohol problem, the trials of which are recounted on his 1978 album *From The Inside*.

Steely Dan's props were intellectual rather than theatrical and they scored first time round with *Can't Buy A Thrill* – a top twenty album in 1972. The album provided two significant hits, *Do It Again* and *Reeling In The Years*, but their biggest single was *Rikki Don't Lose That Number*, from the follow-up album *Countdown To Ecstasy*.

Their highly sophisticated sound, instrumentally perfect and lyrically obscure, made Steely Dan the

thinking fan's favourite band – but in the middle of the decade the group's prime movers, Donald Fagen and Walter Becker, showed their hatred of touring by coming off the road permanently. This ploy did little to reduce the impact of later albums like *The Royal Scam* and *Aja*, both of which went platinum within weeks of release, but it rendered their backing musicians obsolete.

Two decided to throw in their lot with the Doobie Brothers, who also broke through in 1972 with the single *Listen To The Music* and the album *Toulouse Street*. Despite numerous personnel changes and their relative individual anonymity, the Doobies refined their style and increased their following, selling a total of over 30 million records, and in 1979 they were hotter, commercially, than they'd ever been – though in Britain they continue to mean comparatively little.

The Eagles' 1979 album, *The Long Run*, cruised effortlessly up charts all over the world, indicating that their laid-back country rock had lost none of its early appeal, even though spontaneity appeared to have been replaced by formularised technique. After watching *Eagles* and *Desperado* hover in the middle reaches, they saw *On The Border* carry them into the top twenty for the first time, but their most successful period was 1975-76 when three albums, *One Of These Nights, Greatest Hits* and *Hotel California*, and three singles, *Take It To The Limit*, *Best Of My Love* and *Hotel California* all made number one.

Four experienced musicians from diverse reaches of the States, the Eagles first teamed up as Linda Ronstadt's backing group in Los Angeles. All were excellent singers and songwriters and their potential was recognised by Asylum Records, who flew them to London to record with ace producer Glyn Johns.

In January 1974, guitarist Don Felder made the group a quintet and two years later ex-James Gang and Barnstorm leader Joe Walsh came in to replace Bernie Leadon. Founding bassist Randy Meisner, previously with Poco, was replaced in the Eagles by his replacement in Poco, Tim Schmit, and by late 1977, Glen Frey and Don Henley found themselves the sole survivors of the original group. Leadon's and Meisner's solo sorties left both with egg on their faces but, after viewing the rock world from the top, they seemed to place little importance on commercial success.

Left: David Bowie emerged from hibernation in flamboyant style and contrived to stay one jump ahead of the competition throughout the seventies.

The original Eagles, pictured in England during the recording of their second album (left to right: Bernie Leadon, Don Henley, Glenn Frey and Randy Meisner).

Jackson Browne, a very talented singer/songwriter, furnished the Eagles with their earliest hit, *Take It Easy*. After the excellence of his own first albums went largely ignored, Browne hit paydirt with *Late For The Sky*, which preceded two top five albums, *The Pretender* and *Running On Empty*. Over the years, his songs – for instance *Doctor My Eyes*, *Jamaica*, *These Days* and *Rock Me On The Water* – have provided several other artists with hits, but strangely, his own biggest single success was with one of the few non-original numbers he's recorded, Maurice Williams' *Stay* in 1978.

In 1972's American singles chart the Philadelphia soul sound, which the Delfonics and the Intruders had kept bubbling for four years, suddenly boiled over as producers Thom Bell and Gamble and Huff got into their stride. The former was responsible for hits by the Stylistics (*Betcha By Golly Wow* and *I'm Stone In Love With You*) and the Spinners (*I'll Be Around* and *Could It Be I'm Falling In Love*), while Gamble and Huff furthered the careers of Joe Simon (*Power Of Love*), the O'Jays (*Back Stabbers*), Harold Melvin and the Blue Notes (*If You Don't Know Me By Now*), and the chart-topping Billy Paul (*Me And Mrs. Jones*).

The Chi-Lites, a long established soft soul group from Chicago, broke nationally with *Have You Seen Her* and the number one *Oh Girl*; Bill Withers peaked with the funky *Lean On Me* and *Use Me*, which reached numbers one and two respectively; Beatle cohort Billy Preston made number two with *Outa Space*; and veteran gospel group the Staple Singers came through with the chart topping *I'll Take You There* . . . but the most successful new soul practitioner was Roberta Flack, who stayed at number one for six weeks with her smouldering version of *The First Time Ever I Saw Your Face*, *Where Is The Love*, a duet with Donny Hathaway, went top five and she returned to number one with *Killing Me Softly With His Song* (inspired by a Don McLean performance) and *Feel Like Makin' Love*.

Country singer Mac Davis reached the top with *Baby Don't Get Hooked On Me*, and the aforementioned Don McLean left the folk clubs forever when his epic *American Pie* paved the way for a concert hall and television future.

Dr. Hook, originally a dope-oriented comedy and pathos rock band, began a long and continually evolving chart romance with *Sylvia's Mother*, the first of intermittent top ten entries throughout the decade, but Looking Glass were jilted immediately after a brief chart topping flirtation with *Brandy* and the Raspberries, despite two excellent smashes, *Go All The Way* and *Overnight Sensation*, couldn't stay the pace either.

Two fifties rockers made spectacular though short-lived comebacks – Rick Nelson with *Garden Party*, his biggest hit since 1963, and Chuck Berry with his only number one, the uncharacteristic novelty song *My Ding-A-Ling* – but a sixties R&B drop-out was back to stay.

After leaving Them, Van Morrison had gravitated to New York, where numerous sessions with Bert Berns produced only one hit, *Brown-Eyed Girl*, in 1967. When Berns died, Morrison changed musical direction completely, but his brilliant *Astral Weeks* album, released at the end of 1968, attracted scant attention – though constant critical acclaim subsequently ensured steady sales which eventually won it gold status almost ten years later. Three more albums increased his audience before *St. Dominic's Preview* entered the top twenty in 1972.

Always a shadowy, enigmatic figure, Morrison continued to change pace, direction and location, making fleeting appearances and fascinating albums along the way, but despite his many triumphs, he has never relaxed in his search for something more.

Morrison, however, was an exception: self-satisfaction was beginning to take root in America during 1972 . . .

Top: Jackson Browne, an accomplished songwriter.

Top left: Philly soul superstars the O'Jays.

Centre: Folk singer Don McLean became internationally famous as a result of his smash hit *American Pie*.

Above: Van Morrison's refusal to compromise has ensured his continuing success.

Left: The Doobie Brothers have experienced personnel turbulence, but remain a top attraction.

Opposite above: The New York Dolls.

Opposite right: Alice Cooper.

Opposite far right: Ray Sawyer, with Dr. Hook and the Medicine Show, as they used to be known.

Opposite centre: Roberta Flack.

'72 the year

Events

9 Jan. The ocean liner the Queen Elizabeth is destroyed by fire in Hong Kong harbour.

30 Jan. In Londonderry, 13 civilians are shot by troops on 'Bloody Sunday'.

21 Feb. President Nixon meets Mao Tse-Tung in Peking.

29 Mar. Queen Elizabeth opens the treasures of Tutenkhamun exhibition at the British Museum.

15 May Governor Wallace of Alabama is crippled in an assassination attempt.

12 Aug. The last U.S. combat troops leave Vietnam.

4 Sept. Mark Spitz wins a record seven gold medals at the Olympic Games.

5 Sept. Palestinian terrorists kill Israeli Olympic team-members.

10 Oct. Sir John Betjemen becomes Poet Laureate.

7 Nov. Nixon defeats McGovern in a landslide victory and remains President.

Films of 72

Cabaret · Deliverance · Dirty Harry · Fritz The Cat · The Godfather · The Harder They Come · Straw Dogs · What's Up Doc?

Opposite top left: Liza Minnelli and Joel Grey in *Cabaret.*

Opposite top right: Marlon Brando in *The Godfather.*

Opposite below: Troops in Ulster.

U.S. CHART TOPPERS – WEEKS AT TOP

Brand New Key	Melanie
American Pie	Don McLean
Let's Stay Together	Al Green
Without You	Nilsson
Heart Of Gold	Neil Young
A Horse With No Name	America
The First Time Ever I Saw Your Face	Roberta Flack
Oh Girl	Chi-Lites
I'll Take You There	Staple Singers
The Candy Man	Sammy Davis Jr.
Song Sung Blue	Neil Diamond
Lean On Me	Bill Withers
Alone Again (Naturally)	Gilbert O'Sullivan
Brandy	Looking Glass
Black And White	Three Dog Night
Baby Don't Get Hooked On Me	Mac Davis
Ben	Michael Jackson
My Ding-A-Ling	Chuck Berry
I Can See Clearly Now	Johnny Nash
Papa Was A Rolling Stone	Temptations
I Am Woman	Helen Reddy
Me And Mrs. Jones	Billy Paul

U.K. CHART TOPPERS – WEEKS AT TOP

Ernie	Benny Hill
I'd Like To Teach The World To Sing	New Seekers
Telegram Sam	T. Rex
Son Of My Father	Chicory Tip
Without You	Nilsson
Amazing Grace	Royal Scots Dragoon Band
Metal Guru	T. Rex
Vincent	Don McLean
Take Me Bak Ome	Slade
Puppy Love	Donny Osmond
School's Out	Alice Cooper
You Wear It Well	Rod Stewart
Mama Weer All Crazee Now	Slade
How Can I Be Sure?	David Cassidy
Mouldy Old Dough	Lieutenant Pigeon
Clair	Gilbert O'Sullivan
My Ding-A-Ling	Chuck Berry
Long Haired Lover From Liverpool	Little Jimmy Osmond

'73

'Goodbye Yellow Brick Road'

Jim Croce · David Essex · Loggins and Messina · Lynyrd Skynyrd · Mud
Mike Oldfield · Suzi Quatro · Queen · Lou Reed · Todd Rundgren
Status Quo · Thin Lizzy · Wizzard

1973 was undoubtedly the dullest year of the decade, especially in America, where a stodgy complacency, which would effectively stifle most rock development for the rest of the decade, was already setting in. Innovation was out; 'more of the same' was in.

Americans appeared to be more interested in sonic perfection – albums which would sound good on their expensive stereo systems – than in musical excitement – and rock music was becoming progressively blander as a result. This climate was exactly suited to the rise of Loggins and Messina, an increasingly unobtrusive pair of country rockers (Messina had been in the Buffalo Springfield and Poco) whose early spirit soon slipped towards unremitting tedium. Their biggest single, *Your Mama Don't Dance*, a top five hit in 1973, preceded a stream of gold albums which dried up only when the partnership dissolved four years later.

The year's most successful American single was Dawn's *Tie A Yellow Ribbon Round The Old Oak Tree*, closely followed by *Bad Bad Leroy Brown* by the promising Jim Croce, whose plane crash death in September didn't prevent *Time In A Bottle* from reinstating his name at the top of the chart around Christmas time.

Other newcomers to the American singles chart were Stories, who reached number one with their cover of Hot Chocolate's *Brother Louie*, Albert Hammond, a transplanted Londoner who broke through with *It Never Rains In Southern California*, Seals and Crofts, who had two top tenners in *Summer Breeze* and *Diamond Girl*, and Johnny's brother Edgar Winter, who had a massive hit with *Frankenstein*.

Dr. John, also known as hot session man Mac Rebennack, found himself among the hits with *Right Place Wrong Time*, and sixties favourites the Isley Brothers stormed back to prominence with *That Lady*.

Another soul group, the Detroit Spinners made it on both sides of the Atlantic with *Could It Be I'm Falling In Love*, whilst their crosstown rivals the Detroit Emeralds enjoyed far greater popularity in Britain where *Feel The Need In Me* reached number four.

With a style ranging from the most casual to a theatricality bordering on decadence, former Velvet Underground star Lou Reed made an impressive return. *Walk On The Wild Side*, a smash single produced by David Bowie, prepared the way for several big selling albums, including *Transformer* and *Sally Can't Dance*, but as his works became more bizarre his following dwindled to cult level – even though his outrageous public image continued to command considerable press coverage.

The only other American male star to surface was Todd Rundgren, a graduate of blues (Woody's Truck Stop) and psychedelia (The Nazz) who quit group life to concentrate on producing and engineering. However, having quickly acquired a reputation in that field he returned to the road with Runt, an early seventies band who reached the top twenty with *We Gotta Get You A Woman*.

By 1973, he had virtually disbanded Runt and was making albums like *Something/Anything* and *A Wizard, A True Star*, which, as well as displaying his writing and singing skills, showcased his precocious multi-instrumental talents, but abundant critical praise was not reflected in sales. A desire to return to touring induced him to form Utopia, but their infrequent appearances, both live and on record, left adequate time for Rundgren to develop his career as a producer – and artists as diverse as Meatloaf, Steve Hillage, Tom Robinson, Grand Funk Railroad, and Hall and Oates have all benefited from his expertise.

Among 1973's new groups, only Lynyrd Skynyrd showed any enduring quality. Five of the group had been at school together in Florida (while the remaining member, Ed King, had seen flickering fame in the Strawberry Alarm Clock), but it was in the bars around Atlanta Georgia that they worked up their R&B-slanted style.

Their first album, released on Sounds of the South – a label floated by their discoverer Al Kooper, was an immediate success, particularly after the group had been exposed to huge audiences supporting the Who on a nationwide American tour, and by 1977 they had enjoyed several top twenty albums including *Gimme Back My Bullets*, *One More For The Road* and *Street Survivors*. Their aggressive and very loud stage show, fronted by vocalist Ronnie Van Zant, became extremely popular – the high points

Opposite: Still a chart regular in the eighties, Detroit-born Suzi Quatro rocked her way to the top in '73 under the direction of Mickie Most.

Opposite above: The ever-enigmatic 'Godfather of Punk', Lou Reed.

Below: A wizard, a true star? The multi-faceted Todd Rundgren.

Bottom: The first publicity shot of the ill-fated Lynyrd Skynyrd.

'73 the year

Events

1 Jan. Britain becomes a member of the E.E.C.

30 Jan. Liddy and McGord are found guilty of attempting to spy on Democratic headquarters in the Watergate building.

27 Feb. Wounded Knee, South Dakota is occupied for 70 days by the American Indian Movement in protest at federal treatment of Indians.

26 May An Icelandic gunboat shells a British trawler, beginning the 'cod war'.

11 Sept. A military coup in Chile overthrows the left-wing government of President Allende, who dies in the fighting.

20 Sept. Billie Jean King defeats Bobby Riggs in a $100,000 tennis match billed as 'the battle of the sexes'.

11 Oct. The Yom Kippur War begins.

16 Oct. Henry Kissinger receives the Nobel Peace Prize.

14 Nov. Princess Anne and Mark Phillips are married in Westminster Abbey.

17 Dec. Arab terrorists kill 31 at Rome airport.

Films of 73

American Graffiti · Day Of The Jackal · Live And Let Die · Mean Streets · Oh Lucky Man · Paper Moon · Pat Garret And Billy The Kid · That'll Be The Day

Below: Israeli tanks on the Golan Heights. *Opposite bottom:* Cambodian refugees.

U.S. CHART TOPPERS – WEEKS AT TOP

Me And Mrs. Jones	Billy Paul	1
You're So Vain	Carly Simon	3
Superstition	Stevie Wonder	1
Crocodile Rock	Elton John	3
Killing Me Softly With His Song	Roberta Flack	5
Love Train	O'Jays	1
The Night The Lights Went Out In Georgia	Vicki Lawrence	1
Tie A Yellow Ribbon	Tony Orlando and Dawn	4
You Are The Sunshine Of My Life	Stevie Wonder	1
Frankenstein	Edgar Winter	1
My Love	Paul McCartney and Wings	3
Give Me Love	George Harrison	1
Will It Go Round In Circles	Billy Preston	2
Bad Bad Leroy Brown	Jim Croce	2
The Morning After	Maureen McGovern	2
Touch Me In The Morning	Diana Ross	1
Brother Louie	Stories	2
Let's Get It On	Marvin Gaye	2
Delta Dawn	Helen Reddy	1
We're An American Band	Grand Funk	1
Half Breed	Cher	2
Angie	Rolling Stones	1
Midnight Train To Georgia	Gladys Knight and the Pips	2
Keep On Truckin'	Eddie Kendricks	2
Photograph	Ringo	1
Top Of The World	Carpenters	2
The Most Beautiful Girl	Charlie Rich	2
Time In A Bottle	Jim Croce	1

U.K. CHART TOPPERS – WEEKS AT TOP

Long Haired Lover From Liverpool	Little Jimmy Osmond	4
Blockbuster	Sweet	5
Cum On Feel The Noize	Slade	4
Twelfth Of Never	Donny Osmond	1
Get Down	Gilbert O'Sullivan	2
Tie A Yellow Ribbon	Tony Orlando and Dawn	4
See My Baby Jive	Wizzard	4
Can The Can	Suzi Quatro	1
Rubber Bullets	10 cc	1
Skweeze Me Pleeze Me	Slade	3
Welcome Home	Peters and Lee	1
I'm The Leader Of The Gang	Gary Glitter	4
Young Love	Donny Osmond	4
Angel Fingers	Wizzard	1
Eye Level	Simon Park Orchestra	4
Day Dreamer	David Cassidy	3
I Love You Love Me Love	Gary Glitter	4
Merry Xmas Everybody	Slade	2

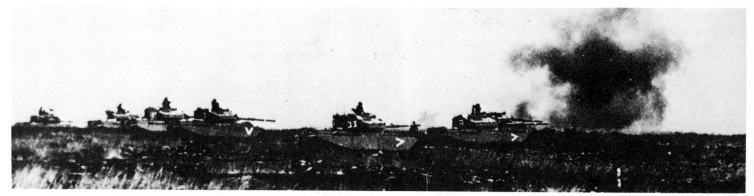

Above: Multi-instrumentalist Mike Oldfield produced the year's most unexpected best seller, *Tubular Bells.*

Far left: Who star Pete Townshend supports Eric Clapton on his celebrated comeback concert at London' Rainbow Theatre.

Left: The outrageous Freddie Mercury, lead singer with Queen.

Below: Status Quo (left to right: Rick Parfitt, Francis Rossi, John Coghlan and Alan Lancaster), back on top after several years in the wilderness.

being their single hit *Sweet Home Alabama* and their triple lead guitar tour de force *Free Bird* – and there was little doubt that Lynyrd Skynyrd were on the way to becoming one of the biggest groups in the world. However, their promising career was tragically ended when their tour plane crashed in late 1977, killing Van Zant and guitarist Steve Gaines and his sister Cassie.

The only female newcomer to make any headway in America was Bette Midler, who worked hard to put show business back into rock, but Detroit-born Suzi Quatro was blowing up a storm in England, where she was one of several new stars jousting with Peters and Lee and Barry Blue to brighten up the singles chart.

A dynamic personality, the leather-clad bass-playing Ms. Quatro gave vivid performances of songs specially written for her by the Chinn and Chapman team: in 1973, *Can The Can* reached number one and *48 Crash* number three, while the following year *Devil Gate Drive* returned her to the top and *The Wild One* to number seven. Though still a sporadic chart visitor during the late seventies, she added a second string to her bow by becoming a television actress, appearing as a regular on *Happy Days.*

Another Chinnichap act was Mud, whose top twenty debut, *Crazy,* heralded a four year singles reign featuring three chart toppers: *Tiger Feet, Lonely This Christmas* and *Oh Boy.* After 15 hits, they divided and fell, though lead singer Les Gray subsequently found regular employment on the revival of Jack Good's *Oh Boy* television series.

Equally bouncy but rather more sinister than Mud were Thin Lizzy, a Dublin trio who re-based in London to crack the singles market with *Whiskey In The Jar,* an uncharacteristic piece of folk-rock which provided them with their first and last hit before *The Boys Are Back In Town* revitalised their flagging spirits in 1976.

Led by their charismatic singing bassist Phil Lynott, Lizzy then proceeded to cut a bloody swath up the album charts, scoring heavily with *Jailbreak,* which remained in the list for nearly a year, *Johnny The Fox, Bad Reputation,* and their first number one, *Live And Dangerous,* a double album of awesome

Left: Alvin Stardust strikes a menacing pose.

Opposite top left: The 1979 edition of Thin Lizzy (left to right: Phil Lynott, Gary Moore, Scott Gorham and Brian Downey).

Opposite top right: After stage and screen success, David Essex became a fully fledged pop star when *Rock On* made the top three in the summer of 1973.

Opposite below: The constantly inventive Roy Wood left the Move and E.L.O. to start Wizzard.

power. Despite several traumatic personnel changes (inevitably involving lead guitarists), the group fought its way to the top, and at the end of the decade Lizzy were one of the five biggest groups in Britain, though their continued failure to break through in America was a cause of much puzzlement and perplexity.

Queen, on the other hand, succeeded first in America, where they were among the best sellers months before achieving significant results at home. The group formed from the remnants of a minor league outfit called Smile, among whose members were guitarist Brian May and drummer Roger Meadows-Taylor, both of whom had forsaken specialist education, May in astronomy and Taylor in dentistry. Recruiting singing clothes-designer Freddie Mercury and electronics graduate turned bassist John Deacon, they struck again as Queen, espousing the current fashion for glitter rock (or 'glam rock' as it had become known by this time) but also embracing heavy metal – though with a great deal more subtlety and complexity than most of their competitors.

Their first two albums sold only moderately in Britain, where they were initially regarded with suspicion – their style of music, clashing with Mercury's onstage prancing, tending to drop them between two stools – but audiences eventually caught up with their consistently inventive output and *Killer Queen* followed *Seven Seas Of Rye* into the top ten, attracting concurrent album interest which belatedly put *Queen II* and the succeeding *Sheer Heart Attack* into the top five.

Their fourth album, *A Night At The Opera*, released in late 1975, became their first chart topper but it was a simultaneous single release, *Bohemian Rhapsody*, which really catapulted Queen into the superstar league – outselling any other British release and cruising the U.S. top hundred for six months. It remains one of the most adventurous singles made during the seventies and though they've been unable to come up with anything of similar stature, Queen have managed to stay on top ever since, outliving most of their new wave detractors and straddling recent chart successes to ride into the eighties a major force.

The same holds true for Status Quo, who found a new lease of life in 1973. After two pseudo-psychedelic hits in 1968, they had watched their popularity deteriorate alarmingly, although they did manage a couple of hits during 1970, one of which, *Down The Dustpipe*, is remembered as a classic.

Around this time, the band decided on a complete change in approach, both musically and visually, replacing their Carnaby Street threads with omnipresent blue denim and their slightly arty songs with heads-down boogie. Slowly, the music industry began to realise it had been wrong to write Quo off, and a triumphant set at the 1972 Reading Festival (the only British festival, by the way, to survive the seventies) finally convinced the doubters.

In 1973, following the acquisition of a new recording contract, they revealed the strength of their new style by releasing three top twenty singles, and two top five albums, the second of which, *Hello*, flew to number one. Since then, they have rarely been absent from charts all around the world – except in America, where audiences seem particularly resistent to the Quo recipe of boogying until the drop. If they remain together until 1982, the band will be able to celebrate their twentieth anniversary – a great rarity in the ephemeral world of rock.

Roy Wood was another whose career received new impetus in 1973. Having established himself as leader of the Move, he elected to drop out of his next project, the Electric Light Orchestra, leaving Jeff Lynne to wield the baton while he formed an excellent Birmingham-based eight piece called Wizzard.

Stage shows were characterised by lunacy, wild costumes and greasepaint, whilst records reflected Wood's current passion for the works of Phil Spector, whose 'wall of sound' technique he employed on the group's six top tenners – including two brilliant number ones, *See My Baby Jive* and *Angel Fingers*.

During the same period, 1973-74, Wood also released four smaller hits under his own name and was active as a songwriter (providing two songs recorded by Elvis Presley), a session musician (playing on a Beach Boys album, among others), and

a producer . . . but this enormous workload eventually got the better of him. When Wizzard folded, early in 1975, he kept a fairly low profile until 1979 when he re-emerged as a solo artist on the newly formed Automatic label – but it remains to be seen whether he will regain the inspiration which created so many rock milestones during the late sixties and early seventies.

No other British group made a lasting impression though Stealers Wheel, containing Gerry Rafferty had a sizeable hit with *Stuck In The Middle With You* and Nazareth began an intermittent chart association with *Broken Down Angel*. Clifford T. Ward was among the solo acts to enter the arena but his first hit, *Gaye*, proved to be his biggest. Alvin Stardust, however, was to be around for a little longer.

Following in the footsteps of Gary Glitter, sixties has-been Shane Fenton remodelled himself for seventies consumption – renaming himself Alvin Stardust and coming on as a black leather glam-rocker.

For two years he was a big star in Britain, reaching the top twenty 6 times with such catchy candyfloss confections as *My Coo-Ca-Choo*, *Jealous Mind* and *You You You*, but following the termination of his partnership with songwriter/producer Peter Shelley he disappeared as quickly as he'd arrived.

One of the brightest new stars was David Essex, the cockney singer who rose to fame in the lead of the London production of *Godspell* and won great acclaim for his portrayal of the searching teenager in *That'll Be The Day*. After numerous totally unsuccessful singles, he had teamed up with American songwriter/arranger/producer/musician Jeff Wayne to create a series of singles which encompassed the requirements of teenybop audiences (Essex possessed all the physical attributes to reduce teenage girls to uncontrollable screaming), the mums and dads (he was wholesome and matey), and the more serious record buyers who wanted a bit of ingenuity in their music.

Hits like *Rock On*, *Lamplight*, *Gonna Make You A Star*, *Stardust* and *Rollin' Stone* established him as one of the hottest properties in the business, but after a second number one, *Hold Me Close*, his chart success began to wane – even though his concert appearances continued to provoke hysteria.

In 1977, Essex decided to return to the theatre, attracting much praise for his performance as Che Guevara in the smash musical *Evita*.

The rock musicals *Godspell* and *Jesus Christ Superstar* both appeared as films during 1973, and the year's most successful album (seven weeks at the top) was a spin off from *That'll Be The Day* – a double album of old hits from the fifties.

The year's surprise album hit was *Tubular Bells*, an instrumental work of symphonic proportions put together by Mike Oldfield, a little-known guitarist who overdubbed practically all the musical parts himself, a practice he continued on subsequent releases including *Hergest Ridge*, *Ommadawn* and *Incantations*. *Tubular Bells*, which was turned down by most major companies before being accepted by the newly founded Virgin label, sold well over five million copies – transforming Oldfield from obscure backing musician into an overnight star.

David Essex, still a sucker for the fun fair.

'74

'When Will I See You Again'

Abba · Bachman Turner Overdrive · Bad Company · Bay City Rollers
Brownsville Station · Cockney Rebel · Ronnie Lane · Gordon Lightfoot
George McCrae · Ted Nugent · Linda Ronstadt · The Rubettes · Leo Sayer
Showaddywaddy · Sparks · Billy Swan · Three Degrees · Barry White
The Wombles

1974 saw the continuing chart dominance of teeny-bop music, especially in Britain. Established artists like Mud, Suzi Quatro, Gary Glitter and Alvin Stardust all enjoyed chart toppers during the year, but their position was challenged by several similarly motivated newcomers – most notably the Wombles and the Bay City Rollers.

Bogus groups were nothing new: the cartoon strip Archies had topped charts all over the world in 1969 and several of Jonathan King's bands were merely figments of his rampant imagination ... but for an act which didn't exist, the Wombles surpassed anything else in the field.

The theme music for the Wombles, furry puppets in a B.B.C. children's series, was composed by Mike Batt, and soon *The Wombling Song* became the first of six top twenty singles within 20 months. At the end of 1975, Batt began an independent career, but seemed typecast as 'the man behind the Wombles' even though he composed and produced Art Garfunkel's massive 1979 hit *Bright Eyes* as part of his score for the film *Watership Down*.

The Bay City Rollers had been trying to establish themselves beyond Edinburgh since the turn of the decade but, though they charted briefly in 1971 (with the Jonathan King-produced *Keep On Dancin'*), it wasn't until 1974 that they began to pull the mantles from Bolan, Cassidy and the Osmonds.

In the meantime, the original group had undergone a transformation under the direction of their astute manager Tom Paton: new members, selected mainly for their teen appeal, were drafted in; tartan was employed liberally in the creation of an easily identifiable image; appropriate writers and producers were brought in, and a huge publicity campaign was set in motion. As a result, the group rode nine singles into the top five between 1974 and 1976, becoming the principal teenybop idols during that time and attracting teen worship reminiscent of Beatlemania.

In Britain, they peaked during 1975, when *Bye Bye Baby* and *Give A Little Love* spent a total of nine weeks at the head of the chart and two albums, *Rollin'* and *Once Upon A Star*, went platinum but by 1977 the group had more or less forsaken their homeland to concentrate on the more lucrative Japanese and American markets, which they conquered with consummate ease.

By the end of that year, however, further personnel changes and increasing internal friction led to the bubble bursting: the hits dried up and the posters came off the walls.

While the Rollers basked in megafame, more deserving acts struggled to survive – though many of 1974's hits were either one-hit wonders or novelties: *Kung Fu Fighting* by Carl Douglas, *Everything I Own* by Ken Boothe, *I Get A Kick Out Of You* by Gary Shearston and *Costafine Town* by Splinter.

A public thirst for catchy pop ditties saw the speedy rise and fall of several groups including Paper Lace (*Billy Don't Be A Hero* and *The Night Chicago Died*), Kenny (*The Bump* and *Fancy Pants*), Pilot (*Magic* and *January*) and the Rubettes (who followed their chart-topping debut *Sugar Baby Love* with a couple of classic pop discs, *Juke Box Jive* and *I Can Do It*).

Rather more successful were Sparks, an Anglo-American group led by the Mael brothers from Los Angeles, and Showaddywaddy, a rock'n'roll revival outfit from Leicester, who burned up the charts after winning a television talent show.

Sparks' first hit, *This Town Ain't Big Enough For The Both Of Us*, was their biggest, reaching number two in May 1974, but they remained popular until their temporary dissolution at the end of 1975. After several tentative stabs, they re-established themselves with *Beat The Clock*, the biggest of three hits from their Giorgio Moroder-produced album, *Number One In Heaven*, in 1979.

After their debut, *Hey Rock And Roll*, Showaddywaddy went from strength to strength. With a musical style and image derived from the fifties, they went on to achieve total singles sales in excess of six million, whilst both their *Greatest Hits* albums were certified platinum. Amongst their 15 hits were re-recordings of Eddie Cochran's *Three Steps To Heaven*, the Kalin Twins' *When* and Curtis Lee's *Under The Moon Of Love*, which took them to number one at the end of 1976.

Though the majority of their fans are totally unfamiliar with the names of the musicians comprising Showaddywaddy, the same could not be said of

A studio creation, the Rubettes were unable to capitalise on their early hit single streak.

Bad Company, a supergroup formed by Paul Rodgers and Simon Kirke from Free, Mick Ralphs from Mott the Hoople and Boz Burrell from King Crimson. Their first eponymous album and its accompanying single, *Can't Get Enough Of Your Love*, were huge hits in America, where the group (who quickly became British tax exiles) predictably achieved their greatest success. Subsequent albums, *Straight Shooter* and *Run With The Pack*, made the top five on both sides of the Atlantic but after the less successful *Burnin' Sky* they remained inactive for two years.

Desolation Angels, their 1979 comeback album, made the top three in America but it was by far their least popular album in Britain where their formularised, riffy music had come to be regarded as somewhat irrelevant.

On the solo front, ex-Face Ronnie Lane reached the charts with *How Come*, whilst former frontmen Leo Sayer and Steve Harley left their respective groups, Patches and Cockney Rebel, to make it on their own.

Sayer's first album, *Silverbird*, and the concurrent single, *The Show Must Go On*, both reached number two, paving the way for ten further hit singles, the most popular of which was *When I Need*

ou, an early 1977 number one, and six more top ten albums.

His initial dramatic rise to fame, assisted by songwriting partner David Courtney and manager Adam Faith, was due not only to the quality of the material, but also to a highly theatrical image and stage act, which involved costume changes and mime. As the seventies progressed, however, he became less dependent on props and allowed his increasingly sophisticated songs to be judged on their own merits.

Whilst Leo Sayer enjoyed a smooth ride through the last half of the decade, Steve Harley chose a considerably bumpier route, leading him to a position where he faces the eighties with some trepidation.

Cockney Rebel, his adventurous and lavishly promoted group had become well-known on the club circuit before *Judy Teen* and *Mr. Soft* propelled them into the top ten, but Harley's increasing dominance resulted in their disbanding at the peak of their popularity. Resurfacing immediately, fronting a completely different group made up of experienced session musicians, Harley flew into the top three with his album *The Best Years Of Our Lives* and to number one in the single charts with *Make Me Smile*.

After a number of less successful ventures, however, he dropped from view, his subsequent comeback attempts being hampered by his somewhat immodest view of his relative merit.

The European scene, rarely relevant outside its own geographical area, seemed to be unusually active during 1974, with Finland (Tasavallan Presidenti), France (Magma), Italy (PFM), and Germany (Faust, Amon Duul, Tangerine Dream and Can) all producing internationally successful album acts. However, it was Holland which, for the second year running, fostered the biggest singles group. In 1973, Focus had impressed Britain and America with *Sylvia* and *Hocus Pocus*, while the following year, Golden Earring enjoyed brief chart activity with *Radar Love*.

The Eurovision Song Contest, usually an abysmally banal affair, was sparkled up by the presence of the Swedish entry, Abba, whose *Waterloo* racked up the winning vote. It was a decisive victory in a career which during the next few years would lead them to become their country's second leading export, outstripped only by the international success of Volvo cars.

Initially compared to the Mamas and the Papas because of their cleverly crafted, classy pop recordings and their two males/two females composition, Abba proved to be somewhat more durable – quickly achieving world superstardom and maintaining it. *S.O.S.* followed *Waterloo* into the top ten in Britain, since when *Mamma Mia*, *Fernando*, *Dancing Queen*, *Knowing Me Knowing You*, *The Name Of The Game* and *Take A Chance On Me* have all reached the top – a total surpassed only by Elvis Presley, Cliff Richard, the Beatles and the Rolling Stones.

Abba's incredible consistency was based on the songwriting skills of the two males, Bjorn Ulvaeus and Benny Andersson, the visual appeal of their wives, Agnetha and Anni-Frid respectively, and the business experience of Stig Anderson, who not only masterminded their rise but had a hand in the composition of many of their hits.

Opposite above left:
Leo Sayer, seen here in his breakthrough clown guise, first attracted attention when Roger Daltry recorded an entire album of Sayer's compositions in 1973.

Opposite below left:
The success of Wombles' records sparked off not only a craze, but a vast industry which saw the market saturated with Womble merchandising.

Opposite above right:
The Bay City Rollers display their Tartan trim trademark.

Opposite below right:
Showaddywaddy, one of the most consistent British hit-makers of the latter half of the seventies.

Above: Ron (left) and Russell Mael, better known as Sparks, left America to break into the charts in Britain.

Far left: Bad Company (left to right: Mick Ralphs, Paul Rodgers, Simon Kirke and Boz Burrell).

Left: Steve Harley sprang to national fame fronting Cockney Rebel.

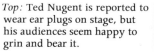

Top: Ted Nugent is reported to wear ear plugs on stage, but his audiences seem happy to grin and bear it.

Above: Abba (left to right: Bjorn Ulvaeus, Agnetha Faltskog, Anni-Frid Lyngstad and Benny Andersson).

Foxy Linda Ronstadt. One of her early seventies backing bands departed to become the Eagles.

Barry White grunted and groaned his way into the dreams of the everyday housewife.

Opposite top: His drug problems behind him, Eric Clapton returned to international prominence with a succession of hit records.

Opposite below: Superstar convention at the premiere of *Born To Boogie* – left to right: Elton John (cameo role), Marc Bolan (star) and Ringo Starr (director).

Strangely, though enormously successful in every other country of the Western world, Abba have yet to conquer America, where *Waterloo*, which reached number six, was their biggest hit until *Dancing Queen* became their only number one in 1977.

The biggest thing to come out of America during 1974 was the corpulent Barry White, a prime mover in the conversion of soul into disco music. His speciality was the intonation of sexually oriented lyrics, half spoken, half sung, to a highly danceable backing and this recipe provided him with a string of smashes including *Can't Get Enough Of Your Love Babe* and *You're My First My Last My Everything*.

The Three Degrees, a soul group of considerable sophistication, broke internationally with *When Will I See You Again* and George McCrae made number one with *Rock Your Baby*, his first and last significant hit. Also in a soul vein, MFSB scored with *TSOP*, Kool and the Gang with *Jungle Boogie*, the Hues Corporation with *Rock The Boat* and the Commodores with *Machine Gun*.

Two new mainstream rock groups came to the fore: Brownsville Station, from Michigan, found mass acceptance with *Smokin' In The Boys' Room* and the Bachman Turner Overdrive, descendants of the Canadian band Guess Who, had a smash with the stuttering *You Ain't Seen Nothing Yet*. Other massive hit singles were *Rock Me Gently* by Andy Kim, *Spiders And Snakes* by Jim Stafford, *Seasons In The Sun* by Terry Jacks, and *I Can't Help* by Billy Swan – but none of the four was able to deliver a follow-up of equal impact.

America's major new white act was Linda Ronstadt, an extremely attractive part-Mexican country singer who had actually been trying to break into the big time since the mid-sixties. Her first group, a folk-oriented trio called the Stone Poneys had an isolated top twenty hit with *Different Drum* in 1967, but her subsequent solo career went nowhere fast until a final contract-fulfilling album for Capitol, *Heart Like A Wheel*, spawned a pair of massive singles, *You're No Good* and *When Will I Be Loved* – and from a position of apparent hopelessness, Linda was suddenly transformed into the top-selling female artist in America.

Her American success continued unabated with top ten albums like *Prisoner In Disguise*, *Greatest Hits*, *Hasten Down The Wind* and the chart-topping *Simple Dreams*, all of which achieved platinum status, and top ten singles like *Blue Bayou* and *It's So Easy*. By the end of the decade, however, Linda appeared to be rather more interested in her romantic attachment to Jerry Brown, Governor of California and prospective President of the United States, than in trying to further her musical career.

Canadian folk singer Gordon Lightfoot also broke through in 1974 after knocking on the door for several years. Many of his compositions, most notably *For Lovin' Me* and *Early Morning Rain*, had been recorded successfully by others and he himself had made the top five with *If You Could Read My Mind* three years earlier – but it was his classic number one, *Sundown*, which really put him on the map.

The Pointer Sisters, Phoebe Snow, Minnie Ripperton, Herbie Hancock, the Average White Band, Maria Muldaur and Ry Cooder all impressed discriminating American record buyers while Ted Nugent was among those catering for the heavy metal market.

Nugent had previously led Detroit powerhouse band the Amboy Dukes, but after a couple of minor hits, several moderately successful albums and innumerable personnel changes, he went solo. Under the motto 'if it's too loud, you're too old', he wreaked havoc on stages across the world, forcing half a dozen albums into the charts during the next few years.

Eric Clapton came back with a smash single, *I Shot The Sheriff*, an equally successful album *461 Ocean Boulevard*, and a new band, whilst fifties R&B pioneers the Drifters made an unlikely return with *Kissing In The Back Row Of The Movies*. Only lead singer Johnny Moore had any connection with the earlier group, which had seen many members come and go over the years, and their renaissance was restricted to Britain, where they based their activities, but during 1974-75, the Drifters enjoyed a constant stream of hits and more live work than they'd seen in the previous 10 years.

In both Britain and America, record sales continued to increase, despite a vinyl shortage created by escalating oil prices, but a slump was predicted for the future as record prices rose.

'74 the year

Events

4 Jan. President Nixon refuses to comply with subpoenas demanding the 'White House tapes'.

4 Feb. Patti Hearst is kidnapped by the Symbionese Liberation Army.

13 Feb. The U.S.S.R. deports Solzhenitsyn; in December he claims the Nobel Prize awarded to him in 1970.

28 Feb. Labour wins the U.K. General Election and forms a minority government.

8 Apr. Hank Aaron of the Atlantic Braves hits his 715th home run, breaking Babe Ruth's record.

13 July West Germany beats the Netherlands 2–1 to win the soccer World Cup.

5 Aug. Nixon admits his complicity in the Watergate scandal and later resigns.

8 Sept. Evil Knievel fails to cross Snake River Canyon, Idaho, on a rocket-bike.

10 Oct. In the U.K., Labour wins a second General Election.

30 Oct. Muhammad Ali knocks out George Foreman in Zaire to regain the World Heavyweight Championship.

Films of 74

Blazing Saddles · Chinatown · The Great Gatsby · Murder On The Orient Express · Serpico · Sleeper · The Sting · The Towering Inferno

Opposite top: The Towering Inferno.

Opposite below left: Alexander Solzhenitsyn receives the Nobel Prize in Stockholm.

Opposite below right: President Nixon meets the Shah of Iran.

Overleaf opposite top: John and Yoko declare peace for Christmas.

U.S. CHART TOPPERS – WEEKS AT TOP

Time In A Bottle	Jim Croce
The Joker	Steve Miller
Show And Tell	Al Wilson
You're Sixteen	Ringo Starr
The Way We Were	Barbra Streisand
Love's Theme	Love Unlimited Orchestra
Seasons In The Sun	Terry Jacks
Dark Lady	Cher
Sunshine On My Shoulder	John Denver
Hooked On A Feeling	Blue Swede
Bennie And The Jets	Elton John
T.S.O.P.	MFSB
The Locomotion	Grand Funk
The Streak	Ray Stevens
Band On The Run	Paul McCartney and Wings
Billy Don't Be A Hero	Bo Donaldson and the Heywoods
Sundown	Gordon Lightfoot
Rock The Boat	Hues Corporation
Rock Your Baby	George McCrae
Annie's Song	John Denver
Feel Like Makin' Love	Roberta Flack
The Night Chicago Died	Paper Lace
You're Having My Baby	Paul Anka
I Shot The Sheriff	Eric Clapton
Can't Get Enough Of Your Love Baby	Barry White
Rock Me Gently	Andy Kim
I Honestly Love You	Olivia Newton-John
Nothing From Nothing	Billy Preston
Then Came You	Dionne Warwick and the Spinners
You Haven't Done Nothing	Stevie Wonder
You Ain't Seen Nothing Yet	Bachman Turner Overdrive
Whatever Gets You Through The Night	John Lennon
I Can Help	Billy Swan
Kung Fu Fighting	Carl Douglas
Cat's In The Cradle	Harry Chapin
Angie Babie	Helen Reddy

U.K. CHART TOPPERS – WEEKS AT TOP

Merry Xmas Everybody	Slade
You Won't Find Another Fool Like Me	New Seekers
Tiger Feet	Mud
Devil Gate Drive	Suzi Quatro
Jealous Mind	Alvin Stardust
Billy Don't Be A Hero	Paper Lace
Seasons In The Sun	Terry Jacks
Waterloo	Abba
Sugar Baby Love	Rubettes
The Streak	Ray Stevens
Always Yours	Gary Glitter
She	Charles Aznavour
Rock Your Baby	George McCrae
When Will I See You Again	Three Degrees
Love Me For A Reason	Osmonds
Kung Fu Fighting	Carl Douglas
Annie's Song	John Denver
Sad Sweet Dreamer	Sweet Sensation
Everything I Own	Ken Boothe
I'm Gonna Make You A Star	David Essex
You're My First, My Last, My Everything	Barry White
Lonely This Christmas	Mud

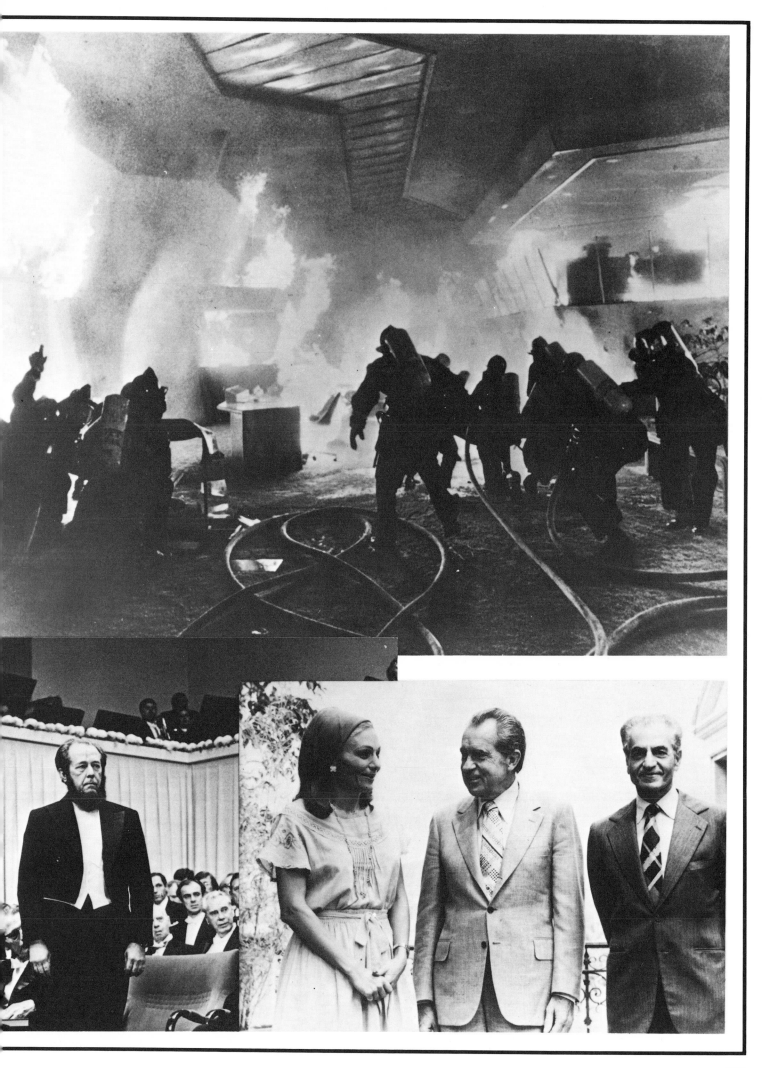

The early
'70s

THE EMPIRE STADIUM - WEMBLEY

ARK MUSIC FESTIVALS LTD.

THE LONDON
ROCK & ROLL SHOW
SAT. AUG 5th 1972
12-30 P.M.

TURNSTILES
H
57
ENTRANCE

THIS TICKET IS SOLD SUBJECT TO THE
PROMOTERS STANDARD CONDITIONS
OF SALE AVAILABLE AT PLACE OF
PURCHASE.

PRICE £1.80

WEST
STANDING
ENCLOSURE

STANDING

TO BE RETAINED   (SEE PLAN AND CONDITIONS ON BACK)

RAINBOW
THEATRE   412

EVENING 8-0
FRIDAY
OCTOBER
5

CIRCLE
£1-10
incl. VAT

TO BE GIVEN UP

RAINBOW THEATRE
FINSBURY PARK

JOHN SMITH PRODUCTIONS presents
LOU REED in Concert
PLUS SUPPORTING ACT
EVENING 8-0 p.m.

FRIDAY, OCTOBER 5th, 1973

CIRCLE
£1-10
incl. VAT

W30

W30

FOR CONDITIONS OF SALE SEE OVER

EMPIRE POOL, WEMBLEY

NOVEMBER
20

Buffalo Concert Presentations Ltd.
In association with Peter Grant
presents
ELECTRIC MAGIC
featuring
LED ZEPPLIN
plus support artistes
SATURDAY, NOVEMBER 20, 1971
at 5 p.m.

SOUTH DOOR

ENTRANCE
64

ROW
E

SOUTH UPPER TIER
75p

SEAT
149

TO BE RETAINED   See conditions on back

DAVID BOWIE

"HOUND DOGS" ELVIS FAN CLUB
P. O. BOX 66231
PORTLAND, OR. 97266 (U. S. A.)

B.E. White
87 Southill Park
Hampstead, London NW3
ENGLAND

PRINTED MATTER

'Sailing'

Ace · Average White Band · Blue Oyster Cult · Dr. Feelgood · Earth, Wind and Fire · Gloria Gaynor · Alex Harvey · Jefferson Starship · Kraftwerk Bob Marley · Ralph McTell · Graham Parker · Rush · Patti Smith Bruce Springsteen

In Britain, 1975 was a wilderness year, with very little substantial talent emerging. The singles chart was populated either by established acts or by passing visitors like Jigsaw, Sailor, Stretch, Pete Wingfield, Fox, Linda Lewis, Andy Fairweather Lowe, Typically Tropical, Laurel and Hardy, Steeleye Span, Billy Connolly, Ralph McTell and Jasper Carrot. Smokie (Chinn and Chapman's latest protégés) displayed a little more staying power with a string of good mainstream pop hits but Bill Nelson's much vaunted Be Bop Deluxe delivered considerably less than they promised.

In an attempt to move 'pub rock' out of the confines of a handful of London bars, the enterprising 'Naughty Rhythms' national tour showcased three of the genre's prime movers, Kokomo, Chilli Willi and the Red Hot Peppers, and Dr. Feelgood, but only Dr. Feelgood were able to capitalise on the ploy. Kokomo ultimately fizzled out and Chilli Willi, together with Brinsley Schwarz, Ducks Deluxe, Bees Make Honey and various other pub bands, simply threw in the towel in the face of too much adversity.

Ace, on the other hand, survived on the success of their excellent first single *How Long*, and moved to California, where they lived in style, and a vital new band, Graham Parker and the Rumour, rose from the combined ashes of the Brinsleys, the Ducks and Bontemps Roulez.

Dr. Feelgood, a brash and energetic R&B quartet from the depressing coastal town of Canvey, conquered audiences with their powerful music and the exciting stage presence of vocalist Lee Brilleaux and manic guitarist Wilko Johnson, but early recordings did little to convey their force. However, a live album, *Stupidity*, released in 1976, flew to the top of the chart and the follow-up, *Sneakin' Suspicion*, also made the top ten. When Johnson left to form his own band, the Solid Senders, it was generally presumed that Dr. Feelgood would fade but Gypie Mayo proved to be a perfect replacement and the group went on to enjoy their biggest single hit, *Milk And Alcohol*, in 1979.

At the other end of the scale, Camel impressed listeners with *The Snow Goose*, an instrumental work inspired by Paul Gallico's novel and Supertramp, a relatively innocuous group from Wales, broke through with the first of four extremely successful albums, *Crime Of The Century*, which topped the U.K. charts and remained on the U.S. chart for eight months. Supertramp initially formed at the end of the sixties as a result of the patronage of an eccentric millionare, but their achievements were less than remarkable and prior to *Crime*, founder members Rick Davies and Roger Hodgson had spent considerable time rebuilding and remodelling the group. Further dividends appeared in the shape of *Crisis? What Crisis?* and

Graham Parker and the Rumour (left to right: Martin Belmont, Brinsley Schwarz, Bob Andrews, Graham Parker, Steve Goulding and Andrew Bodnar) established themselves as one of the finest groups of the late seventies.

Dr. Feelgood's interests focussed on blues, booze and birds. Left to right: the Duchess of Canvey Island (an admirer). The Big Figure, Lee Brilleaux, John B. Sparks, Wilko Johnson plus omnipresent barman.

Pioneer queen of the discotheque, Gloria Gaynor.

the concurrent *Dreamer*, which provided them with their first hit single.

After relocating in America, they promoted their 1977 album, *Even In The Quietest Moments*, with a world tour lasting the entire year, but their later album, *Breakfast In America*, was their most successful to date, reaching the top in America and providing several hit singles on both sides of the Atlantic: *The Logical Song*, *Breakfast In America* and *Goodbye Stranger*. By the end of the decade, Supertramp had become extraordinarily popular throughout the world, though internal dissent was said to be inhibiting further progress.

The year's other British 'newcomers' came from Scotland. Glasgow's Alex Harvey, a professional musician since the fifties, drove audiences wild with his vivid, violent stage act and Dundee's Average White Band, a six-piece soul outfit domiciled in Los Angeles, topped the U.S. chart with their tightly disciplined *Pick Up The Pieces*, the danceability of which was its most significant feature.

In America, a specific 'disco' style of music, soul with a clipped beat, emerged. 'Disco' music, so named because it was devised for and played in discotheques, became enormously popular. Since it was meant to be danced to in noisy conditions, its main characteristic was a loud, rhythmic beat, and, in fact, the music and lyrics of disco music were always less important. Surprisingly, many talented black artists began playing it. An outstanding female trio was Labelle, combining strong vocals with stunning presentation, and even more exciting was Earth, Wind and Fire, who by 1975 had become a major headlining attraction with four gold albums under their belts.

Earth, Wind and Fire was the brainchild of Maurice White, a multi-talented entrepreneur who had paid his dues drumming for John Coltrane, Muddy Waters and the Ramsey Lewis Trio, and as well as masterminding their progress he successfully produced hits for the Emotions and Deniece Williams. By 1977, every release by Earth, Wind and Fire seemed guaranteed of a high chart placing, including the double platinum album *All'n'All*; *Best Of, Volume One*; *I Am* and a series of top thirty singles in America and Britain. Currently among the top half dozen black acts in the world, they continue the tradition of James Brown and Sly and the Family Stone, combining musical quality with a large cast and a multitude of special effects.

America's dominant new female singer was Gloria Gaynor, the 'Queen Of The Discotheque'. She had been recording without success since the mid-

Top: All-conquering Earth, Wind and Fire

Above: The Bee Gees (left to right: Maurice Gibb, Robin Gibb and Barry Gibb).

Above right: Jefferson Starship, more successful than their precursors, Jefferson Airplane. Seen here left to right: Craig Chaquico, Grace Slick and Pete Sears.

sixties but at the end of 1974 she conspired with a group of studio experts to come up with the top ten single *Never Can Say Goodbye*. She continued to provide vocal lines to immaculately crafted, rhythmically perfect disco-backing tracks, succeeding particularly well with *I Will Survive*, an early 1979 chart topper in both Britain and America, but those experts who have followed the lady's career since before she became a hitmaker almost unanimously agree that, although she is consistently successful in her disco guise, it has been at the expense of almost all her individuality as a soul singer.

Disco music's major champions were the Bee Gees, now reunited and living happily in California. After the lull following their sixties successes, they had got back on their feet with two U.S. hits in 1971, *Lonely Days* and *How Can You Mend A Broken Heart*, but had then foundered until 1975 when the million-selling *Jive Talkin'* gave them the biggest hit of their career.

Since then, almost everything they have touched has turned to platinum, including four albums, *Children Of The World, Here At Last . . . Bee Gees . . . Live, Spirits Having Flown* and *Greatest Hits*, and numerous singles among them *How Deep Is Your*

Love, Stayin' Alive, Night Fever and *Too Much Heaven.* The group was also featured strongly in the incredibly successful *Saturday Night Fever* movie, which catapulted almost everyone connected with it, especially the Bee Gees and John Travolta, to superstardom.

Having made the transition to disco, it remains to be seen if the Bee Gees will develop and survive when the craze inevitably wanes.

The Bee Gees were not the only group to evince a spectacular revival in 1975. The Jefferson Airplane, rebuilt and restyled as the Jefferson Starship, came back stronger than ever with a massive single, *Miracles*, and a number one album, *Red Octopus.* Revolving around the original core of Grace Slick, Martyn Balin and Paul Kantner, they remained successful until the middle of 1978 when internal disputes erupted and splintered the band once more. A top twenty compilation, *Gold*, was released as a holding action in 1979, but a question mark still hangs over the group's future.

Among the new acts keeping *Miracles* company in the singles chart were the Captain and Tennille, who had the year's biggest-selling single in *Love Will Keep Us Together*, Barry Manilow, who floated the new Arista label with his chart-topping *Mandy*, the Ozark Mountain Daredevils, who secured their greatest hit with *Jackie Blue* and two country stars, Freddy Fender and Tammy Wynette.

Fender, a maverick bar singer from South Texas, had to wait almost 20 years for national success, which came with two smash hits in 1975, *Before The Next Teardrop Falls* and *Wasted Days*

And Wasted Nights, since when he has taken up permanent residence in the U.S. country charts. Tammy Wynette had worked as a beautician before being signed to Epic Records in 1967, soon after which time she became a favourite of country and western audiences, who identified with her songs, most of which reflected a highly traditional and moral view of woman's role. Periodically her records crossed into the national chart, as in 1969 with *Stand By Your Man* (which, when re-released in Britain, rose to number one in 1975) and in 1975 with *D.I.V.O.R.C.E.*

Kraftwerk, a West German synthesiser-based group, made the American chart with *Autobahn* and Jamaican reggae star Bob Marley finally broke through with his *Natty Dread* album.

Reggae, which originated in the West Indies, was protest music with religious overtones. It was music for the underprivileged, and although its distinctive rhythms and West Indian patois made it almost unintelligible to whites, it was adopted by white skinheads as well as young blacks. The biggest reggae star was undoubtedly Bob Marley. The half-caste son of a Jamaican mother and a white English father whose seafaring career had taken him to the Caribbean, Marley had become a local star by the late sixties, when he was in a highly talented trio, completed by Peter Tosh and Bunny Livingstone, known as the Wailers. Soon after this, he had also become associated with the American singer Johnny Nash, who used Marley compositions to score several hits, and with Island Records head Chris Blackwell (whose family were pillars of the white community in Jamaica), who began to record and distribute Wailers material on a worldwide basis.

Earlier recordings had often been fairly straightforward soul performances, but by 1972 Marley was heavily involved in the Rastafarian movement, a religious organisation which held that all black-skinned people would one day return to their origins in Africa, and which recognised Emperor Haile Selassie of Ethiopia as the reincarnation of Christ, and later albums reflected his beliefs. (The Rasta style involved clothing incorporating the colours red, green and gold, and plaited hair known as 'dreadlocks', and after Marley became popular, dreadlocks became a significant fashion, even among white people).

Catch A Fire, the first Wailers album released by Island, became an immediate cult success and though his cohorts left for solo careers, Marley recruited new musicians and stormed on to superstar status. His 1977 album, *Exodus*, reached the top twenty in America and the top ten in Britain, where the title track, *Waiting In Vain* and *Jamming* were all singles hits.

Marley's outspoken religious and political views (a late seventies assassination attempt was almost successful) have to some extent restricted his potential audience but he remains the most successful artist to have emerged from the West Indies.

Heavy metal was still attracting a growing patronage in 1975, but the only noteworthy new group was Rush, a trio from Toronto. Formed in 1969, they spent several years evolving their 'myths and monsters/swords and sorcery' line of attack, eventually recording an album at their own expense

Jamaican superstar Bob Marley.

Rush (left to right: Alex Lifeson, Geddy Lee and Neil Peart).

Tammy Wynette, the Queen of Nashville.

after building a strong local following. Released commercially, the album was a great success, edging Rush into the international spotlight. At this point, the original drummer left to be replaced by Neil Peart, not only a more adept percussionist but also an ingenious lyricist, and he, along with guitarist Alex Lifeson and bassist/vocalist Geddy Lee, consolidated Rush's frontline position with a series of big-selling albums including *2112*, *All The World's A Stage* and *A Farewell To Kings*.

Despite criticism concerning Peart's apparent plagiarism of the ideas of Tolkien and far-right authoress Ayn Rand, the band remained unassailable heavy metal giants as the decade drew to a close.

America's three other main arrivals all came from the East Coast: Bruce Springsteen from New Jersey, and the Blue Oyster Cult and Patti Smith from New York. In fact, Patti had been born in Chicago but had moved east in 1967 to engage in various

'75 the year

Events

11 Feb. Margaret Thatcher becomes leader of the Conservative Party.

17 Apr. Pol Pot takes power in Cambodia, as the previous Government surrenders.

30 Apr. South Vietnam surrenders to the Communists.

5 June The U.K. votes in a referendum to remain in the E.E.C.

12 June In India, Indira Gandhi is convicted of election violations.

31 July Former teamsters Union President Jimmy Hoffa is reported missing.

18 Sept. Patti Hearst is arrested by F.B.I. agents.

30 Oct. Prince Juan Carlos of Spain becomes King.

4 Dec. Two groups of South Moluccan terrorists seize a train and the Indonesian consulate in Amsterdam.

Films of 75

Day Of The Locust · The Exorcist · The Godfather Part II · Jaws · Monty Python And The Holy Grail · Nashville · Rollerball · Tommy

Opposite top: the Who.

Opposite below left: a Skinhead.

Opposite below right: The Exorcist.

U.S. CHART TOPPERS – WEEKS AT TOP

Song	Artist	Weeks
Lucy In The Sky With Diamonds	Elton John	2
Mandy	Barry Manilow	1
Please Mr. Postman	Carpenters	
Laughter In The Rain	Neil Sedaka	
Fire	Ohio Players	
You're No Good	Linda Rondstadt	
Pick Up The Pieces	Average White Band	
Best Of My Love	Eagles	1
Have You Never Been Mellow	Olivia Newton-John	1
Black Water	Doobie Brothers	1
My Eyes Adored You	Frankie Valli	1
Lady Marmalade	Labelle	1
Lovin' You	Minnie Ripperton	1
Philadelphia Freedom	Elton John	2
Another Somebody Done Somebody Wrong Song	B. J. Thomas	1
He Don't Love You	Tony Orlando and Dawn	3
Shining Star	Earth, Wind and Fire	1
Before The Next Teardrop Falls	Freddy Fender	1
Thank God I'm A Country Boy	John Denver	1
Sister Golden Hair	America	1
Love Will Keep Us Together	Captain and Tenille	4
Listen To What The Man Said	Paul McCartney and Wings	1
The Hustle	Van McCoy	1
One Of These Nights	Eagles	1
Jive Talkin'	Bee Gees	2
Fallin' In Love	Hamilton, Joe, Frank and Reynolds	1
Get Down Tonight	K.C. and the Sunshine Band	1
Rhinestone Cowboy	Glen Campbell	2
Fame	David Bowie	2
I'm Sorry	John Denver	1
Bad Blood	Neil Sedaka	3
Island Girl	Elton John	3
That's The Way	K.C. and the Sunshine Band	2
Fly Robin Fly	Silver Convention	3
Let's Do It Again	Staple Singers	1

U.K. CHART TOPPERS – WEEKS AT TOP

Song	Artist	Weeks
Lonely This Christmas	Mud	2
Down Down	Status Quo	1
Ms. Grace	Tymes	1
January	Pilot	3
Make Me Smile	Steve Harley and Cockney Rebel	2
If	Telly Savalas	2
Bye Bye Baby	Bay City Rollers	6
Oh Boy	Mud	2
Stand By Your Man	Tammy Wynette	3
Whispering Grass	Windsor Davies/ Don Estelle	3
I'm Not In Love	10 cc	2
Tears On My Pillow	Johnny Nash	1
Give A Little Love	Bay City Rollers	3
Barbados	Typically Tropical	1
I Can't Give You Anything	Stylistics	3
Sailing	Rod Stewart	4
Hold Me Close	David Essex	3
I Only Have Eyes For You	Art Garfunkel	2
Space Oddity	David Bowie	2
D.I.V.O.R.C.E.	Billy Connolly	1
Bohemian Rhapsody	Queen	5

Blue Oyster Cult (left to right: Eric Bloom, Donald Roeser, Allen Lanier, Albert Bouchard and Joe Bouchard). Their pre-fame group names included the Stalk Forrest Group and Soft White Underbelly.

Bruce Springsteen, the most charismatic and influential American artist of the late seventies.

New Wave explorer Patti Smith drew attention to the fermenting subterranean scene in New York.

artistic pursuits, the most successful of which were as rock journalist and poet.

In early 1973 she teamed up with rock writer/guitarist Lenny Kaye to piece together a rock group over the next couple of years. Growing local acclaim was rewarded by a contract with Arista and the release in 1975 of *Horses*, a top fifty album which gave rise to the question of whether energy and undoubted enthusiasm can atone for substandard musicianship.

Oblivious to criticism Patti increased her following with American and European tours and her third (and most competent) album, *Easter*, together with the extracted single *Because The Night*, took her to the peak of her career in 1978. The response to her fourth album, *Wave*, was considerably cooler and in 1979 she granted her group a year's leave while she disappeared with her rumoured husband Fred 'Sonic' Smith, late of the MC5.

Patti's previous beau, Allen Lanier, was keyboard player in the Blue Oyster Cult, a heavy metal band with artistic but commercial aspirations, who signed with Columbia in 1972. However, it was not until the release of their live double album *On Your Feet Or On Your Knees* in 1975 that they began to be widely recognised. Their next album, *Agents Of*

Fortune, made the top thirty in both Britain and America but, more importantly, spawned their first hit single, the excellent *(Don't Fear) The Reaper* which made the top twenty in America during 1976 and in Britain two years later, when it was reissued to coincide with a European tour.

Each of their subsequent albums has charted in America, where many believe that their finest work is yet to come.

September 1975 saw the 'arrival', after two years of minority acclaim, of singer/songwriter Bruce Springsteen, a particularly gifted artist whose first two albums, *Greeting From Ashbury Park* and *The Wild, The Innocent, And The E Street Shuffle*, had peaked at numbers 60 and 59 respectively. After being styled 'the new Dylan', he was saddled with a further albatross when Columbia's overkill publicity campaign for his third album, *Born To Run*, was headed by the quote from his producer, respected rock critic John Landau, 'I have seen the future of rock'n'roll and his name is Bruce Springsteen'. The album rose swiftly to number three and Springsteen became an 'overnight' superstar, consolidating his breakthrough with extensive American and European tours.

His ingenious melodies and brilliant lyrics combined with his romantic image as an inner city street underdog, captured the imagination of millions but a legal dispute between Springsteen and his manager, Mike Appel, prevented any further recording until 1978, when he began to regain lost ground with *Darkness On The Edge Of Town*. Undoubtedly one of the major talents to have surfaced over the last ten years, Springsteen looks certain to maintain his position through the eighties.

In Britain, no such titanic act emerged. By the end of the year, rock music had reached its lowest ebb. Energy and commitment had gone out of the window to be replaced by contrivance, formula and repetition. A revolution was inevitable, but nobody had yet realised.

Meanwhile, a new group had just made their debut at a London art school and were looking forward to establishing themselves over the next few months. They were called the Sex Pistols.

'76

'Dancing Queen'

Aerosmith · Joan Armatrading · The Bellamy Brothers · George Benson
Boston · The Damned · Peter Frampton · Emmylou Harris · Hall and Oates
Heart · Kansas · Dolly Parton · Iggy Pop · The Ramones · Jonathan Richman
The Runaways · Bob Seger · The Sex Pistols · Slik · Bonnie Tyler

While everything was quite normal in America during the Bicentenniel, the rock industry experienced its strangest period in Britain. In a year when even veteran guitarist Bert Weedon found himself at number one, the biggest-selling album artists were Abba, the Beach Boys, Slim Whitman, Demis Roussos, Glen Campbell and Queen – in that order – yet fermenting in the subterranean depths of London's new underground was a movement which would soon create havoc with established values and turn the record business upside down.

By the end of the year, after acres of sensationalist newsprint had alarmed the silent majority and media coverage in general had reached saturation point, nobody in Britain could fail to have been familiar with the word 'punk'.

Although the London S.S. and the Hollywood Brats were subsequently found to have been operating in a similar field at the same time, the prime instigators of punk were the Sex Pistols, who by late 1975 were developing under the guiding hand of an extremely astute entrepreneur, Malcolm McLaren.

McLaren, the proprietor of a bizarre Chelsea boutique called 'Sex', had recently returned from America where he had been managing the ailing New York Dolls, and had made careful note of prevailing and interesting trends. Particularly fascinating had been Television, a struggling New York group whose singing bassist, Richard Hell, wore short spiky hair (at a time when long hair was de rigeur for rock musicians) and deliberately torn and ragged clothing held together with safety pins.

It wasn't long before McLaren's boutique was doing a roaring trade promoting this image a modified version of which had now been adopted by the Sex Pistols.

Though Glen Matlock (bass), Steve Jones (guitar) and Paul Cook (drums) proved to be adequate, the group still needed a charismatic frontman if they were to succeed commercially, and after Richard Hell, among others, had turned down an invitation to join, McLaren, attracted by his imbecilic screaming and obnoxious behaviour, brought in John Lydon, an exceptionally down at heel youth who often hung around 'Sex'.

Lydon (now rechristened Johnny Rotten) and his cohorts, playing as many London area gigs as they could (either legitimately or by gate crashing), were soon regarded as the most vile and unmusical group ever to set foot on a stage – an image Rotten fostered by spitting, swearing and stubbing out cigarettes on his bare arm.

The music industry's initial reaction was one of horror and revulsion but a growing section of the

Johnny Rotten sings in San Francisco during the American tour which fragmented the Sex Pistols.

The ever flamboyant Elton John began to devote less time to rock music, and more to his commitments as Chairman of Watford soccer club.

rock audience, disillusioned and dispirited by the current scene, lauded the Sex Pistols as their champions. Here was a loud, arrogant, disorderly group not only challenging authority but succeeding with limited resources: fans began to realise that you didn't need a million watt p.a. system, a bank of synthesisers and a degree in music to get somewhere ... anyone could start a group!

By the end of 1976 it was obvious that they had become a very strong and influential force ... and the industry shuddered as they signed a long and lucrative contract with E.M.I. The contract was hastily terminated, however, when the group, interviewed on a teatime trivia programme, outraged televiewers with a deliberately obtuse display of apathy and swearing which catapulted them to national notoriety. Their only E.M.I. single, *Anarchy In The U.K.*, was withdrawn after pressure from employees and stockholders, even though it had risen into the top forty.

At this point Sid Vicious (né John Ritchie), a friend of Rotten's, came in to replace Matlock (who went off to form the Rich Kids – a short-lived band which perennially promised more than it delivered) and the Pistols signed a new deal with A. & M. in a moronic ceremony outside the gates of Buckingham Palace. The company tolerated their presence for only a few days, however, and McLaren and the group were said to have been £75,000 richer as a result of advances forfeited by E.M.I. and A. & M. when they chose to break their contracts.

By this time, it had become virtually impossible for the Sex Pistols to perform anywhere in Britain but the intrepid Virgin strode in where other labels feared to tread and they were able to maintain their enormous popularity with a string of successful records. *God Save The Queen*, a typically irreverent Pistols original which attracted the loathing of royalists across the country and was banned by the B.B.C., reached number two during the Jubilee celebrations of June 1977 and *Pretty Vacant* and *Holidays In The Sun* also made the top ten during the year.

Their debut album, *Never Mind The Bollocks, Here's The Sex Pistols*, topped the charts for two weeks, despite its provocative title and it was assumed that having achieved commercial success the group would modify its stance to prolong their active life. The first step in this direction was an American tour, an ill-received shambles following the completion of which, in January 1978, Rotten unexpectedly left the band. After little over two years, the group was in tatters.

Of the army of bands following in the Pistols' footsteps, the Damned were the most immediately successful – due primarily to their marketing and management. Adopting the same anti-social attitude, they made their name in the subterranean London clubs where their overtly unmusical mayhem won a contract with Stiff, a new record label specialising in perverse talent.

Their debut single, *New Rose*, was the first punk hit, paving the way for *Damned Damned Damned*, the first punk album to chart, and the members of the group, Dave Vanian, Captain Sensible, Bryan James and Rat Scabies became pop-press celebrities for their wayward behaviour as much as their musical achievements.

Sex Pistols Johnny Rotten (left) and Sid Vicious (right) attract the attention of the forces of law and order in Portobello Road, London.

Curiously enough, Elton John's only British chart-topping single was *Don't Go Breaking My Heart*, his duet with his protegée Kiki Dee.

After a year, the bubble burst. Tepid reviews and underattended concerts led them to dissolve in early 1978, after their second album had failed to live up to expectations, but individual ventures fared dismally and at the end of the year three of the original members re-formed the Damned. A 1979 single, *Love Song*, took them to their highest chart

ollowing in the footsteps of
oldie and the Gingerbreads
nd Fanny, were all-girl
roup, the Runaways (*above*).

ave Vanian (left) and Cap-
in Sensible of the Damned
iscuss Einstein's theory of
elativity (*above right*).

1976, Joan Armatrading
und the love and affection
e'd craved (*far right*).

oadrunner Jonathan Rich-
an demonstrates the dance
eps to his 1977 hit,
gyptian Reggae (*right*).

position and they are currently trying to establish
themselves as something more than a dated novelty
act.

Most of the musical inspirations for the early British punk groups derived from American sources:
the Velvet Underground, Patti Smith and the
Dolls from New York, and the MC5 and the Stooges
from Detroit. Of these groups, only Patti Smith's
was currently functioning on a full-time basis,
however, and during 1976 two major new influences emerged: the Ramones and Jonathan
Richman.

Jonathan Richman's band, the Boston-based
Modern Lovers, were exceptional enough to have
been courted by America's most distinguished label
chiefs, but ethical considerations, rare in rock
music, caused the band to self-destruct before an
album could be released. Nevertheless, a collection
of demos issued by Berserkeley in 1976 as *The
Modern Lovers* made a strong impression on
musicians and audiences alike.

Richman's subsequent solo single, *Road Runner*,
was an immediate favourite and with a new group of
Modern Lovers he toured Britain to great acclaim
during 1977-78, achieving two more hits in quick

succession. By 1979, however, he had become a solo
acoustic performer more noted for his whimsicality
and weirdness than for the strength of his material.

The Ramones, a model for hundreds of imitators,
developed their unique approach in the clubs of
New York before signing with Sire Records early in
1976. Their first appearance in Britain, on
Independence Day that year, influenced everyone
who saw them but the impact of their non-stop
high-speed barrage of short, simple songs dwindled
annually as they refused to deviate from their
original formula. Practically all Ramones releases
have sold better in Britain than in America where
their brash, essentially monotonous style does not
conform to many listeners' requirements.

The same was true for the Runaways, a raunchy
Los Angelean group of teenage girls who were
popular in Europe for a couple of years. It was said
that their mentor, Kim Fowley, selected the mem-

209

Iggy Pop, seen here during a typically uninhibited 1970 Stooges gig, inspired a generation of punk rockers with his uncompromising vision.

bers for their ability to fake orgasms whilst playing their instruments with minimal expertise and, once this had become public knowledge and photographs of the group had been circulated, the music became almost incidental. Naturally, the enormity of their live following was never reflected in album sales.

After languishing in poverty for most of the decade, erstwhile Stooge Iggy Pop suddenly found himself a figurehead of the burgeoning punk movement in Britain when several of its leading spokesmen declared their respect and admiration for his uncompromising line of attack.

In fact, during their career the Stooges had been regarded as virtually unemployable due to Iggy's stage antics, which included smashing himself with his microphone until his face bled and allowing molten candle wax to cascade down his bare chest, and practically unlistenable to because of their instrumental ineptitude – but even long after they'd broken up they enjoyed vociferous cult worship.

In the wake of this new-found adulation, Iggy toured Britain to fevered response and a new album, *The Idiot*, marked the start of a fresh recording career.

Despite all the media fuss, on neither side of the Atlantic was punk music taken seriously during 1976 – like rock'n'roll 20 years earlier, it was thought, by the powers-that-be, to be a passing fad – and its influence certainly wasn't felt in the year's charts.

In Britain, the singles lists were still clogged with such trite dross as *Save All Your Kisses For Me* by the Brotherhood Of Man, *No Charge* by J. J. Barrie and *Combine Harvester* by the Wurzels. Slik, a Scottish hypergroup tipped to draw fan adoration from the Bay City Rollers, reached the top with *Forever And Ever* but, after a relatively poor follow-up, were never heard of again. But 1976's singles charts really favoured the girls.

Chirpy cockney Tina Charles, who had impressed audiences with her *Two Ronnies* television sho appearances and her lead vocal on 5000 Volts' 197 hit *I'm On Fire*, reached number one with *I Love Love* and Yvonne Elliman, after playing Mar Magdalene in the stage and film versions of *Jesu Christ Superstar*, reached number six with *Love M*

Welsh cabaret singer Bonnie Tyler hit the b time with her catchy *Lost In France* and sub sequently achieved a worldwide breakthrou with *It's A Heartache*, a top five single in bot Britain and America, which won her gold discs i 12 countries around the world.

The year's most successful arrival, however, w Joan Armatrading, a West Indian who had moved Britain as a child. Her initial career was spent i partnership with another black lady, Pam Nesto who co-wrote the songs which appeared on her fir solo album, *Whatever's For Us*, in 1974. It was not great success and the pair split up, Nestor going ground for several years and Armatrading pressin on under the patronage of a new record compan

Late in 1976, her third album, *Joan Armatradin* reached number 12 while a single *Love Ar Affection*, climbed into the top ten. Her subseque album, *Show Some Emotion*, was even more succes ful and she was able to see out the seventies as headlining concert attraction.

In the American singles chart disco mus prospered though it was becoming increasing mechanical, formularised and dull. Rick Dees an His Cast Of Idiots, Silver Convention, Johnn Taylor, Wild Cherry and the Sylvers were amon the most successful of a growing number recordin singles with the words 'boogie', 'funky' or 'disc included in the title.

Vocal duos were also very popular, with th Bellamy brothers, England Dan and John For Coley, and Daryl Hall and John Oates all achievin high placings. The Manhattans made the top wit *Kiss And Say Goodbye* as did the Starland Vocal Ban with *Afternoon Delight*. Dorothy Moore scored h iggest hit with *Misty Blue*, and John Sebastian, a are chart visitor since his Lovin Spoonful days, had is first number one in ten years with *Welcome ack*, the theme song from a high-rating television eries starring John Travolta.

Other ex-group members going solo included ormer Raspberries frontman Eric Carmen, who eached number two with *All By Myself*, Sha Na Na efugee Henry Gross, who took *Shannon* to number ix, and Gary Wright from Spooky Tooth, who egan an intensely successful sweep with a number wo single *Love Is Alive*.

C. W. McCall shunted off all competition on the ountry front with his truck-driving epic *Convoy*, vhich was subsequently stretched out into a full ength movie, directed by Sam Peckinpah and tarring Kris Kristofferson. Maverick country ingers Waylon Jennings, Willie Nelson and Jerry eff Walker also crossed over to a wider market, articularly through album sales, but theirs had een longer journeys than those of their female ounterparts, Jessi Colter, Tanya Tucker, Emmylou Iarris and Dolly Parton.

Miss Parton, boasting a blonde wig of prodigious roportions and a chest to match, started her career s featured singer in Porter Wagoner's show during he sixties but in early 1974 a minor hit single, *olene*, boosted escalating solo album sales. In 1977 he reached the U.S. top ten for the first time with *Iere You Come Again*. (She had already visited the ritish top ten a year earlier with the reissued *olene*.) Although she has released over 15 country lbums (some featuring Mr. Wagoner), Dolly Parton as, over the last few years, been steering her career owards the rock market – as the style of her late 979 release, *Great Balls Of Fire*, attests.

Emmylou Harris, though a regular country-chart opper, has always been regarded as a rock artiste. In the suggestion of two Flying Burrito Brothers, vho 'discovered' her playing in a bar in Vashington D.C., she teamed up with Gram arsons, who was attempting to get his solo career ff the ground. The efficacy of the partnership was isplayed on the two excellent albums Parsons ompleted before his death, following which mmylou struck out on her own.

Touring with her Hot Band (so-called because it boasted some of the finest country musicians available) including guitarist James Burton, she quickly established herself as a headlining act and her second album, *Elite Hotel*, carried her into the U.S. top thirty and the British top twenty. A follow-up, *Luxury Liner*, achieved similar placings but then her once novel approach seemed to lose much of its impact and the sales of subsequent albums were relatively disappointing.

However, this may not be a cause of concern to Emmylou as, by 1978, she had married her record producer, Brian Ahern, and seemed rather more interested in a career as a wife and mother than in the music which had originally brought them together.

Other girls to break through in 1976 included two pairs of sisters. The McGarrigles, Kate and Anna, from Canada, were outstanding in the folk field, while the Wilsons, Nancy and Ann, were the focal points in the Seattle-based Heart, one of three major new rock groups to achieve platinum albums during the year.

Heart's debut album, *Dreamboat Annie*, released on the small Canadian label Mushroom, was an unexpected smash hit, reaching the American top ten and selling over two million copies – a feat equalled by their first C.B.S. Portrait release, *Little Queen*, in 1977.

The comparative failure of *Dog And Butterfly*, which just scraped into the top twenty in 1978, indicated that their streak of fortune may be wearing thin, whereas Aerosmith seemed set for a successful transition to the eighties.

A Massachusetts band, formed in 1970, Aerosmith acquired a recording contract after three years, and their second album, *Get Your Wings*, went gold just as their third, *Toys In The Attic*, was released. *Toys*, the fifteenth best-selling album of 1976, preceded *Rocks* and *Draw The Line* into the platinum bracket to set a pattern for the rest of the decade and the group's Mick Jagger-lookalike vocalist, Steven Tyler, became one of the biggest stars in rock'n'roll.

In late 1979, lead guitarist Joe Perry un-expectedly left the group but, despite his pre-dominant role in their ascent, his departure appeared to do little damage to the group's reputation.

Boston, a rather more calculated and sophisti-cated heavy metal unit from the same part of the country, was the brainchild of Tom Scholz, whose job as a research technician for the Polaroid Corporation had earned him enough money to indulge his desire to make a record. Having completed the album, on which he played and sang everything, he sought a label to release it and Epic Records, amazed by the ingenuity and technical brilliance of the work, signed him immediately.

Scholz then recruited various friends with whom he'd played in bar bands and the resultant group, named Boston, theoretically re-recorded his original demos in accordance with union regulations, though much of the final album, titled *Boston*, is thought to comprise the original tapes. When it was released during the latter half of 1976, it became the biggest-selling debut album of all time, accumulat-ing sales in excess of six million within two years.

Dolly Parton, the truckers' pin up, wasn't just a pretty face . . .

Three singles from the album also made the charts, the biggest being *More Than A Feeling*, though British reaction to the group was generally unenthusiastic – as it was to both Heart and Aerosmith. *Don't Look Back*, a follow-up album over two years in the making, easily attained platinum status despite its inferiority and Boston entered the eighties one of the most successful, albeit unprolific, groups in the world.

Kansas, another band whose name reflected their origins, hauled around the mid-West to little effect until they eventually attracted the attention of Don Kirshner, the publishing mogul who had 'invented' the Monkees 10 years earlier. An overblown dinosaur band with no pretension to do anything other than play interminable songs at very high volume, Kansas soon became exceedingly popular across America.

Their 1976 breakthrough came with *Leftoverture*, which took five months to creep up to number five. It was followed into the top ten by *Point Of No Return* and after a succession of further hits, including their 1979 epic, *Monolith*, Kansas find themselves facing the eighties as yet another megaplatinum heavy metal act – even though it is doubtful whether 95% of the record-playing public would recognise them in the street.

A huge local star for over 10 years, Bob Seger, from Detroit, meant little nationally – even though he had a top twenty hit, *Ramblin' Gamblin' Man*, in 1969 – and at one point he was depressed enough to leave the music business for two years in order to gain outside qualifications. In 1976, however, a double album, *Live Bullet*, took him into the top forty for the first time, and his considerable hard-rocking talent began to be recognised.

A classic single, *Night Moves*, also released in 1976, took him into the top five and its eponymous parent album subsequently made the top ten. His 1978 album *Stranger In Town*, together with the concurrent single *Hollywood Nights*, firmly established him at the top of the tree.

Opposite above left:
Faceless mid-Westerners Kansas.

Opposite above right:
After years of obscurity in East Coast folk clubs, Emmy-lou Harris rose to fame partnering Gram Parsons.

Opposite centre:
Heart never recaptured the success they found with their first multi-platinum album.

Opposite bottom:
Boston (left to right: Barry Goudreau, Sib Hashian, Fran Sheehan, Tom Scholz and Brad Delp).

Aerosmith (*right*), led by dynamic vocalist Steven Tyler (*above*) were pre-eminent among mid-seventies hard rock groups, as a succession of platinum albums demonstrated.

'76 the year

Events

16 Mar. James Callaghan succeeds Harold Wilson as U.K. Prime Minister.

10 May Jeremy Thorpe resigns as head of the Liberal Party.

24 May Concorde begins regular flights between London and Washington.

16 June 175 are killed in riots in Soweto, South Africa.

4 July The bicentennial of the Declaration of Independence is celebrated in the U.S.A.

17 July In Montreal, the Olympic Games begin.

9 Sept. Mao Tse-Tung dies in Peking.

2 Nov. Jimmy Carter is elected President, defeating Gerald Ford.

Films of 76

All The President's Men · Mahogany · Network · The Omen · One Flew Over The Cuckoo's Nest · Return Of The Pink Panther · The Shootist · Taxi Driver

U.S. CHART TOPPERS – WEEKS AT TOP

Saturday Night	Bay City Rollers
Convoy	C. W. McCall
I Write The Songs	Barry Manilow
Theme From 'Mahogany'	Diana Ross
Love Roller Coaster	Ohio Players
Fifty Ways To Leave Your Lover	Paul Simon
Theme From 'S.W.A.T.'	Rhythm Heritage
Love Machine	Miracles
December 1963	Four Seasons
Disco Lady	Johnnie Taylor
Let Your Love Flow	Bellamy Brothers
Welcome Back	John Sebastian
Boogie Fever	Sylvers
Love Hangover	Diana Ross
Silly Love Songs	Paul McCartney and Wings
Afternoon Delight	Starland Vocal Band
Kiss And Say Goodbye	Manhattans
Don't Go Breaking My Heart	Elton John and Kiki Dee
You Should Be Dancing	Bee Gees
Shake Your Booty	K.C. and the Sunshine Band
Play That Funky Music	Wild Cherry
A Fifth Of Beethoven	Walter Murphy and the Big Apple Band
Disco Duck	Rick Dees and His Cast of Idiots
If You Leave Me Now	Chicago
Rock'n'Me	Steve Miller Band
Tonight's The Night	Rod Stewart

U.K. CHART TOPPERS – WEEKS AT TOP

Bohemian Rhapsody	Queen
Mamma Mia	Abba
Forever And Ever	Slik
December 1963	Four Seasons
I Love To Love	Tina Charles
Save Your Kisses For Me	Brotherhood of Man
Fernando	Abba
No Charge	J. J. Barrie
Combine Harvester	Wurzels
You To Me Are Everything	Real Thing
The Roussos Phenomenon	Demis Roussos
Don't Go Breaking My Heart	Elton John and Kiki Dee
Dancing Queen	Abba
Mississippi	Pussycat
If You Leave Me Now	Chicago
Under The Moon Of Love	Showaddywaddy
When A Child Is Born	Johnny Mathis

Left: an over-enthusiastic Punk.

Opposite top: Concorde.

Opposite bottom left: Jack Nicholson in *One Flew Over The Cuckoo's Nest.*

Opposite bottom right: Roger Daltry of the Who goes punk

215

If Seger's climb to stardom was tortuous, George Benson's was even tougher. Though his guitar playing was readily appreciated, his vocal attributes were almost totally overlooked during a long jazz career which led him to play with innumerable greats, including Jack McDuff,

Freddie Hubbard, Herbie Hancock and Miles Davis

This Masquerade, written by Leon Russell, became a top ten single in Summer 1976 and soon afterwards *Breezin'* rose to number one to become the biggest selling jazz album of all time. After two further smash albums, *In Flight* and *Weekend In L.A.*, Benson was described not only as 'the leading crossover jazz artist of the decade' but also as 'the greatest living jazz guitarist', even though his musical horizons had broadened immensely by then.

At the head of the American chart, *Breezin'* fought a tenacious battle with Peter Frampton's double set *Frampton Comes Alive*, which it deposed twice between July and September, when it finally gave up the ghost. In fact, Frampton's album went on to become the best-selling album of the year as well as the biggest dollar grossing album to date.

A survivor of the Herd and Humble Pie, Frampton had struggled to make a name for himself since leaving the latter in 1971, but his first four albums made no significant chart inroads, even though his live following was rabid. *Frampton Comes Alive*, coupled with the top ten single *Show Me The Way*, turned him into a superstar and his next album *I'm In You*, reached number two, selling a million copies within days.

By the end of the seventies, however, a catalogue of turmoils, incorporating the extravagant financial demands of his former girlfriend, his unfortunate connection with the abysmal *Sergeant Pepper* movie and disappointing sales for his latest album, had weakened his position and his popularity appeared to be ebbing.

Not so Fleetwood Mac, who, after nine years on the road, were just getting into their stride in 1976

Peter Frampton (*above*) and George Benson (*below*) jostled for album chart honours during the summer of 76.

'77

'Anarchy In The U.K.'

Boney M. · Boomtown Rats · Bootsy's Rubber Band · The Clash
Elvis Costello · Firefall · Foreigner · The Jam · Tom Robinson
Kenny Rogers · Rose Royce · Boz Scaggs · The Stranglers · Donna Summer
Talking Heads · Television

By the beginning of 1977, the British punk industry was in full swing, turning out posters, fanzines, appropriately decorated t-shirts, zip-strewn jackets, bondage trousers, razor blade pendants, safety pins for insertion in cheeks and ears, badges and all the other paraphernalia lapped up by a growing army of meat heads. Like all previous rock revolutions, punk had mellowed into commercialised comedy.

However, though already passé, punk rock had sparked off a more musical trend which had broadened into what was now known as the 'new wave'. Bringing raw energy, controversy and new blood, it swept the rock business to the extent that almost all the year's major newcomers were representatives of the fashion. New wave was essentially urban music, reflecting the cynical and violent times, and its most immediately successful exponents were the Stranglers, the Jam, the Tom Robinson Band, the Boomtown Rats, the Clash and Elvis Costello.

The Stranglers, originally known as the Guildford Stranglers after the city where they formed, were the first to reach the charts when *(Get A) Grip (On Yourself)* crept into the top fifty during the early part of the year. *Grip* preceded a trio of top ten singles, *Peaches*, *Something Better Change* and *No More Heroes*, while their first two albums, *Rattus Norvegicus IV* (the sleeve picture was of a rat) and *No More Heroes*, both made the top five, establishing them as one of the most important groups of the late seventies.

By no means typical of the genre, the Stranglers were older, worldlier and more accomplished musically, drawing inspiration from sixties groups (principally the Doors and Captain Beefheart) their peers professed to loathe. While their American success has been minimal, they have managed to remain exceedingly popular in Britain through their intelligent reading of the scene.

Springing from the same geographical area were the Jam, three disciples of the mid-sixties 'mod' movement, whose musical and fashion styles they plundered unashamedly. To a generation of fans unfamiliar with the originals, the Jam sounded vigorous and fresh and the songs of 18 year old lead guitarist/lead singer Paul Weller soon began to find their way into the lower reaches of the charts – starting with the excellent *In The City*.

Whilst quickly evolving their own style, they amassed a considerable live following – although their records were seldom more than moderate hits – but by 1979 they appeared to be losing ground, their exclusivity having been usurped by a flood of similarly motivated mod bands who were able to

The Stranglers in action (left to right: Jet Black, Dave Greenfield, Hugh Cornwell (top) and Jean-Jacques Burnel). Their performance at an open-air concert in London's Battersea Park during the summer of 78 (*left*) was relieved by the presence of several strippers and the odd exhibitionist.

The Jam (left to right: Rick Buckler, Bruce Foxton and Paul Weller) relax in San Francisco.

By 1977, Diana Ross had become a top box-office attraction in the film world with starring roles in *Mahogany* and *Lady Sings The Blues* under her belt.

The Boomtown Rats, led by the loquacious Bob Geldof (left) were the first New Wave group to reach the top of the British singles chart, with *Rat Trap* in 1978. The following year, they returned to number one with their imaginative headline grabber *I Don't Like Mondays*.

attract more publicity. However, at the end of the year their eighties prospects were rekindled by the success of a new single, *Eton Rifles*, and a new album, *Setting Sons*.

After his acoustic harmony group Cafe Society had sunk without trace, Tom Robinson suddenly resurfaced with one of the year's most individual singles, *2-4-6-8 Motorway*, a top five hit which afforded a platform for his social conscience. His outspoken support of myriad minority groups, including strikers, dubiously convicted criminals, 'Rock against Racism', and particularly homosexuals (Robinson himself was a self-proclaimed bisexual) won him a large audience, but by the latter part of 1979, after two successful but patchy albums, both the public and his band appeared to be tiring of his diatribes.

Equally eloquent, but considerably sharper, was Bob Geldof, an ex-journalist from Dublin, who led

his band, the Boomtown Rats, to instant victory with *Looking After Number One*, the start of an unbroken run of top twenty singles. With a vitality reminiscent of the early Stones, the Rats gnawed their way to national fame, climaxing their rise with a pair of brilliantly crafted chart toppers, *Rat Trap* and *I Don't Like Mondays* – the latter remaining at number one for four weeks during the summer of 1979, to become the year's biggest seller.

Despite their failure to crack the American market, their obvious ability and ingenuity make the Boomtown Rats odds-on favourites for global superstardom during the eighties.

The Clash, fronted by vocalist/rhythm guitarist Joe Strummer and lead guitarist Mick Jones, presented a very charismatic image though their early recordings were marred by poor production. This did not prevent their first album, *The Clash*, reaching number 12 within days of release, however, although two superb singles, *Clash City Rockers* and *White Man In Hammersmith Palais*, failed to punctuate the top thirty. After the solution of managerial disputes which had hampered their progress considerably, the Clash got into their stride in late 1978, reaching number two with their second album, *Give Em Enough Rope*. Two singles, *Tommy Gun* and *I Fought The Law*, provided further impetus, though much of 1979 was spent in America, where their cult status was only just beginning to expand.

The first new wave artist to make significant

headway in the States was Elvis Costello, whose exceptional material and offbeat appearance was recognised by the burgeoning Stiff label after he'd been turned down by many major companies. Under the astute guidance of manager/label boss Jake Riviera, Costello released three highly acclaimed chart failures before *Watching The Detectives* took him into the top twenty in late 1977 when he and four other Stiff acts (including his gifted producer Nick Lowe) toured Britain in a spectacular package show.

Costello's debut album, *My Aim Is True*, which had reached number 14 in Britain, made the upper regions of the chart in America, where he toured consistently to expose himself to maximum advantage, and his 1978 album, *This Year's Model*, a top five in Britain, was regarded as one of the year's finest.

In 1979, his third album, *Armed Forces*, combined with the single *Oliver's Army* to cement his worldwide success and at the turn of the eighties, when established artists were covering his songs and lesser talents were plagiarising his idiosyncratic style, Costello was being tipped as one of the brightest hopes for the future.

The Adverts, another group originally launched by Stiff, hit the charts with *Gary Gilmore's Eyes* but delivered nothing of significance thereafter – finally becoming one of the new wave's early casualties when they split up in late 1979.

Whilst acting as a flushing oil, cleansing the rock system of many of the characterless bands clogging the gig circuit, the punk/new wave movement was responsible for comparatively little chart activity during 1977 and established artists like 10cc, Yes, Emerson, Lake and Palmer, Queen, Leo Sayer, Rod Stewart and Pink Floyd, who all enjoyed undiminished success, felt no sense of threat or alarm.

The year's best-selling British single was *Don't Cry For Me Argentina*, the show-stopping song from *Evita*, sung by Julie Covington, while the Shadows' *Twenty Golden Greats* outstripped any other album.

The rock scene was radically different in America, where a great diversity of successful new acts sprang up during 1977.

In the singles field Shaun Cassidy and Andy Gibb, the younger brothers of established acts, both reached number one – with *Da Doo Ron Ron* and *I Just Want To Be Your Everything* respectively – and Pat's daughter, Debby Boone, was responsible for

Son of a dance band singer, Elvis Costello (né Declan McManus) was one of the most exciting and cryptic stars of the New Wave.

Tom Robinson's spectacular emergence preceded a two-year hiatus at the end of the decade.

Peaking 10 years after their inception, Fleetwood Mac (left to right: Lindsey Buckingham, Mick Fleetwood, Stevie Nicks, Christine McVie and John McVie) released the year's biggest selling L.P. *Rumours*.

Having survived numerous traumas, the Clash (left to right: Mick Jones, Joe Strummer, Topper Headon and Paul Simonon) finally realised their full potential with the release of their *London Calling* double album in late 1979.

the year's walkaway smash, *You Light Up My Life* which topped the singles chart for a record 10 weeks.

Starsky And Hutch heart-throb David Soul made an equivalent impact on vinyl, hitting the top with *Don't Give Up On Us Baby* (a feat he repeated with *Silver Lady* in Britain, where an equally fine actor Kermit the Frog, topped the album chart with *The Muppet Show*) and the screen success of *Star Wars* was reflected in its theme music, which reached number one at the hands of Meco. Mary MacGregor Alan O'Day, Bill Conti and the Emotions were also among 26 different singles artists to reach the top in the U.S.

On the album front, the chart was dominated by the Eagles, Barbra Streisand, Linda Ronstadt and Stevie Wonder, but primarily by Fleetwood Mac, whose *Rumours* held the number one position for 29 weeks.

After an early seventies slump, they had returned to prominence with their twelfth original album *Fleetwood Mac*, which introduced new members Lindsey Buckingham and Stevie Nicks, who contributed to their astonishing revival. Despite a top hundred tenure exceeding three years, that album produced three hit singles, while *Rumours* produced four – including the chart-topping *Dreams* Recording a follow-up to such an unprecedentedly successful album took the group some two and a half years but *Tusk*, a double album reputed to have cost one million dollars to produce, reinforced their position as one of the finest groups in the world.

By the end of the decade, after a career spanning more than 12 years, they were confronted with the choice of whether to retire at the top or face an inevitable decline.

The eighth best-selling album of 1977 was by Boz Scaggs, who had slowly refined his style since leaving the Steve Miller Band nine years earlier. An increasingly sophisticated approach culminated in *Silk Degrees*, but after the rather less successful *Down Two Then Left* Scaggs dropped from public view for the rest of the decade.

Randy Newman, another who believed in quality rather than quantity, released his sixth album, *Little Criminals*. Though just as subtle and acerbic as the previous five, which had been little more than cult items, the album reached the top ten while a concurrent single, *Short People* made Newman an overnight star and the bane of short people everywhere.

Subtlety was not the province of Z. Z. Top, an ultra-loud Texan trio whose stage act incorporated bison and other beasts indigenous to their home state, nor was it prevalent in the music of Styx and Montrose, the year's heavy metal messiahs. By contrast, Foreigner, a New York-based Anglo-American sextet, knew the value of peppering their mainstream stew with melodic interludes.

After spending a year holed up in rehearsal, they watched their debut album, *Foreigner*, climb to number four whilst three singles reached the top ten, and numerous publications voted them the best new group of 1977. Their calculated formula paid even greater dividends second time around when *Double Vision* and a simultaneous single, *Hot Blooded*, both made the top three and after languish-

220

ing in minor bands since the sixties, the members suddenly found themselves riding a winner.

Similarly exalted were the components of Firefall, who had banded together after the dismal failure of previous ventures. Under the leadership of former Burrito Brother Rick Roberts they found a huge market for their bland, undemanding country mush and by 1979 their three albums, *Firefall*, *Luna Sea* and *Elan*, had all risen to the top thirty.

Exploring similar territory were Dan Fogelberg and Stephen Bishop, both scoring with beautifully produced, innocuous wallpaper music, and Jimmy Buffet, a genuine but underrated talent whose mastery was widely recognised when *Margarita-ville* made the top ten, and its parent album, *Changes In Latitudes*, *Changes In Attitudes*, the top twenty.

Kenny Rogers, a Texan-born country artist, who during the late sixties had led the First Edition to a series of hits (the biggest of which were *Just Dropped In* and *Ruby, Don't Take Your Love To Town*), scored his greatest success in 1977. *Lucille* reached the U.S. top five and became a chart topper in Britain – according Rogers a pre-eminent position as a country music superstar.

Muddy Waters, Chuck Berry's original inspiration over 20 years earlier, had long been regarded as one of the most important blues artists in the world but during the early seventies had been down on his luck, suffering physically as well as financially. In 1977, however, his career was revived when Johnny Winter produced a fine album, *Hard Again* which put Muddy back on the map.

In America, the 'new wave' meant comparatively

little and musical experimentation in that area was confined to underground clubs, the most celebrated of which was CBGB's in New York's Bowery district. After providing a launch pad for Patti Smith and the Ramones during the previous year, CBGB's performed a similar service for Television and the Talking Heads during 1977.

Television, led by innovative singer/songwriter/guitarist Tom Verlaine, secured a contract with Elektra, after attracting attention with *Little Johnny Jewel*, a limited edition single released on a small local label. Their first album, though a dismal seller in conservative America, did well in Britain, spawning two top thirty singles in *Marquee Moon* and *Prove It*, and the pattern was repeated in their second release, *Adventure*, which, while reaching

Top left: Foreigner.

Top right: William 'Bootsy' Collins, protegé of George Clinton's Academy of Funk.

Bottom right: Tom Verlaine, formerly the leader and inspiration of Television, left the group for a solo career.

number seven in Britain, failed even to enter the U.S. top 200. In August 1978, some 4½ years after they'd formed, Television could tolerate their frustration no longer and split up – Verlaine opting for a solo career and his co-guitarist forming the Richard Lloyd Quartet.

Three friends from the Rhode Island School of Design moved to New York to form the Talking Heads in early 1975, playing their first gig (as support act to the Ramones) six months later. The unique songs of leader David Byrne and the charm of girl bassist Tina Weymouth soon won them a solid local following and by the beginning of 1977 they were recording their first Sire album, which took them into the lower half of the chart. The considerably more successful *More Songs About Buildings And Food* established them as one of 1978's more talked-about acts and their later album, *Fear Of Music*, finally transformed them into a top twenty band.

Whilst the new wave struggled, disco music ran amok. The key to much of the activity was the release of *Saturday Night Fever*, a film starring John Travolta as a New Yorker living for his evenings on the discotheque floor while merely existing for the rest of the time. As well as shooting Travolta to stardom, the film advanced the careers of the Bee Gees, Tavares, Walter Murphy and Yvonne Elliman, who all reached the charts after exposure on the soundtrack.

Some good music was played by William 'Bootsy' Collins. Collins was formerly a member of the Parliafunkadelicment Thang, a bizarre collection of black musicians under the leadership of one George Clinton, who had contrived to acquire two separate recording contracts – one under the name of Parliament, a soul group, the other as Funkadelic, a more jazz-oriented band which basically contained similar personnel. Bootsy's Rubber Band was one of several splinter groups to emerge from this confusion, reaching the top twenty with their second album, *Aah . . . The Name Is Bootsy, Baby* in 1977 and repeating the process with *Bootsy? Player Of The Year* in 1978.

Even more successful were Rose Royce, a nine-piece group formed in California during 1973 under the name of Total Concept Unlimited. They toured as backing group to several soul artists including the Temptations and Edwin Starr before being signed by ex-Motown mastermind Norman Whitfield, under whose guidance they came to prominence when they provided the music for the film *Car Wash*. The title track became one of only two platinum singles awarded during 1977 (the other achieved by Debby Boone), while *I Wanna Get Next To You* also made the top ten.

Since that first breakthrough, Rose Royce have been chart regulars: singles like *Wishing On A Star* and *Love Don't Live Here Anymore* have been massive sellers, and albums like *Rose Royce Strikes Again* and *Rainbow Connection IV* have consolidated their position. While Norman Whitfield continues to function as their producer and source of material they will undoubtedly flourish but as the group remain individually anonymous, their reliance on him is almost absolute.

Donna Summer's incredible rise to fame was also the result of her involvement with an imaginative production team, that of Giorgio Moroder and Peter Bellotte, whom she met while appearing in the German production of the musical *Hair*. Her first hit, *Love To Love You Baby* was a blueprint for much of what was to follow in the field of recorded disco music – a repetitive and very danceable backing track over which the singer moans in ecstasy or torment.

The single, which reached the top five on both sides of the Atlantic, was the first of many hits in a career which appeared to peak in late 78 when her revival of *MacArthur Park* headed the singles list while *Live And More* topped the album chart. However, she was able to repeat the feat during Summer 79 when *Bad Girls*, the single and the album, monopolised the number one spots for five weeks.

Without any doubt, much of the Boston girl's success was due to the facilities available in Germany: writers, producers, expert musicians and engineers, and ultra-modern studios – all of which combined to turn out records so technically perfect that they often sounded as if they had been made by machines.

Another act to profit greatly from working in Germany was Boney M, a three girl/one man singing group with Caribbean origins. Their records were masterminded by Frank Farian, who, in his quest for perfection, sometimes went to the lengths of supplying the vocal lines himself.

After minor success with early recordings, the group had a bonanza year in 1977 when four of their singles made the top ten in Britain – a success story which has continued more or less unabated ever since, although the formula was beginning to sound tired by the end of the decade. In 1978, their greatest glory came when *Rivers Of Babylon* and *Mary's Boy Child* each spent a month at the top of the U.K. singles chart, but though they were the biggest-selling singles act of the year in Britain, their achievements in America were relatively insignificant.

The year's saddest news came on 16th August, when it was learned that Elvis Presley had died from heart failure linked to multiple drug abuse.

In the eyes of rock'n'roll fans his brilliance had dimmed in the early sixties when he plumped for a Hollywood career – since when his massive output had comprised a succession of artless films, equally weak soundtrack and studio albums, and a stream of inferior singles with only the occasional jagged rock protruding from the syrup. Nevertheless, Presley, with an unsurpassable total of over 100 gold discs, undoubtedly remained the King of Rock'n'Roll. Only 42 when he died, he had sold more records than anyone else in history and his name was seldom absent from the chart for 21 years.

His death resulted in a near standstill in the city of Memphis, as fans thronged at the gates of his home and thousands of weeping mourners filed past the open coffin, where he lay in state like a real king.

Within days, 19 of his albums and 11 of his singles entered the charts in Britain, where the Elvis Industry got into full swing, turning out every conceivable 'tribute' from solid gold medallions to plaster busts.

The continuing story of rock'n'roll: if there's public interest, milk it for all it's worth.

It was Randy Newman's diatribe *Short People* which elevated him from cult status to international stardom – if only for a few months.

Kenny Rogers consolidated his reputation as America's most popular country singer with four top twenty singles during 1979.

Events

20 Jan. Jimmy Carter is sworn in as 39th President of the U.S.A.

6 Feb. Elizabeth II observes the 25th anniversary of her accession.

20 Mar. In India, Morarji Desai defeats Indira Ghandi to become Prime Minister.

2 Apr. Red Rum wins the Grand National for the third time.

22 May The Orient Express makes its last run across Europe.

20 June The 8000-mile long trans-Alaskan oil pipeline is opened.

1 July Virginia Wade wins at Wimbledon, as does Bjorn Borg for the second year.

U.S. CHART TOPPERS – WEEKS AT TOP

Tonight's The Night	Rod Stewart
You Don't Have To Be A Star	Marylyn McCoo and Billy Davis Jr.
You Make Me Feel Like Dancing	Leo Sayer
I Wish	Stevie Wonder
Car Wash	Rose Royce
Torn Between Two Lovers	Mary McGregor
Blinded By The Light	Manfred Mann's Earth Band
New Kid In Town	Eagles
Evergreen	Barbra Streisand
Rich Girl	Darryl Hall and John Oates
Dancing Queen	Abba
Don't Give Up On Us	David Soul
Don't Leave Me This Way	Thelma Houston
Southern Nights	Glen Campbell
Hotel California	Eagles
When I Need You	Leo Sayer
Sir Duke	Stevie Wonder
I'm Your Boogie Man	K.C. and the Sunshine Band
Dreams	Fleetwood Mac
Got To Give It Up	Marvin Gaye
Gonna Fly Now	Bill Conti
Undercover Angel	Alan O'Day
Da Doo Ron Ron	Shaun Cassidy
Looks Like We Made It	Barry Manilow
I Just Want To Be Your Everything	Andy Gibb
Best Of My Love	Emotions
Star Wars Theme	Meco
You Light Up My Life	Debby Boone
How Deep Is Your Love	Bee Gees

U.K. CHART TOPPERS – WEEKS AT TOP

When A Child Is Born	Johnny Mathis	2
Don't Give Up On Us	David Soul	4
Don't Cry For Me Argentina	Julie Covington	1
When I Need You	Leo Sayer	3
Chanson D'Amour	Manhattan Transfer	3
Knowing Me Knowing You	Abba	5
Free	Deniece Williams	2
I Don't Want To Talk About It	Rod Stewart	4
Lucille	Kenny Rogers	1
Show You The Way To Go	Jacksons	1
So You Win Again	Hot Chocolate	3
I Feel Love	Donna Summer	4
Angelo	Brotherhood of Man	1
Float On	Floaters	1
Way Down	Elvis Presley	5
Silver Lady	David Soul	3
Yes Sir I Can Boogie	Baccara	1
Name Of The Game	Abba	4
Mull Of Kintyre	Wings	4

26 Sept. Laker Airways begin cheap London-New York flights.

Films of 77

Annie Hall · A Bridge Too Far · Close Encounters · King Kong · New York, New York · Rocky · The Spy Who Loved Me · Star Wars

Left: Elvis Presley (1935–1977).

Opposite from top: President Jimmy Carter talks to the Press; *Star Wars*; a programme for Gloria Mundi; the concert at Blackbushe by Bob Dylan.

Talking Heads (left to right:
Jerry Harrison, Chris Frantz,
David Byrne and Martina
Weymouth) (*above*).

Dramatic visual appeal and
singalong songs combined to
make Boney M the top-selling
singles act in Britain (*left*).

In 1979, less than three years
after her breakthrough,
Donna Summer scored five
top five hits (*right*).

Rose Royce, fronted by Gwen
Dickey (second from right).

'You're The One That I Want'

Kate Bush · The Buzzcocks · Cars · Cheap Trick · Commodores · Darts
Devo · Ian Dury · Andy Gibb · Nick Gilder · Billy Joel · Kiss · Nick Lowe
Meatloaf · Tom Petty · Gerry Rafferty · Sham 69 · The Tubes

Whatever feelings the name of Johnny Rotten evokes, few would dispute that his influence on the British scene in 1976-77 was considerable – yet, by and large, punk rock turned out to be a lot of fuss about nothing. Most of the young lions who had challenged the status quo, including the Cortinas, the Models, Cocksparrer, Eater, London and the Vibrators, had already fallen by the wayside while others like the Only Ones, the Lurkers, Chelsea, and Adam and the Ants were plugging on to little effect.

Following the Pistols' debacle, Rotten resurfaced as leader of Public Image, whose creditable first single, *Public Image*, appears to have been their creative peak, while a Pistols copy-group, Sham 69, led by the garrulous Jimmy Pursey, found their feet with *Angels With Dirty Faces*, the first of several rabble-rousing hits, including *If The Kids Are United*, *Questions And Answers* and *Hersham Boys*. In 1979 after disruptive elements in their following had ruined many gigs with stage invasions and acts of violence, Pursey disbanded the group to join the surviving Sex Pistols, but the failure of that coalition saw the speedy resuscitation of Sham 69, who are hoping for a more rational audience response in the eighties.

The Buzzcocks, also inspired by the Pistols, were the only other punk band to blossom during 1978. Their local Manchester reputation had spread nationally after the release of *Spiral Scratch*, pressed on their own label (this self-sufficiency was an important aspect of the late seventies scene, with many groups attracting publicity as a result of such enterprise), and although charismatic leader Howard Devoto left to form the mildly successful Magazine, the remaining four prospered. Their first release, *Orgasm Addict*, came nowhere but eight subsequent singles and three albums, *Another Music In A Different Kitchen*, *Love Bites* and *A Different Kind Of Tension*, all charted – though few achieved significant positions. Unless they can impress a wider audience, the Buzzcocks seem doomed to extinction within the next few years, having achieved an apparent ceiling in Britain.

Of all so-called 'new wave' artists, it was mainstream veterans like Nick Lowe and Ian Dury who made the strongest contribution and gathered most acclaim. Both ex-pub rockers, they shared the energy and enthusiasm of the punk pedlars but were somewhat superior musically.

For a year following Brinsley Schwarz's dissolution, Nick Lowe spread his time between producing records by other artists and writing songs, two of which appeared on the first single issued by Stiff

Ian Dury (*above*) and Chic (*bottom left*).

Sham 69, led by Jimmy Pursey (second from right).

Above: Ian Dury found reasons to be cheerful when his tenacity finally paid off in 1978.

Above centre: Unable to decide whether to be a singer, a songwriter, a producer or a bass player, Nick Lowe compromised and became all four simultaneously.

Above right: After years of seclusion, Dave Edmunds returned to the boards as leader of Rockpile.

Right: Mancunians the Buzzcocks achieved five hit singles during 1978.

Records in August 1976. Treating his own performing career somewhat whimsically, he concentrated his activities in the studio, producing albums by Graham Parker, the Damned, Doctor Feelgood and Elvis Costello, among others, until *I Love The Sound Of Breaking Glass*, his first single for another new label, Radar, took him into the top ten in Spring 1978. A simultaneous album, *Jesus Of Cool*, was equally well received and Lowe returned to performing in earnest, touring Europe and America with Rockpile, a band he fronted with Dave Edmunds.

During 1979, Lowe, backed by Rockpile, created

a stir with *Crackin' Up* and *Cruel To Be Kind*, whi Edmunds, also backed by Rockpile, won hig placings with *Girls Talk* and *Queen Of Hearts*. The union has resulted in greater acclaim than either ha previously experienced and, as a new decade open Rockpile is regarded as one of the best groups in th world.

In common with Lowe, Ian Dury's early wor was appreciated only by a discerning few. Wit income earned as an art teacher, he subsidise various line-ups of his idiosyncratic group Kilbur and the High Roads for intermittent perioc between 1970 and 1976, although a succession misfortunes prevented the release of a repr sentative album. Seen as being too bizarre to brea beyond cult status, Dury was turned down by som 18 labels before being signed by the ubiquitou Stiff, who enabled him to showcase his talents c the celebrated 'Live Stiffs' package tour, fro which he emerged a star.

A meticulously crafted album, *New Boots An Panties*, entered the chart at the beginning of 197 and remained all year, peaking at number five an turning Dury and his superb band, the Blockhead into a major headlining attraction. *What A Wast* his first single featuring the Blockheads, precede *Hit Me With Your Rhythm Stick* (a chart topper) an *Reasons To Be Cheerful (Part Three)* into the top te and a second album, *Do It Yourself*, reached numb two only days after release.

The fact that his songs are very British in terms lyrical content has not hampered his progress Europe, but America has yet to fall under his spe

Lowe and Dury were not the only old campai ners to break through after years of minorit acclaim. Elkie Brooks, the raunchy vocalist fro Vinegar Joe, enjoyed chart action with a ne sophisticated image; Renaissance, a respecte mainstream album group, had their first top te single with *Northern Lights* and Frankie Miller, tenacious Glaswegian, had a similar success wit *Darlin'*.

Another Scot, Gerry Rafferty, who had been Bil Connolly's partner in a folk duo called th Humblebums before an abortive run with th briefly successful Stealers Wheel, returned with bang in 1978 when *Baker Street* reached the to three on both sides of the Atlantic. A concurre album, *City To City*, sold over a million copies ar

fter waiting in the wings for more than 10 years
afferty suddenly found himself at centre stage,
howered with praise. Despite his low public profile
nd hatred of publicity, he has retained his
nagnetism, the quality of his second album, *Night
wl*, convincing listeners that he is here to stay.

Considerably less durable were several other
hart newcomers, including Althia and Donna,
rian and Michael, Yellow Dog, Marshall Hain,
onight, and Jilted John, who all scored one big hit.
acey, a pop group in the tradition of early Sweet,
ad their first success with *Lay Your Love On Me*,
nd the Motors, who rose from the ashes of pub-
ock practitioners Ducks Deluxe, took off with
irport.

Justin Hayward, one of several specialists assem-
led by producer Jeff Wayne to wage his star-
tudded *War Of The Worlds*, had his biggest single
ince the Moody Blues' 1970 hit *Question* when
orever Autumn* reached number five. The parent
lbum, a musical interpretation of H. G. Well's
ovel, was among the year's best sellers and another
lassic, Emily Brontë's *Wuthering Heights*, inspired
he spectacular debut of Kate Bush.

Her distinctive singing and songwriting initially
aught the attention of the Pink Floyd's Dave
Gilmour, who helped her to cut some demos which
esulted in a recording contract in 1976 – but Ms.

Gerry Rafferty swam against
the prevailing tide to break
through with *Baker Street*.

Freely tipped as a major star
of the eighties, Kate Bush.

Bush was not to be rushed and spent the next two years improving her technique, as well as studying dance and mime.

Kate's eventual unveiling was stunning. *Wuthering Heights*, a unique single, reached number one and the album on which it appeared, *The Kick Inside*, made the top three. *The Man With The Child In His Eyes* provided a second top ten single in 1978 and the following year her success rate escalated with further hits and a very ambitious tour which allowed her to flaunt her newly acquired skills. At a time when the majority of new artists had the utmost difficulty in following up their initial breakthrough, Kate Bush was a notable exception, her musical and visual appeal making her one of Britain's brightest hopes for the future.

The Darts, too, were here to stay. A nine-piece group comprising a front line of four singers plus five backing musicians (three formerly were in the John Dummer Blues Band), the Darts were pure entertainment, basing their style on slick new versions of fifties doo-wop material. Their first single, *Daddy Cool* (originally recorded by the Rays on the back of their 1957 hit *Silhouettes*), reached the top ten at the start of 1978 and was followed into the chart by a series of smashes including *Come Back My Love*, *The Boy From New York City* and *It's Raining*.

By the end of the decade they had demonstrated their resounding popularity with two gold albums, *Darts* and *Everybody Plays Darts*, and a television-advertised compilation double, *The Amazing Darts*, which went platinum.

Jeff Lynne (*left*), leader of the all conquering Electric Light Orchestra, pictured (*centre* and *right*) in concert at Wembley Arena.

Despite vast American acclaim, Britain remained steadfastly underwhelmed by the spectacle of the Tubes, fronted by Fee Waybill (*right*).

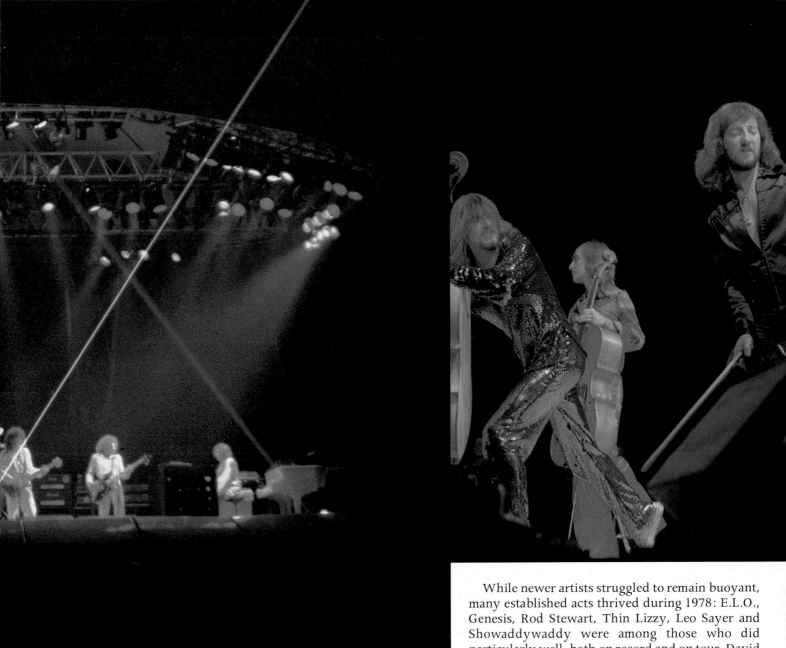

David Bowie maintained his remarkable popularity and inspired a constant spate of imitators.

While newer artists struggled to remain buoyant, many established acts thrived during 1978: E.L.O., Genesis, Rod Stewart, Thin Lizzy, Leo Sayer and Showaddywaddy were among those who did particularly well, both on record and on tour. David Bowie's concert return showed him maintaining a one-step lead over his imitators and the live double album, *Stage*, cruised effortlessly into the top five, but the most comprehensive 'comeback' was by the Rolling Stones.

In fact, since their dramatic entry in 1963, the Stones had never really been away. They had reached the top four with all 17 of their albums, eight of which had topped the chart, but doubts were hovering over their ability to maintain this sustained creativity, which must have surely been sapped by various marital and drug problems.

As if to silence their critics, they bounded back with *Some Girls*, a brilliant album which reinstated their reputation as the best rock'n'roll band in the world, and *Miss You*, which became their biggest British single since *Brown Sugar* in 1971.

In America, too, the Stones reigned supreme, *Some Girls* being voted Album of the Year. Among the runners-up in this category were two other British efforts, *This Year's Model* by Elvis Costello and *Misfits* by the Kinks, plus *Darkness On The Edge Of Town* by the revitalised Bruce Springsteen and *Bat Out Of Hell* by an extraordinary newcomer calling himself Meat Loaf.

Bat Out Of Hell, which by the end of the decade had racked up sales exceeding six million, was the

231

end product of several years of work by Mr. Loaf (real name Wilbur Aday) and his collaborator, songwriter/keyboard player Jim Steinman, who managed to convince a new company, Cleveland International, of their commercial potential. Steinman's surreal lyrics and Wagnerian music, Meat Loaf's remarkable delivery and Todd Rundgren's excellent production combined to make it one of the most successful debut albums ever – and subsequent concert appearances by the outrageous and overweight singer added to the clamour. A follow-up, *Bad For Good*, had still not been completed at the end of the seventies, although *Bat Out Of Hell* was still in the L.P. charts two years after its initial release.

Two other acts whose enormous success was boosted by fantastic theatrical presentation were the Tubes from San Francisco and Kiss from New York.

Having established themselves locally, the Tubes' reputation began to spread as a result of sensational publicity surrounding their satirical show, which involved a large cast, many props and costume changes, and several musical styles. Undeterred by the failure of others to capture a primarily visual band adequately on vinyl, A.&M. signed them in 1975, releasing an album a year for the rest of the seventies. *White Punks On Dope* and *Don't Touch Me There* were highlights on their early releases, none of which sold substantially enough to support the bacchanalian propensities of their 20-strong touring party and, faced with splitting up or pruning down, they chose the latter.

Concentrating more on musical presentation, a trim eight-piece line-up broke through with a live double album, *What Do You Want From Live*, which became their biggest seller until supplanted by *Remote Control* in 1979, and with a concurrent hit single, *Prime Time*, to their credit the Tubes at last found commercial justification for their overblown image.

Aspiring to stretch Alice Cooper's precedents to the limit in their quest to become larger than life rock idols, Kiss, a heavy metal quartet formed in 1973, adopted instantly recognisable identities by the use of grease paint – each member keeping to his own bizarre facial design. Additionally, they evolved a powerhouse stage show which was elaborate and flamboyant in the extreme – possibly to disguise the fact that their music was of a fairly simple, fundamentalist character – and they set out to conquer the world.

Their battle plan was very successful. Burgeoning public interest resulted in their fourth album, *Alive*, released in 1975, reaching the top ten and accumulating sufficient sales to be declared double platinum. A follow-up, *Destroyer*, brought them equal success in 1976, when they also had a million-selling single in *Beth*.

Rock And Roll Over, *Love Gun*, *Alive II* and the prophetic *Double Platinum* all devastated the album charts and by 1978 they were the biggest heavy metal act in the world. A unique Kiss Marvel comic and their cinematic debut, *Kiss Meets The Phantom Of The Park*, preceded the release of four solo albums, all of which reached the top fifty despite the fact that without their make-up the members remain completely anonymous.

The perennial Rolling Stones, led by Mick Jagger (*top*) returned to prominence with *Some Girls*.

Meat Loaf perspires as on-stage stooge Karla DeVito rejects his unwelcome advance

Darts (left to right: Den Hegarty. Hammy Howell, Griff Fender, John Dummer, Rita Ray, George Currie, Bob Fish, Thump Thompson and (front) Horatio Hornblower).

Anonymity never troubled the Commodores, who since their 1974 hit *Machine Gun*, had become one of Motown's most significant late seventies acts, scoring top tenners with *Sweet Love, Just To Be Close To You, Easy* and *Brick House*, before achieving their first worldwide number one with *Three Times A Lady* during 1978.

Roger Daltrey (left) and Keith Moon of the Who. Moon, one of rock's most colourful characters, succumbed to his excessive life style in September 1978.

The year's other hot American singles included *Life's Been Good* by Joe Walsh of the Eagles, *Instant Replay* by Dan Hartman, *Hot Child In The City* by Nick Gilder, *Kiss You All Over* by Exile, *Shadow Dancing* by Andy Gibb and a plethora of smashes from the soundtrack of *Grease*, an overwhelmingly successful film vehicle for John Travolta and Olivia Newton-John. They streaked up the chart together with *Summer Nights* and *You're The One That I Want*, and individually with *Sandy*, *Greased Lightnin'* and *Hopelessly Devoted To You*,

while former Four Season Frankie Valli had a number one with the title song.

Some strong new talents emerged in country music, including Crystal Gayle, Joe Ely, Ronnie Milsap and veteran Don Williams; and Nicolette Larsen was voted 'Female Singer Of The Year'.

Representing an expanding American trend known as A.O.R. (Adult Oriented Rock) were clean-sounding singer/songwriters Dean Friedman, Andrew Gold and Billy Joel. Of these, Joel was the most interesting (and successful), his sophisticated

Comic book heroes Kiss lobotomise yet another willing audience.

Right: Firing on all cylinders Cars (left to right: Elliott Easton, Benjamin Orr, Richard Ocasek).

Below: Motown's new stars of the seventies, the Commodores.

album, *The Stranger*, producing a memorable single in *Just The Way You Are* and paving the way for a solid selling follow-up, *52nd Street.*

Falling into the new wave category were the Cars, Devo, Tom Petty and the Heartbreakers and Cheap Trick. Devo, a superintelligent outfit from Ohio, made a spectacular entry – much of the groundwork being laid in Britain, where they achieved instant stardom due to Stiff's patronage and publicity – but after securing unprecedented monetary advances, lost much of their impetus and, despite interesting musical ideas, faded quite alarmingly.

Cheap Trick, on the other hand, had built their reputation very slowly since their inception in 1972 and seem poised to become a major world class group in the early eighties. An instant hit in Japan, where they were regarded as heroes as soon as they got off the plane, they drew only a modicum of American acclaim for their first albums, *In Colour*

and *Heaven Tonight*, but *Live At Budokan*, released in late 1978, reached the top five, indicating that Cheap Trick had finally arrived.

Two hit singles, *I Want You To Want Me* and *Ain't That A Shame*, exposed them to a wide audience who were able to witness the group's considerable visual appeal, and their last seventies release, *Dream Police*, became one of the year's fastest-selling albums.

Like Cheap Trick's, Tom Petty's music had its feet in the sixties – as his most well-known song, the Byrds-like *American Girl*, attests – though he had developed a distinctive style of his own before signing with Shelter Records in Los Angeles. Originally from Florida, Petty had moved west in

search of gold but a hit single, *Breakdown*, and a well received second album, *You're Gonna Get It*, preceded business problems which not only impeded his progress to the first division but left him officially bankrupt. In the final months of 1979, he was able to pick up the pieces and a new album, *Damn The Torpedoes*, was tipped to elevate his status substantially.

The Cars, comprising the depressed remnants of various ill-fated Boston groups, concocted a musical formula which catapulted their debut album into the top twenty to make them the year's most promising newcomers. The principal assets behind their rapid rise were the songs of leader Ric Ocasek, the production of Roy Thomas Baker, and an intuitive feel which was even more evident in their second release, *Candy-O*, which reached number three. (In Britain, where singles still proved the ideal medium for breaking new groups, the competition was fiercer than ever in 1978 and promotional devices such as coloured vinyl and elaborate sleeves proliferated. A Cars single, *My Best Friend's Girl*, was the first widely publicised picture disc – a factor which quickly lifted it into the top three.)

Other noteworthy artists to surface in America included Warren Zevon, who, besides scoring with *Werewolves Of London*, saw Linda Ronstadt turn his *Hasten Down The Wind* into platinum; George Thorogood, a powerful blues specialist; and Steve Forbert, a singer/songwriter reminiscent of the early Bob Dylan.

Dylan himself re-emerged for a triumphant world concert tour, reportedly undertaken to recoup financial losses on his film *Renaldo And Clara*. A series of great albums, including the exceptional *Blood On The Tracks*, had maintained his superstardom throughout the seventies although his relatively naive 1978 release, *Street Legal*, and his 1979 L.P., *Slow Train Coming*, which evinced his recent conversion to Christianity, raised a few questioning eyebrows amongst even his most devoted followers.

Devo frontman Mark Mothersbaugh gets paid for doing this?

Cheap Trick (left to right: Bun E. Carlos, Tom Petersson, Robin Zander and Rick Neilsen), stars in America, have yet to achieve similar fame in Britain.

Bob Dylan forgot his domestic and financial troubles, and embarked on a highly successful world tour.

'78 the year

Events

17 Mar. The oil tanker Amoco Cadiz breaks in half off Brittany.

6 June California mandates tax cuts under Proposition 13.

25 June Argentina beats the Netherlands 3–1 to win the soccer World Cup.

25 July The world's first test-tube baby, a girl, is born in England.

17 Aug. Three U.S. hot-air balloonists successfully cross the Atlantic in Double Eagle II.

15 Sept. Muhammad Ali defeats Leon Spinks to become Heavyweight Champion for the third time.

16 Oct. Karol Wojtyla of Poland becomes John Paul II, the third Pope in two months.

17 Oct. Anatoly Karpov defeats the Soviet defector Viktor Korchnoi to remain World Chess Champion.

30 Nov. *The Times* and *Sunday Times* suspend publication.

Films of 78
Animal House · Death On The Nile · Grease · Lord Of The Rings · Renaldo And Clara · Saturday Night Fever · Superman · A Wedding

U.S. CHART TOPPERS – WEEKS AT TOP

How Deep Is Your Love	Bee Gees
Baby Come Back	Player
Stayin' Alive	Bee Gees
Love Is Thicker Than Water	Andy Gibb
Night Fever	Bee Gees
If I Can't Have You	Yvonne Elliman
With A Little Luck	Wings
Too Much Too Little Too Late	Johnny Mathis and Deniece Williams
You're The One That I Want	John Travolta and Olivia-Newton John
Shadow Dancing	Andy Gibb
Miss You	Rolling Stones
Three Times A Lady	Commodores
Grease	Frankie Valli
Boogie Oogie Oogie	A Taste of Honey
Kiss You All Over	Exile
Hot Child In The City	Nick Gilder
You Needed Me	Anne Murray
MacArthur Park	Donna Summer
You Don't Bring Me Flowers	Barbra & Neil
Le Freak	Chic

U.K. CHART TOPPERS – WEEKS AT TOP

Mull Of Kintyre	Wings	4
Uptown Top Ranking	Althia and Donna	1
Figaro	Brotherhood of Man	1
Take A Chance On Me	Abba	3
Wuthering Heights	Kate Bush	
Matchstick Men	Brian and Michael	3
Night Fever	Bee Gees	2
Rivers Of Babylon	Boney M	5
You're The One That I Want	John Travolta/ Olivia Newton-John	9
Three Times A Lady	Commodores	5
Dreadlock Holiday	10 cc	1
Summer Nights	John Travolta and Olivia Newton-John	7
Rat Trap	Boomtown Rats	2
Do Ya Think I'm Sexy?	Rod Stewart	1
Mary's Boy Child	Boney M	4

Left: Luque, Kempes and Bertoni celebrate Argentina winning the World Cup.

Opposite top left: John Travolta in *Saturday Night Fever.*

Opposite top right: Christopher Reeve in *Superman.*

Opposite centre: Olivia Newton-John and John Travolta in *Grease.*

Opposite bottom: the Amoco Cadiz oil tanker breaks up.

'79

'I Don't Like Mondays'

Blondie · Chic · Dire Staits · Generation X · The Knack · Lene Lovich
Madness · Gary Numan · Police · Pretenders · Siouxsie and the Banshees
Sister Sledge · Specials · Squeeze · Undertones · Van Halen
Village People

During 1979, the rock scene was more active and varied than in any other year of the decade.

It was a year when many seasoned campaigners girded their loins for a fresh chart assault. The Eagles, Led Zeppelin, James Taylor, Roxy Music, the Beach Boys, Jethro Tull, the Kinks and the Allman Brothers all returned to prominence, proving that even if, in some cases, there wasn't much life left in the old dog there was still plenty of sales potential. All had originally entered the arena full of fire and spirit; all had now completed their smooth transition into the establishment.

Other campaign veterans who had good reason to feel pleased with themselves included Eric Clapton, Cliff Richard, Supertramp, the Bee Gees, the Doobie Brothers, Elton John, Rod Stewart, the Who, the Electric Light Orchestra, Stevie Wonder, Dr. Hook, Art Garfunkel, Neil Young, Wings, Fleetwood Mac and Abba.

Of the ever-increasing British new wave progeny, the Ruts, the Skids, the Tourists, the Pretenders, the Jags, the Members, Joe Jackson, Siouxsie and the Banshees, XTC, Stiff Little Fingers and Penetration were among many making their presence felt in the charts, which like teen-oriented radio and television programmes, were finally beginning to reflect the musical changes.

The Undertones, an effervescent bunch from Northern Ireland, showed great promise with no less than five hit singles during the year and *Lucky Number*, a smash single for Lene Lovich, started her on the road to stardom.

Generation X, who had been contenders in the first punk onslaught of 1976, came through with *King Rocker*, a hit from their second album, *Valley Of The Dolls*, but they failed to capitalise on its popularity, choosing instead to hibernate for most of the year. Meanwhile, the remains of the Sex Pistols, further depleted by the drug-induced death of Sid Vicious, who had been out on bail after being charged with the New York murder of his girlfriend Nancy Spungen, staggered on aimlessly, obviously missing the leadership of Johnny Rotten. Nevertheless, their following was still considerable, as was shown by the success of an album, *The Great Rock 'n'Roll Swindle* – the soundtrack of an unreleased film, and two top three singles, *Something Else* and *C'mon Everybody* – both Eddie Cochran hatchet jobs. All had been recorded in 1978, however, and lacking anything more substantial to keep the cash flowing, their record company scraped the barrel with a hotch-potch album of odds and ends called *Some Product* . . . which is unlikely to be the last we shall hear of the Sex Pistols.

Keeping the heavy metal flag flying were Judas

Detroit-born Lene Lovich emerged from the late 1978 Stiff Train Tour as a leading contender for stardom. Hit singles in the shape of *Lucky Number* and *Say When* further established her unique talent.

Banshees leader Siouxsie achieved instant record success after being turned down by several labels.

Top left: Police (Sting, Stewart Copeland and Andy Summers).

Squeeze (*centre*) and Dire Straits (*right*), put the name of Deptford, a south-east London suburb, on the map.

Top right: Generation X (left to right: Mark Laff, Derwood Andrews, Billy Idol and Tony James).

Centre right: Joe Jackson was a hit in America, but took somewhat longer to be recognised in his native Britain.

Far right: Richard returned to number one with *We Don't Talk Anymore*, his first chart-topper in more than 14 years.

Priest, AC/DC, Rainbow, Whitesnake, Gillan, Motorhead and a slew of new groups who proved that, though passé, their favoured music was far from dead.

The singles chart introduced several newcomers including Judy Tzuke, the Korgis, Bill Lovelady, the Buggles, Sad Cafe, B. A. Robertson and M, although the most successful new acts were Police, Dire Straits, Squeeze and Gary Numan.

Police, a dynamic and powerful trio, comprised

It took 18 months of intensive gigging before Squeeze achieved their national breakthrough with *Take Me, I'm Yours*.

drummer Stewart Copeland, formerly with Curved Air, guitarist Andy Summers, whose long apprenticeship involved spells with Zoot Money, the Animals and the Soft Machine among others, and singer/songwriter/bassist Sting, who had arrived in London to seek a worthy band after the failure of several Newcastle-based outfits. Although they gained a significant following from their extensive live work during the new wave heydays of 77, neither their early singles, *Fall Out* and *Roxanne*, nor their debut album, *Outlandos d'Amour*, attracted more than minimal attention in Britain.

In 1978, they decided to try their luck in America, where they covered prime markets in the lowest of low budget tours, their impecuniosity allowing only the cheapest transport and accommodation. Their persistence paid off when *Roxanne* and the album made impressive showings on the American charts, thereby creating renewed interest in Britain, where both records began selling, making the top twenty during the first half of 1979. *Can't Stand Losing You*, another single from the album, climbed to number two and Police were suddenly stars – Sting, in particular, being accorded saturation media coverage.

Towards the end of the year they released a second album, *Regatta De Blanc*, and a new single, *Message In A Bottle*, and watched both reach number one in a matter of days.

1979 style Who (left to right: John Entwistle, Kenny Jones, Roger Daltrey and Pete Townshend).

Squeeze, sharing the same managerial stable a Police, also started their vinyl career on a small labe before being signed by A. & M. and reaching the to twenty with *Take Me I'm Yours* in 1978. When tw follow-ups were comparative failures, it was widel assumed that they would fade but their secon album, *Cool For Cats*, produced three major hi singles in the title track, *Up The Junction* and *Sla And Tickle*. Their very cute English style has mad them one of the most popular groups in Britain, bu their appeal has so far proved rather too insular t attract American audiences.

Dire Straits' sensational emergence paralleled tha of Police. A South London four-piece, they, too won an avid but meagre audience as they paid thei dues in small clubs and poured their hearts into a original and innovative album which did nothing

In America, however, *Dire Straits* was im mediately acclaimed a masterpiece, reaching the to three while a single, *Sultans Of Swing*, did likewise British record buyers re-investigated and, mor than a year after their release, both records becam substantial U.K. hits. A second album, *Communique* was less successful because of its basic similarit and this, to some extent, detracted from thei startling rags to riches fairytale, but singer songwriter/lead guitarist Mark Knopfler and drum mer Pick Withers were invited by Bob Dylan to pla on his *Slow Train Coming*, so they couldn't feel to piqued.

Dire Straits' was presumed to be the 'Overnigh Success' story of the year, but that was before th triumphant entry of Gary Numan, who had spen much of the late seventies fronting unsuccessfu punk bands. In late 1978, following a couple of non selling singles, the latest of these bands, Tubewa Army, released a similarly unregarded album on th small Beggar's Banquet label – and Numan was mor or less written off as a down-market Bowie imitato

By the middle of 1979, however, critics wer being forced to eat their words: Tubeway Army – o at least Numan – had become instantly famous. second album *Replicas*, and a novel single, *Ar Friends Electric*, both rode to the top of the charts i double quick time ... and three months later ye another album, *The Pleasure Principle* – release under Numan's name – went straight in at numbe one, while another single, *Cars*, also reached the to to seal a remarkable run of success.

It remains to be seen whether his magic will wor in the States but his influence in Britain has alread led to the formation of many similar groups, most c whom claim that they adopted their electroni synthesis before him. With their dyed and blow waved hair, Numan clones began to proliferate i concert audiences, though their numbers were fe in comparison with punks – still the predominar street style – and mods.

The mod cult, dormant since the mid-sixties bu reactivated by the Jam in 1976, received a shot i the arm when the Who returned to active service i 1979. Recruiting Small Face Kenny Jones to replac Keith Moon, who had died the previous year, the struck out for their first live gigs in several yea but, more importantly, saw the first fruits of the film company. *The Kids Are Alright*, a light-hearte documentary detailing aspects of their illustriou career, included historic footage from their earl ears – whilst *Quadrophenia*, based on their album ne of several milestones, including *Tommy* and *Who's Next*, issued between 1969 and 1973), was a dramatic celebration of the mod era. More films are planned but meanwhile the group, now free of the anxiety they felt during the punk boom, seem to have regained their taste for rocking.

Having made the lucrative assumption that a mod revival could spark a sales boom, the rock industry steered the market in that direction – much to the horror of the pre-boom nucleus who saw their exclusivity vanish as a uniformed army of mods appeared overnight. Arriving too was an abundance of groups wearing appropriate apparel and playing appropriate music – though compared with the sixties originals, most were fairly feeble.

The Merton Parkas, the Chords and the Purple Hearts achieved a modicum of success but the leader of the pack was Secret Affair, who rose from the ashes of a punk rock called the New Hearts to score a hit with *Time For Action*.

Rather less contrived was a parallel ska/blue beat revival activated by a multi-racial Coventry group called the Specials, who set up their own Two-Tone label with money borrowed from a local businessman. Their first record, *Gangsters*, reached the top ten when Chrysalis picked up Two-Tone for national distribution and the label's second release, *The Prince* – a tribute to their mentor, Prince Buster – was a hit for North London group, Madness. A third single, *On My Radio*, gave the Selector a top tenner and the Specials' follow-up, *A Message To You, Rudy*, maintained their label's 100% hit record.

Demonstrating just how swiftly their style was sweeping the country, the Specials' debut album (produced by Elvis Costello) leapt into the album chart at number four while the first album by Madness (now signed to Stiff) crashed in a few places lower.

In America, Adult Oriented Rock and disco music continued to rule the roost. In the former category, two mainstream rock outfits, Toto and Journey, made the most progress while the Pointer Sisters and Rickie Lee Jones broke through with fine singles, *Fire* and *Chuck E's In Love* respectively. John Stewart, who had begun his professional career in the late fifties, was rewarded for his unflagging optimism when *Gold* became a top five single and *Bombs Away Dream Babies* a top ten album.

On the disco front, Anita Ward, Amii Stewart, McFadden and Whitehead and also the Crusaders all came up with winners but it was the Village People, Chic and Sister Sledge who really set the dance floors alight.

The idea for the Village People was conceived by Jacques Morali, a Frenchman who had moved to New York and was fascinated by the visual appeal of the ordinary working people he saw around Greenwich Village. After finding six suitable actors, he dressed them as a policeman, a construction worker, a biker, a serviceman and, to colour the proceedings, a cowboy and a Red Indian chief. The overall effect was bizarre – and Morali provided them with material to match. In 1977, *Macho Man* was the title of their first platinum album and their first top ten single – but their success was comprehensively eclipsed in 1979 when *Cruisin'* achieved triple platinum status and spawned the massive hit single *Y.M.C.A.*, which sold over 12 million copies worldwide. A follow-up single, *In The Navy*, also topped the chart while two further albums, *Go West* and *Live And Sleazy*, added to their platinum haul. Some observers feel that the Village People, with their gay overtones and banal songs, are a joke which has long since worn thin but their multitudinous fans will appreciate *Can't Stop The Music*, a 'fictionalised documentary' which details their meteoric rise to fame.

While for the Village People it is open to question, for Chic the future seems assured: unless something unforeseen occurs they will become the biggest black act of the early eighties. Led by bassist Bernard Edwards and guitarist Nile Rodgers (a veteran of the houseband at the famous Apollo Theatre in New York), Chic burst upon the scene in late 1977 when *Dance Dance Dance* became the first in a long line of hit singles. Hit follow-ups included *Everybody Dance*, *Le Freak*, *I Want Your Love* and *Good Times*. The albums, *Chic*, *C'est Chic* and *Risqué* have also been worldwide smashes, their sophisticated sound and technically perfect production impressing even the most ardent disco hater.

Rodgers and Edwards were also responsible for the swift escalation of Sister Sledge's fortune. A four-girl vocal group, they actually started before Chic but, since being patronised by the Chic Organisation, have produced a million-selling album, *We Are Family*, and three big hit singles in the title track, *He's The Greatest Dancer* and *Lost In Music*.

The year's other American hitmakers included Charlie Daniels, Randy Vanwarmer, Teddy Pendergrass, Peaches and Herb, Leif Garrett and Styx – one of several hugely popular heavy metal bands. Also making giant strides in this field were Molly Hatchet, a boogie band from Florida, REO Speedwagon from the mid-West, and Van Halen, whose second album *Van Halen II* (the title is as imaginative as their music) remained in the top ten for several months.

Overleaf opposite top left: a disco, late seventies-style.

Overleaf opposite top right: the Ramones.

Overleaf bottom: 'Godfathers of Punk' – the Velvet Underground plus Iggy Pop.

Van Halen demonstrated that there was still a market for raw and basic heavy metal.

The late '70s

'79 the year

Events

1 Feb. Ayatollah Khomeini returns to Iran after 14 years of exile.

17 Feb. China invades Vietnam.

26 Mar. Presidents Sadat and Begin sign an Egypt-Israeli peace treaty in Washington.

11 Apr. Tanzanian forces invade Uganda, overthrowing Amin.

4 May Margaret Thatcher is elected the U.K.'s first female Prime Minister.

7 July Bjorn Borg wins the Wimbledon Men's Singles for the fourth successive time.

27 Aug. Earl Louis Mountbatten and three others are killed by an I.R.A. bomb.

4 Nov. Iranian students storm the U.S. embassy and take over 60 Americans hostage.

15 Nov. Professor Anthony Blunt publicly confesses to spying for the U.S.S.R.

21 Dec. A constitutional settlement and ceasefire is agreed to for Zimbabwe-Rhodesia.

U.S. CHART TOPPERS – WEEKS AT TOP

Too Much Heaven	Bee Gees
Le Freak	Chic
Do Ya Think I'm Sexy?	Rod Stewart
I Will Survive	Gloria Gaynor
Tragedy	Bee Gees
What A Fool Believes	Doobie Brothers
Knock On Wood	Amii Stewart
Heart Of Glass	Blondie
Reunited	Peaches and Cream
Hot Stuff	Donna Summer
Love You Inside Out	Bee Gees
Ring My Bell	Anita Ward
Bad Girls	Donna Summer
Good Times	Chic
My Sharona	The Knack
Sad Eyes	Robert Johnson
Don't Stop Til You Get Enough	Michael Jackson
Rise	Herb Alpert
Pop Music	M
Heartache Tonight	Eagles
Still	Commodores
No More Tears	Barbra Streisand and Donna Summer
Babe	Styx
Escape	Rupert Holmes

U.K. CHART TOPPERS – WEEKS AT TOP

YMCA	Village People
Hit Me With Your Rhythm Stick	Ian Dury and the Blockheads
Heart Of Glass	Blondie
Tragedy	Bee Gees
I Will Survive	Gloria Gaynor
Bright Eyes	Art Garfunkel
Sunday Girl	Blondie
Ring My Bell	Anita Ward
Are Friends Electric?	Tubeway Army
I Don't Like Mondays	Boomtown Rats
We Don't Talk Anymore	Cliff Richard
Cars	Gary Numan
Message In A Bottle	Police
Video Killed The Radio Stars	Buggles
One Day At A Time	Lena Martell
When You're In Love With A Beautiful Woman	Dr. Hook
Walkin' On The Moon	Police
Another Brick In The Wall	Pink Floyd

Films of 79

Alien · Capricorn One · The Chess Players · The Deer Hunter · The Europeans · Love At First Bite · Manhattan · Quadrophenia

Left and opposite top left: 1979 saw roller disco becom a craze.

Opposite top right: Alien

Opposite bottom right: Pope John Paul II.

Opposite bottom left: the Mods made a come-back.

Neil Young enjoyed another good year; *Rust Never Sleeps* and *Live Rust* providing further evidence that he was one of the seventies' most vital artists; erstwhile guitar hero Eric Clapton released another top ten album in *Backless*, proving that in his seventeenth year as a professional musician he was enjoying his greatest popularity since the demise of Cream in 1968.

After years of suppression, new wave music was beginning to gain momentum but apart from the odd exception it remained at cult level. When they did get as far as releasing albums, most acts – for instance the Pop, the Screams, the A's, and the Motels – were weak compared with the English models whose ideas they plundered. The year's biggest breakthroughs were by the Knack and Blondie.

Produced by Mike Chapman (of Chinnichap fame), the Knack were an uptempo pop group from Los Angeles. Their debut album, *Get The Knack*, rocketed to number one, where it stood for five weeks, a feat surpassed by their first single, *My Sharona*, which topped the chart for six weeks during the summer. However, their spectacular entrance was dimmed by the rather less successful *Good Girls Don't*.

The focal point of Blondie, a six-piece from New York City, was the extremely attractive Debbie Harry, who had begun her recording career with a hippie group, Wind In The Willows, during the late sixties. In 1973, she and guitarist Chris Stein formed

Paul McCartney wonders what John Lennon's doing these days (*far left*).

Madness (*above*), together with former labelmates the Specials, the Selector, the Beat, helped to make Two Tone Records the most consistent independent British label of the year.

Gary Numan (*left*) was the biggest solo star of the year.

The Village People extol the virtues of a life on the ocean wave (*left*).

Blondie's Debbie Harry (*righ*) became the decade's most celebrated pin-up.

the Stilettos and this group evolved into the prototype Blondie a year later.

By 1976 Debbie and Chris, the only remnants of the original group, had been joined by new cohorts and a re-shaped Blondie securing a recording deal with Private Stock. Their first album was not a resounding success but, certain of their potential, Chrysalis bought out their contract for a reported half million dollars and set about bringing their talents to the public' notice.

Long before gaining acceptance at home, Blondie cracked the British market: their second album, *Plastic Letters*, was one of 1978's best sellers and two tracks, *Denis* and *(I'm Always Touched By Your) Presence Dear*, became top ten singles. Later that same year *Parallel Lines*, produced by the ubiquitous Mike Chapman, flew to number one in Britain and three singles from it, *Picture This*, *Hanging On The Telephone* and *Heart Of Glass*, all made the top ten – the last becoming the group's first number one, a position it also achieved in America, where it became their first substantial hit.

Sunday Girl, which also reached number one, became the fourth U.K. hit from the album, by which time a new L.P. was almost ready for release. Issued in late 1979, *Eat To The Beat* entered the U.K. chart at number one, while a single, *Dreaming*, peaked at number two. Without doubt, Blondie, are one of the major success stories of the late seventies, their musical and visual appeal combining to make them certain front runners over the coming years.

American audiences, who had long since developed an aversion to anything unpolished or raw, felt most comfortable with familiarity, for which

The Knack's *My Sharona* was the biggest American hit single of 1979, remaining at number one for six weeks.

reason the Eagles and Led Zeppelin both topped the chart even though their albums were markedly inferior to their earlier classics. E.L.O. and Fleetwood Mac were also welcomed back with open wallets and Paul McCartney made excellent progress in his quest to become the richest rock star in the world – despite his refusal to become a British tax exile. Overall, however, sales had slumped and the turn of the eighties saw the record industry reeling from too much ill-considered investment and drastically decreasing profits.

Of the pioneers who featured in chapter one, 25 years ago, Hank Ballard, Chuck Berry, Pat Boone, Ray Charles, Bo Diddley, Fats Domino, the Drifters, Bill Haley, Etta James and B. B. King are still rocking, although time has turned them mellow. The rest have either given up or died.

Nevertheless, rock'n'roll is here to stay, just like the man said, and every year brings fresh stars. As long as the world keeps spinning, there are going to be people out there turning music into gold.

Wings 1979 (left to right: Lawrence Juber, Linda McCartney, Paul McCartney, Steve Holley and Denny Laine).

Index

250